CONTROLLING WOMEN

SANDRA HEMPEL

Controlling Women

*The Untold Story of Britain's
First Female Police Force*

HURST & COMPANY, LONDON

First published in the United Kingdom in 2025 by
C. Hurst & Co. (Publishers) Ltd.,
New Wing, Somerset House, Strand, London, WC2R 1LA
© Sandra Hempel, 2025
All rights reserved.

Distributed in the United States, Canada and Latin America by
Oxford University Press, 198 Madison Avenue, New York, NY 10016,
United States of America.

The right of Sandra Hempel to be identified as the author
of this publication is asserted by her in accordance with the
Copyright, Designs and Patents Act, 1988.

A Cataloguing-in-Publication data record for this book
is available from the British Library.

ISBN: 9781911723967

This book is printed using paper from registered sustainable
and managed sources.

www.hurstpublishers.com

Printed and bound in Great Britain by Bell & Bain Ltd, Glasgow

CONTENTS

PART IV

PART V

ACKNOWLEDGEMENTS

I am extremely grateful to the Society of Authors for their award. It was, of course, a great support during the research and writing, but also a fantastic endorsement from such a respected body.

Huge thanks to my wonderful agent Jon Curzon. I was extremely fortunate to be taken on by Jon. He believed so strongly in the book and has been an invaluable source of advice, encouragement and reassurance during the writing. And his skill and experience during the discussions with potential publishers resulted in another brilliant result for me, namely Hurst Publishers.

When I read the response to the proposal from Hurst senior editor, Lara Weisweiller-Wu, I was elated. Lara was, like Jon, so enthusiastic about both the story itself and the way that I wanted to tell it. It seemed clear that this would be another perfect fit for me, and so it proved. Lara's editing skills are phenomenal and I felt entirely confident in such safe hands. Her comments and revisions were invariably insightful, as well as sympathetic to the tone and style of the book.

I am also very grateful everyone who helped me with the research, in particular: Dr Clare Smith, Curator of the Metropolitan Police Museum for her knowledge and guidance; the staff at the British Library, particularly the great team in the Rare Books and Music Reading Room; everyone at the National Archives, Imperial War Museum archives and the Women's Library at the London School of Economics; Richard Ward at the Parliamentary Archives; and Emily Cameron, archivist to the Kelburn Estate.

PART I

1

NO NICE WOMAN

July 1913, thirteen months before the outbreak of war. Two hundred Members of Parliament and their guests sit taking tea on the terrace in the light summer breeze. Behind them in Pugin's great gothic House, the business of the day rumbles sleepily on.

No one took much notice at first as the little steam launch headed upriver, but when the skipper throttled up and made straight for the terrace, heads began to turn. The vessel pulled up alongside the terrace and a middle-aged woman with the air of a reproving nanny clambered up onto the cabin roof. Fortunately, Nina Boyle was armed with nothing more menacing than a megaphone, for the police patrol boat was nowhere to be seen. She began by telling the politicians that she had no intention of berating them, before going on to deliver a lengthy scolding on the subject of women's suffrage. The MPs were more than happy to accept women's help when it came to canvassing in elections, she told them, but as soon as the Members won their seats they were quite prepared to refuse to give women the vote. They might not all be fools and rogues, she conceded, but they certainly appeared so to the public.

It was some twenty minutes before a police boat nosed its way out from under Westminster Bridge, at which point the protestors shot off in their nippy little craft, easily outpacing the ponderous police vessel. The politicians were amused but the men from Thames Division failed to see the joke. The *Manchester Courier* published the story under the headline "Suffragist Comedy: Police Outwitted at Westminster". It wasn't a stunt that would endear Boyle to the Commissioner of the Metropolitan Police when she could have done with his support a few months later but despite her impeccable establishment credentials, challenging authority was Boyle's favourite sport, and she did it rather well.

* * *

That same summer and it's business as usual at the Bailey. A young girl is weeping in the witness box as the counsel for the prosecution takes her through her story of sexual assault. The thirteen-year-old had been home alone when the lodger, Robert Crawford, returned from work and found her in the bedroom. Now Minnie Pittaway is reliving her ordeal before an audience of men: the judge, the lawyers, the reporters, the officers of the court, the jailors, the police, the spectators in the public gallery—leering youths and drooling old men was how one onlooker described them—and, of course, the gentlemen of the jury. The women had been banished from the courtroom before the case began, sent off with the usual usher's cry of "Females out". Among them was Minnie's mother.

Today, though, there is one other female present. A tall, striking 26-year-old with a disconcerting gaze and thick chestnut hair sits bent over a notebook, head down, scribbling furiously. When the defence lawyer rises to cross-examine the child, the woman glares up, waves her pencil in the air and fixes him with her wide dark eyes. The lawyer begins his question, hesitates, stumbles over his words and trails off. He pulls himself together and starts again but he has lost some of his edge; the old hands at the Central Criminal Court are used to having an easy run when they're tearing into a terrified witness.

Edith Watson had been a familiar figure around the London courts since the previous summer when she had marched into the offices of the suffragette paper *The Vote*, edited by her friend Nina Boyle, and thrust a newspaper into Boyle's face. It carried a report of a man who had been sent to prison for two months for a savage physical attack on a woman. "If he'd stolen a loaf because he was starving, they'd have given him six months," she told Boyle, adding that "Something ought to be done about it." Boyle looked at her silently for a moment and then rummaged about in her desk drawer for a press card. "All right, go and do something about it. Hear those cases and write them up for *The Vote*. Go to the courts, say you're press and walk in."

And so the suffragette became a crime correspondent. She was baffled by the court procedure at first, but she sat and listened and learned. She was helped in this by her fierce intelligence and also by an interpreter at Marlborough Street Magistrates Court—"a very handsome man"; Watson had an eye for them—who took it upon himself to instruct her. The result was a regular column in *The Vote* called "The Protected Sex", an ironic reference to the widely held view that women didn't need the vote because they had men to protect them. How much that protection was worth was clear from the routine day-to-day sentencing that Watson was exposing in a series of snapshots from the Old Bailey and Clerkenwell Magistrates Court.

John O'Brien was found guilty of wounding Martha French, assaulting Eliza French and stealing a suitcase. He had been in a drunken fight in the street when he stabbed a bystander, Martha, causing her to lose an eye. He was given six months in prison for injuring Martha and fifteen months for stealing the suitcase.

James Neil, who had a history of extreme violence, was sentenced to eight months with hard labour for assaulting two policemen. On the same day in the same court Ada Drummond was also given eight months with hard labour, in her case for soliciting.

James R.G. was bound over for £5 for wounding his wife while attempting to cut her throat. E.J. received six months in prison, also for trying to cut his wife's throat. It was his third attempt. Peter M., on the other hand, received nine months with hard labour for stealing half a pint of milk, while Ellen R. was given eighteen months for stealing three brooches.

But it was what were known as the indecency cases like Minnie's that most shocked Watson. She had had to fight to stay in the courtroom while they were being heard, but after she had been thrown out a few times, Boyle decided to ask for a legal opinion. It turned out that trials had to be held "in the presence of the public" and as there was no mention of women not being members of the public, the next time Watson was ordered to leave she refused.

"The door-keeper stood irresolute," Watson recalled. "'Come along now, you don't want to hear the sort of things that will be said'. I replied that if the poor witness could bear to recount it then I could surely bear to listen to it. And I stayed." The lawyers and court officials were aghast at the sight of this seemingly well brought-up young lady listening to such filth. After all, she might have been their wife or daughter—it was a job that no nice woman would want to do, an usher told her—but it appeared that their hands were tied.

The evidence made for hard listening as the door-keeper had predicted, but just as upsetting for Watson was the way in which the alleged victims were treated. Women and girls, some of them as young as seven, stood in the witness box weeping with fear and shame and humiliation. It was traumatic enough to describe the attack in front of a crowd of strangers, some of whom were obviously enjoying themselves, but when the defence counsel then rose portentously to his feet, the accuser faced a bout of bullying as vicious as it was gratuitous. One lawyer's sole defence strategy was to accuse a child again and again of having sex with schoolboys, while another simply bellowed that the girl was a notorious liar in the certain hope that she would break down.

Watson was outraged. Here was another appalling injustice, but one hidden from public scrutiny.

Unusually, in Minnie Pittaway's case, the jury believed her and they found Robert Crawford guilty; perhaps Watson's attempts at disruption had had some effect. In passing sentence, Mr Justice Rentoul, a former Presbyterian church minister from County Donegal, stressed the importance of protecting girls before sending Crawford to prison for just four months.

2

THE MOST AWFUL COCKNEY

The doorman at the Old Bailey was more perceptive than he knew when he tried to warn off Edith Watson. Sitting in court day after day, listening to women's testimony, Watson was able to empathise deeply with the victims, but it came at a cost and she began to find her peace of mind increasingly disturbed. She had waved the official airily away, confident in the belief not only that she was as tough as the men, but that her own story was firmly stuffed down into a black hole, never to resurface.

* * *

Watson had not had an easy childhood. Born Edith Ward in 1888 to a single mother in the Hackney Workhouse Infirmary, she had grown up in poverty with a mother she found cold and domineering and a stepfather who believed that a child born out of wedlock was the Devil's spawn. She would never refer to him by name. Her first memories were of a small back room in Poplar with a box for a table, sleeping on the floor under a huddle of old coats and running down three flights of stairs to a communal tap and privy in the tiny back yard. As an adult she would be furious when she heard people say, "At least they [the poor] could be clean. It's easy enough to be clean."

"The room was cold and always dark," Edith would recall. "At night we had only a candle. By day the small window let in very little of the murkiness that was London's dockland daylight." Her mother was a home-worker, sewing buttons onto shirts, what was known as one of the sweated trades. It wasn't as bad as making sacks or pulling fur, but the pay was just as wretched. Watson remembered seeing her mother whipping her needle in and out several times for each button, twirling the cotton round the threads and biting it off because it was quicker than scissors. By working very fast she could finish two dozen shirts a day, seven buttons on each, for which she was paid four pence a dozen. As well as helping her mother by tearing the buttons off the cards and threading the spare needle, the child ran errands for neighbours: "A penny a day bought a farthing bundle of wood, an ounce of sugar and half a loaf of stale bread."

Then came a miraculous break. A wealthy woman came across Edith by chance and, impressed by her determination and sharp intelligence, paid for a few years' decent education at a private girls' school in Marylebone which, Edith asserted, changed her life. She learnt music and French as well as the basic subjects, but at the same time she found to her horror that she spoke "the most awful cockney": "I remember my agonised efforts to say Wales instead of Wai-ils and cake instead of cai-ik." She left school at fourteen and went to work as a sales assistant at a Bayswater department store, but her resourceful mother soon wangled her an office job at the Salvation Army headquarters in north London, an impressive achievement for a slum child, even one with an education. Just as the teenager seemed to be making good, however, she had a massive fall from grace. She was caught stealing from two of her colleagues. They were young women of her own age and she resented the fact that for them the pay was pin money, while she had to hand over her wages to her mother each week. After being sacked on the spot without a reference—she was lucky that the police weren't called—her future looked wretched.

Edith finally found a job as a live-in servant to an upstanding but mean-minded elderly couple in North London. The memory of those few life-draining weeks would stay with her. "No-one outside my generation and class can have any conception of what domestic servants of that time had to endure," she would later write. "And not from Simon Legree masters [the cruel slave owner in *Uncle Tom's Cabin*], but from respected churchgoing ordinary men and women with a few pounds a year to spare for the employment of a female slave." The Salvation Army had given up trying to persuade prostitutes to leave the streets because their efforts usually proved futile, she said. "And indeed how could it be otherwise? What had virtue to offer?"

After her miserable experience with the old couple, she found a slightly better job as a waitress in a boarding house. It was here that a South African couple asked her to go back with them as nursemaid to their two children; she was delighted. Here was a route out of penury and disgrace, the prospect of adventure and a new life far away from the filthy London lanes, her stepfather's blows and her mother's carping and complaints. But things didn't work out quite as she had hoped. While she was in South Africa, something happened that would haunt her for years to come.

* * *

She was still little more than a child herself, intelligent and inquiring and beginning to question the attitudes and assumptions that she had grown up with, to such an extent that in South Africa she had had an electrifying religious revelation that sent her running into the street shouting, "I'm free! I'm free!". No longer was God a ghastly old tyrant glaring down at her from behind a cloud, she announced, but a loving, humane presence at the centre of her being. She decided to devote her life to Him.

It was a raw overwrought passion, quickly spent, but strong enough at the time to cause her to throw up her nursemaid's job in order to join the Salvation Army, perhaps a surprising choice given her experience with the organisation in London. The Army welcomed her. She was given some training in Cape Town and then sent off to a remote small-town mission station to set up a new corps. She settled in well, became friends with her young woman assistant, and for a while was comfortable and happy. She was at her desk one afternoon when a Captain Smith arrived to collect some money. He quickly sent her assistant off on an errand and Edith found herself alone with him. It was decades before she was able to describe what happened next, and even then she would choose to write it down rather than to verbalise it.

"Suddenly he was standing over me. I looked up and he bent down swiftly and kissed me. I got up intending to go quietly out of the door but he came after me and imprisoned me by the door with his arms around me." At first she was angry rather than frightened. "I said, 'Don't be silly captain. What do you think you're doing?' I dodged my head from side to side to avoid his mouth with the thick ugly lips. He jammed me hard against the door and took my jaw in a cruel grip. When I struggled I really thought he would break my jaw. He was giving me savage kisses when I went limp and sank to the floor.

"He seemed to go quite mad then. He seized me by one arm and my hair and pulled me across the room, down the passage to the bedroom and over to my bed. He sat down on the low camp bed and tried to pull me up but I was still on the floor and stayed there. By chance I had taken up the one position that could help me. I was kneeling with my knees well under the bed and all his pulling merely wedged them tighter. My arms were crossed, my face down on the bed. Had he punched me he would have knocked me out but he didn't; he just clutched and clawed, trying to get my blouse off. I didn't scream or fight, I just knelt there and prayed to him and to heaven, a jumble of prayer and plea, until with a sigh he stopped clawing at me and said in a queer voice, 'It's all right. I was mad. You're quite safe. You can get up now'."

Shaking and crying, bruised and battered, she staggered to her feet and Smith begged her not to report him. Years later in her memoirs, looking back with experienced eyes, she would describe his pleading as "the usual story". It was all her fault, he told her. By staying there alone with him he naturally assumed that she wanted him to kiss her. "He said I didn't know what I did to a man, it wouldn't happen again, etcetera, etcetera." Worn-down and in shock, Edith agreed not to tell anyone what had happened, provided that Smith left at once and never came back. A few weeks later she received a summons to head office in Johannesburg, where she was taken to the adjutant's office and asked if Captain Smith had ever annoyed her. She hesitated, remembering her promise. The adjutant then told her a sickening story that consumed her with guilt. Smith had gone on to attack another young woman and this time he had left her seriously injured. She was now in hospital, and he was on the run.

Edith stuttered out a vague account of what had happened to her and was promptly accused of leaving Smith free to attack another girl. "I wonder how many other girls haven't reported him?" was the adjutant's first thought. It clearly didn't occur to him to ask Edith why that might be, nor did he, or anyone else, show her the slightest sympathy or concern. When the dressing-down was over, she was dismissed and sent back to the mission to carry on as though nothing had happened. The incident was never referred to again and she never discovered if Smith was ever brought to justice.

Years on, as Nina Boyle's court reporter, Edith would find the memories pushing their way up to haunt her: "Again and again I heard a girl lose her case because she had not screamed or made an immediate complaint. 'Why didn't you scream?'. Because you need that breath to fight. Because obscurely you don't want to be found in that condition. You want to get out of it cleanly and without embarrassment and the more people know about it, the more you feel soiled. It is all too shocking and you are ashamed and embarrassed and want to abolish the very memory of it."

* * *

Back in London in 1909, she managed to talk her way into a job in a telephone exchange near Oxford Street, despite never having used a phone in her life. She also discovered some cheap ways of spending her evenings—anything to delay the commute back to the East End and her parents' joyless home. On one of these expeditions Edith found herself at Speakers' Corner in Hyde Park and was instantly dazzled. Edwardian London was heady with revolutionary ideas if you knew where to look.

The solid, reassuring, unassailable Victorian principles that had held sway for more than half a century were coming under fire from all sides, and Edith was captivated. "I listened avidly to everything. Socialism, women's suffrage, atheism, free love, dress reform, anti-vivisectionism, free trade, the abolition of the Poor Laws, Catholicism. Everything."

She was listening to an impassioned speech on socialism at Speakers' Corner one night when she met someone else who was to mark her life. "I felt someone looking at me. I turned and met a pair of vivid blue eyes in a most handsome face topped by a plume of black hair. In a few minutes we were standing side by side." He turned out to be a postal worker, a passionate socialist called Eustace

Watson. As well as his charming face, Edith was taken with his unconventional appearance, particularly his daring fashion statement of not wearing a hat.

By then she had slammed out of her parents' home after the latest in a series of boiling rows with her stepfather, and was renting a comfortable little room in St John's Wood for ten shillings a week, breakfast and tea included. Within weeks of meeting Eustace, however, she had moved into a bedsitter in Camden Town with him, rejecting marriage in favour of what was then known as free love, very much the vogue in left-wing intellectual circles, although the couple would marry two years later.

Eustace might have been flamboyantly good-looking—Edith described seeing other women looking at him, asking themselves, or so she imagined, what he could possibly see in her—but he was also to emerge as an introspective, unpredictable, self-centred character, prone to depression and mood swings. The pair were clearly obsessed with each other, however, and their relationship quickly settled into years of what was to become a monotonous pattern of misery, separation and wild reconciliation. By the time Edith began writing her courtroom column for Nina Boyle's *The Vote*, she and Eustace would be living apart.

3

VIXENS IN VELVET

Nina Boyle was a serious-minded woman entirely unencumbered by elegance or style. By the time of the 1913 river boat protest, when she was forty-eight, she had acquired the reassuring demeanour of a kindly, pragmatic aunt, albeit one who came with a searing wit and a joyous flair for causing trouble. She was too busy fighting causes to have much time for frivolity, but her warmth and sense of fun—the Thames shenanigans had been her idea—were hard to resist. One of her favourite ploys was to address men in power like naughty schoolboys. Standing in the dock at Bow Street a few months after the river prank—this time she got caught—having been charged with obstruction for chaining herself to a door at Marlborough Street Magistrates Court, she scolded the judge for disallowing a question: "Now, now Mr Campbell; you must not do it. It's naughty"; lectured the prosecution counsel on his delivery: "Would you mind not talking down to your waistcoat but speak up so that we can hear"; and urged a police sergeant, "I know it's not fashionable in this court to tell the truth, but do try."

The upbraided Mr Campbell sentenced her to a forty-shilling fine or seven days in the second division, which meant being treated as a common criminal rather than what was known as a person of standing. She chose prison. It wouldn't be her first trip to Holloway.

Had she cared enough to do so, Boyle could have traced her ancestors back to the Norman family of De Boyville from Caen, at least one of whom came over to England with William the Conqueror. The De Boyvilles went on to become the lairds of the wild green coastal lands of Kelburn in North Ayrshire, and the line continues today. Patrick Boyle, the 10th Earl of Glasgow and chief of the clan, still calls Kelburn Castle home. When Nina's paternal grandfather died in 1853, the land, titles and most of the money had passed not to her father but to his half-brother Patrick. Even so, hers was a background that carried some serious privilege. Her uncles included a vice-admiral and the Dean of Salisbury, while a cousin, the 7th Earl, became governor of New Zealand. A fierce opponent of universal suffrage, he had the chagrin of seeing New Zealand women win the right to vote on his watch, twenty-five years before their compatriots in Britain.

Nina Boyle was born in 1865 in the then village of Bexleyheath in Kent, the fifth of six children of army officer Robert Boyle and Frances Sankey, a surgeon's daughter from Hampshire. This much is known. However, from her early childhood until her mid-thirties, she vanishes. There is no meaningful mention of Boyle in any surviving papers, whether official records, letters or diaries. After the early death of her father, when she was two, she is hidden for three decades. When she finally re-emerges into the daylight at the end of the century, aged thirty-four, it is as one of a new breed of women who were rewriting the old Victorian credo of who they were and how they should live.

Seemingly oblivious to her connections, but blessed with all the casual confidence of the upper classes, she came with a knee-jerk distrust of authority and a compulsion to challenge inequality wherever she found it. How she became that woman, however—the individuals and events that shaped her—remains a mystery. If she had attended a finishing school like many women of her class, then the money had been wasted, for she had acquired no husband, produced no heir and was presiding over no smart household. But there was enough cash in the family to shield her from having to work for a living. In fact, Nina Boyle would only ever drift around town from one rented flat to another, an aristocratic vagabond with an agenda. It was this way of life that in 1899 left her free to embark on a dusty, blood-stained adventure on the other side of the world.

* * *

The British Army was fighting a brutal messy guerrilla war against the Boers in South Africa and in their ranks was Nina's younger brother Lieutenant Cecil Boyle. With the death and injury rates on the rise, the call went out for medical volunteers. For Nina, the prospect of a gruelling mercy mission in deadly conditions thousands of miles from home was irresistible. The surgeon Sir Frederick Treves, best known for rescuing the "Elephant Man" Joseph Merrick from life in a freak show, worked alongside nursing aides like Boyle in the makeshift operating theatres behind the lines where each night the ox wagons loaded with the dead and the barely alive rumbled in from the battlefield. "These ill-housed women," Treves wrote, "seemed oblivious to hunger or any need for sleep … the heat was intense … the thirst incessant … Their ministrations to the wounded were … beyond all praise." One of Boyle's colleagues described coping with scorpions, tarantulas and "flies as thick as sand"; nursing soldiers suffering from typhoid and dysentery; and the living crammed into canvas tents alongside the dying and the dead. Boyle also faced a dreadful personal tragedy in South Africa. Cecil was taken prisoner by a rogue Boer commander, hustled off to a desolate farm and shot in the back. When his body was found two years later, Boyle was asked to identify him. She was only able to do so by his gold tooth.

She stayed on after the war and it was here that she first became involved with the women's rights movement, setting up the Johannesburg branch of the Women's Enfranchisement League and trying to raise awareness among working women by organising small meetings in supporters' homes. It proved a largely fruitless task, however, and she was long gone before the first women won the vote in 1930. It would be another fifty years before black women joined them. On her return to Britain, Boyle was commended by the commander of the British forces, Field Marshal Frederick Roberts, for her unselfish and patriotic work. She accepted his thanks but turned down his offer of a medal.

Ironically, the adult Boyle made her first appearance on the official records in 1911 when she took part in a census boycott. This was organised by the suffrage movement under the slogan "If women don't count, neither shall they be counted." She spent the night with a group of resisters in an apartment block in Westminster. When Mr Eckerton turned up to collect the form, he found it blank except for a defiant scrawl: "No Votes. No Census. Votes for Women", and was forced to obtain his information from the maid.

The census was another of many splits Boyle would see in the women's movement, for not all of the suffragists in Britain backed the boycott. This exercise was specifically devised to take a snapshot of social conditions to guide the government's efforts to clear the rancid slums and tackle the appalling child mortality rates. It had been designed by the head of the Local Government Board, John Burns, who had himself been born into a family of eighteen children, nine of whom died in infancy. It was not an uncommon story in late Victorian and Edwardian Britain. Burns waved the boycott airily away, calling its effects negligible and dubbing the protesters "vixens in velvet". Only four thousand people took part, none of whom were prosecuted. Nevertheless, the campaign has lived on in feminist history thanks to its most famous participant, Emily Wilding Davison, who hid in a cupboard in the House of Commons overnight. Davison would die dreadfully two years later in a suffrage protest, her skull crushed under the hooves of the king's horse on Derby Day.

* * *

By the time Edith Watson first came across her, in London in 1909, Boyle was a key figure in the campaign group known as the Women's Freedom League. The WFL was born in 1907 at the Eustace Miles vegetarian restaurant in Covent Garden, an area popular with sex workers at night and hardline suffrage territory by day. Emmeline Pankhurst was running the Women's Social and Political Union (WSPU) from an apartment in the towering Clement's Inn building behind Kingsway. A minute's stroll away, off the arc of the Aldwych, was the decorative Arts and Craft frontage of The Gardenia, another fashionable vegetarian eatery where suffragettes sat at marble tables eating cheese fritters and French bean omelettes. Behind the stylish leisurely scene, however, another scenario was playing out.

In 1912, a dressmaker called Lilian Ball, who had volunteered to take part in a WSPU protest, received a letter from Mrs Pankhurst asking her to call at the Gardenia at 6pm. Security was tight and Ball was led through a series of doors, each time having to show her pass, before finally being waved into a large upstairs room. A dashing woman in her thirties, well-educated and—the dressmaker thought—somewhat peremptory in her manner, handed her a hammer, told her to put it up her sleeve and ordered her to go to the United Service Museum in Whitehall Yard and break a window. Ball had asked for a crime that wouldn't result in more than a week in prison, as she couldn't afford to miss work, but she received two months with hard labour.

The Eustace Miles, just around the corner, hosted the breakfasts held to celebrate a hunger striker's release from Holloway. Sadly, many of those being fêted were themselves unable to eat, due to the wreckage that force-feeding had made of their digestion. With George Bernard Shaw as a shareholder and Ellen Terry's daughter, the theatre director Ellen Craig, selling *Votes for Women* from a stand on the pavement outside, the place had a certain celebrity cachet. It also had plenty of space with two floors of dining halls. At its zenith, the place was serving 1,000 meals a day.

On the Saturday in September 1907 when the Women's Freedom League was born, the Eustace Miles had been heaving, not with early morning revellers this time but with incredulous WSPU members, furious at Pankhurst's latest power grab. Their leader had just announced her intention to take control of the organisation's governing body and cancel their upcoming conference. The group was also disturbed by her increasing use of violence as a political strategy. Her daughter Christabel would later explain the rationale: "If men use explosives and bombs for their own purpose they call it war, and the throwing of a bomb that destroys other people is then described as a glorious and heroic deed, why should a woman not make use of the same weapons?" In 1907, however, many members were already unhappy with the direction in which the organisation appeared to be going and decided to take a stand. Pankhurst was given three days to back down, and when the deadline came and went, the dissidents voted to set up a new organisation. Run on strictly democratic lines, it would be committed to non-violence, and in order to make this point they chose a pacifist as their leader.

The sixty-three-year-old wealthy widow Charlotte "Lottie" Despard was a Sinn Féin supporter who ran a soup kitchen in the slums of Battersea, a rigid-backed, rock-featured, sandal-wearing woman who stared beadily out at the world from beneath a black lace mantilla. Yet her smile melted her face like a girl's, and she had another life as the writer of novels with titles like *The Rajah's Heir* and *Chaste as Ice, Pure as Snow*. Unlike Emmeline and Christabel, Despard had no fondness for dictatorship nor for throwing bombs. During the First World War, she would campaign on behalf of the conscientious objectors while her brother was commanding the British forces on the Western Front.

The group spent some time discussing names—The Women Emancipators was one suggestion—before settling on the Women's Freedom League (WFL). The chosen motto was "Dare to be Free"; the telegraphic address: Tactics, London.

* * *

After discovering the radicals at Speakers' Corner, Edith Watson also began going to suffrage meetings and it was here in 1909 that she met Boyle. Boyle was an excellent speaker, engaging, articulate and amusing, and Watson was as impressed with the woman as she was with the cause. She promptly joined the WFL where, she said, she found the perfect outlet for her thoughts, feelings and energies. Of Boyle, she would write in her memoirs: "She was everything that is [meant by] the word 'lady' and I became her devoted admirer."

The WFL's first meetings had been held in Buckingham Street, a little 17th-century thoroughfare running from the Strand down to the Embankment Gardens and the river. Their office equipment consisted of two chairs, a table and a typewriter on loan. Within a year, however, they had taken a lease at No. 1 Robert Street, a tall gracious terraced house two blocks away, and it was here that in 1913 Nina Boyle got her sensibly shod feet under the desk, not only as editor of *The Vote* but as head of the League's political and militant department.

4

THE CONSOLATION WHICH ONE FEMALE
MIGHT GIVE ANOTHER

Back twenty-four years, to the sunny early summer of 1890 and a routine shift at Hyde Park Police station. Just after midnight, PC Lee trundles in with thirty-year-old Bessie Moncrieff on a trolley. Despite being strapped down and with two of Lee's fellow officers hanging onto her, the prisoner is still managing to put up a fight.

Moncrieff is, according to Inspector Allison, an infamous local prostitute, one of their regular customers, and Constable Lee had had something of a battle on his hands when he tried to arrest her. He says that he found her accosting men in Rotten Row and ordered her to leave Hyde Park, at which point she used "the most filthy language I have ever heard". He seized her—his words—and was leading her away when according to him she threw herself to the ground and tried to bite him. A trill on his whistle brought a sergeant and several members of the public running to his aid, and between them they wrestled Moncrieff onto one of the handcart ambulances that were intended for taking the injured to hospital, but more often than not were used for transporting drunks.

At the station, Moncrieff was charged with being drunk and disorderly and put into a cell to await the magistrate in the morning. Nearly all of the women that the Hyde Park officers arrested were accused of being drunk and disorderly or soliciting or both, and the area around the great hulk of the cavalry barracks in the park, home to the 450 officers and men of the Royal Horse Guards, had always been a trouble spot.

What happened to Bessie Moncrieff while she was in custody is a matter of dispute. According to *The Standard*, she proceeded to strip nearly naked before being held down and forcibly dressed by a scrum of constables. So far, so unremarkable. The incident wouldn't normally have raised any eyebrows; tellingly, *The Standard* didn't present it as an exposé of the treatment of a half-naked, out-of-control, lone woman by a bunch of men but as a quirky anecdote about an outrageous female. However, the story happened to catch the eye of the radical Liberal MP Henry Wilson, and he had a couple of questions for the Home Secretary, Henry Matthews. First, was the story true? And if so, was a matron present while this fracas was playing out? In a written reply, Matthews quoted from Inspector Allison's version of events. Moncrieff had not stripped off, merely removed her skirt, a black bodice and one petticoat, "having then on her under-linen, stays and a stripped flannel petticoat". She was given a blanket and then "used the vilest language, shouting and 'halloaing' all through the night," according to Constable Lee who, for a policeman patrolling the night streets of central London, seemed to have had a low threshold when it came to swearing. The next morning Moncrieff put her bodice back on, but not the rest of her clothes, and so was taken to court in a cab rather than being walked through the streets in the usual manner. No force was used to make her dress, according to the inspector, but he confirmed there had been no matron on hand, only the men.

Moncrieff stood in the dock in her bodice and petticoat and told the court that she had only just arrived in the capital from Cornwall, and had entered the park together with a respectable laundress when Constable Lee came up and began insulting her friend. "I told him he had no right to call her such a name when he turned upon me and struck me in the eye and tore my clothes to pieces." However, the magistrate had none of it and fined her seven shillings.

Whatever happened in the cell at Hyde Park that night, the scenario of male officers grappling with women prisoners was being played out on a daily basis at police stations across Victorian Britain. The gradual introduction of matrons in the 1880s was a tentative attempt to remedy the situation. They were overwhelmingly recruited from police officers' wives: middle-aged, dependable and heavy on common sense. Their status and pay were low and their powers slight—Herbert Asquith, who succeeded Matthews as Home Secretary in 1892, likened their status to that of paid nurses, servants

CONSOLATION ONE FEMALE MIGHT GIVE ANOTHER

or ladies' maids—but their emergence marked women's first unsteady steps into police stations as anything other than detainees.

By the time Bessie Moncrieff fell foul of Constable Lee, a few stations were employing matrons on a casual basis, sending for them as and when the superintendent felt that a woman's presence was required. They were the result of pressure not so much from women's rights activists but from the moral purity campaigners, who saw it as preposterous that men should be dealing with women who were drunk, distressed, pregnant or ill. It didn't happen in prisons or workhouses or hospitals, so what made it acceptable in police stations?

At first the police were none too happy at the thought of matrons interfering with their routine, putting a dampener on the atmosphere of male camaraderie in the stations and generally making a nuisance of themselves. A quick canvas of superintendents in the Met in 1889 produced a long list of objections, mostly the standard get-outs about the lack of suitable accommodation and the prohibitive cost of having to provide it, but the superintendents also said that women were not to be trusted with the keys to the cells nor with the safety of the prisoners. Some worried that it would be a demoralising job for a respectable woman, while the head of Marylebone division felt that the question was an irrelevance because "Female prisoners of good social position are but rarely detained in cells during the night."

Not all of the senior officers agreed. Superintendent Chisholm of Thames Division was using matrons to good effect at Waterloo Pier station, he said. When a woman was pulled out of the river after trying to drown herself, which was a sadly frequent occurrence, his officers always sent for a matron. Attempted suicide was a criminal offence, so the woman had to be arrested, but once at the station, the matron would help her out of her wet clothes, give her a bath and put her to bed. It was a homely, comforting picture, charmingly at odds with the hurly-burly of life at an inner-city police station. And Acting Superintendent Ferrett in Hampstead said that a matron should always be called "to attend on female prisoners who might require assistance which it would be unseemly or indelicate to be given by police constables or where feelings of commiseration for the prisoner would appear to call for the consolation which one female might give another in time of trouble."

Many of the critics then changed their minds when the first matrons took up their duties, for not only was it quickly apparent that they were well able to cope, but the constables' lives were so much easier when they no longer had to deal with rampaging females like Bessie Moncrieff, fighting and swearing and removing their skirts. Matthews decided that he would introduce matrons at some London stations on a permanent basis, paid one shilling an hour. Soon the Metropolitan Police Commissioner Sir Edward Bradford was telling the Home Secretary that the system was working very well; in fact, there was talk of expanding it. "From my conversations with Miss B. and other ladies I have no doubt that they desire the employment in the capacity of matrons, women who have had the training of nurses, and they also wish that matrons should wear a distinctive uniform and be invested with the powers and responsibilities of police officers," Bradford reported in 1895. When his note reached the Home Office, a civil servant underlined the remarks in red and put an exclamation mark in the margin.

Bradford's "other ladies" came from a slew of campaigning organisations including the National Union of Women Workers, led by someone who would go on to become a key figure in this story, the widow of the former Bishop of London, Louise Creighton. But the most active group was the British Women's Temperance Association, whose president, the reclusive Lady Isabella Somerset, directed operations from Eastnor Castle, a massive 19th-century pile in Herefordshire complete with watch towers and keep. "Miss B." was Lady Isabella's second in command, Florence Balgarnie, the thirty-eight-year-old daughter of a Congregational church minister, who had taken up the cause of women's suffrage at the age of seventeen, and was, unlike Lady Isabella, incapable of keeping still.

Apart from her involvement in the National Union of Women's Suffrage Societies, the People's Suffrage Federation, the International Arbitration and Peace Association, the British Anti-lynching League, the Society for Promoting the Return of Women as County Councillors, the Personal Rights Association, the Moral Reform Union, the Women's Trade Union League and the Men and Women's Club, Balgarnie makes regular appearances in the Home Office and Metropolitan Police files from the 1890s, attending high-level meetings about matrons and writing letters to ministers and officials bemoaning the lack of action. She strode out into the world clear-eyed and brandishing a morality-fuelled compassion for the Victorian underclass that was entirely untainted by sentimentality. She also had a stomach as unflinching as a surgeon's, which allowed her to delve around in the most unsavoury places. Travelling across the country, visiting what she described as some of the lowest haunts of vice in order to talk to women about their experiences in police cells, she noted that the difficulty in writing up her findings was not the lack of material, "but rather a superfluity of horrible detail, a repetition of which would be a sin against the most elementary ideas of good taste."

By the time Boyle and Watson began their campaign in 1914, police matrons were widely established across Britain; however, most did little more than to search a woman when she was brought in and take a quick glance at her in the cell, and none had anything like the training, authority or responsibility for which the energetic Miss B. had been calling.

A BODY OF UNIFORMED, TRAINED WOMEN

An evening in late August 1914, three weeks into the war. The heavy doors of the train swing open as the engine shudders to a halt, venting steam. The disorientated Belgians, white-faced and shaking from trauma and a rough channel crossing, step down onto the platform clutching eiderdowns, cooking pots and anything else they had been able to grab as they fled the smoking ruins of their homes. Some are wearing carpet slippers. Families huddle together, bedraggled and exhausted, and in among them are a few lone travellers. Farmhands in corduroy trousers carry their hoes and rakes, and there is a smattering of single girls and women.

Volunteers in large hats hand out sandwiches and tea, and a line-up of officials and charity workers stands ready to usher their charges out to the buses. The new arrivals will be processed at the chaotic War Refugees' Committee in the Aldwych, and then, sanctioned by paperwork, they will set off on the last leg of their journey to a place of safety. On the fringes of North London, Dr Herbert Cuff is busy turning the grand halls of Alexandra Palace into vast dormitories, with neat rows of tightly-packed beds and washing lines strung up amidst the classical statues. For those with a little money, however, the greeters are armed with lists of cheap respectable hotels, as well as the private homes of members of the public, horrified at the newspaper reports of German atrocities against "plucky little Belgium".

At a London station that night was a forty-one-year-old slightly built woman with wispy fair hair, pale blue eyes and a sharp little face. Margaret Mary Damer Dawson and her friends Lady Lyttelton and Annie St John Partridge had persuaded some of their Chelsea neighbours wealthy enough to own motor cars to help with the refugee effort. With ten vehicles at her disposal and bearing the grand title of Head of Transport, Damer Dawson's job was to collect the single women and girls and settle them into suitable lodgings. But as she waited for her charges to emerge from the train, she noticed another woman on the platform. There was something familiar about her, and something not quite right. Then it dawned upon her: she had seen the woman twice before that day but each time wearing a different dress and with different coloured hair.

As she assembled her bewildered little group and began to lead them out to the waiting cars, Damer Dawson caught sight of the woman again, now trying to home in on two of her girls. She remembered something else; a couple of weeks earlier she had lost two of her charges under what she had thought at the time were suspicious circumstances. In a public place that was heavy with officialdom, traumatised young women were being targeted by a procuress and the little Chelsea charity was unwittingly delivering them into her hands.

* * *

As the ambulances carrying the first tranche of war wounded shuttled to and fro along the Strand to Charing Cross Hospital, around the corner at the Women's Freedom League, Edith Watson and Nina Boyle were working on a plan. Their original idea had been to put an end to the shameful scenes in the courts on which Watson was now reporting, but they quickly found something else in the criminal justice system that needed fixing, namely police brutality towards women.

Just days earlier they had experienced it for themselves in the action at Marlborough Street Magistrates Court, which would lead Boyle to chastise those arresting her. Along with three other Women's Freedom League protestors, she and Edith had padlocked themselves to the doors of the grubby white court building off Oxford Street. They had chosen Marlborough Street because the magistrate there, the ageing, fractious Frederick Mead, was a dedicated misogynist whose idea of a good time was seeing suffragists and women brought before him on soliciting charges in the dock. A former prosecution barrister at the Old Bailey, Mead also had some trouble in shaking off the habit of trying to convict people, and he had been known to take over the cross-examination of a suffragette himself if he thought the lawyer charged with the task wasn't putting enough energy into it.

The police cut through the women's locks and chains easily enough, but when Boyle and her friends refused to disperse, the constables grabbed them like parcels and threw them hard down the steps into the street. One landed badly and nearly broke her neck, according to Boyle. Women, she told Watson later, would have handled this very differently. And women would also bring empathy and understanding to the victims of sexual assault and exploitation. They should be brought in as soon as a complainant came forward, comforting her, taking her statement, collecting the evidence with sensitivity and supporting her in the witness box. Yet this was no role for sympathetic amateurs. It was a heavyweight job that called for trained professionals, handpicked and with status and authority. In other words, police officers.

Since the latter part of the 19th century, supporters of what was known as the moral purity movement had been pushing for women to have a role in the criminal justice system. Only one month before war was declared, one group had been given a hearing at the Home Office, but the official who received them thought their plans vague and ill-thought-out. The demand for a female force patrolling the streets was totally unreasonable, he said, although perhaps it wouldn't be a bad thing if the London County Council employed a few female parkkeepers.

Then, Boyle and Watson were facing the small matter of convincing the Home Office, the Commissioner of the Metropolitan Police, and chief constables across the country to consent to a plan that they refused to consider. Now, however, with the outbreak of war, Nina Boyle thought they might just be in with a chance.

* * *

While Boyle and Watson were conspiring in Charing Cross, three miles to the west along the banks of the Thames, Margaret Damer Dawson was at home in Chelsea, pondering how best to protect her refugees. Cheyne Row runs north-to-south through Chelsea in a straight neat line down to the river, and No. 10 is a three-storey 18th-century mid-terrace of red and amber bricks. A plaque now marks the house but—unlike the smart blue plates that pepper the adjoining Cheyne Walk commemorating the likes of George Eliot, Algernon Swinburne and Dante Gabriel Rossetti—this one is a crude affair in rough grey cement, saying simply, "Margaret Damer Dawson Lived Here".

Damer Dawson was a supporter of The National Vigilance Association, whose mission statement was "The enforcement and improvement of the laws for the repression of criminal vice and public immorality". Operating out of an old carpet warehouse in the Strand, the association had sprung up in 1885 after a national scandal when W.T. Stead, the boisterous editor of the *Pall Mall Gazette*—written "by gentlemen, for gentlemen"—published a sensational exposé of child prostitution. In introducing his scoop, Stead issued a tantalising health warning: "All those who are squeamish, and all those who are prudish, and all those who prefer to live in a fool's paradise of imaginary innocence and purity … will do well not to read the Pall Mall Gazette."

To give clout to his campaign, Stead had bought a chimney sweep's daughter, thirteen-year-old Eliza Armstrong, for five pounds in what was possibly Britain's first media sting. The girl was duly handed over by her mother, taken to a brothel and drugged to wait for him. When the story hit the newsstands, copies of the *Gazette* changed hands for twenty times their face value, the publication was banned by the newsagents W.H. Smith, and the printers ran out of paper. The incident had inspired George Bernard Shaw to write *Pygmalion* (1912), sanitising the story but calling his main character Eliza. As Stead had failed to get the consent of the child's father and had only a verbal agreement with her mother, Eliza's parents weren't charged with any offence. He, on the other hand, went to prison for three months for abduction. As dramatic in death as he was in life, Stead went down on the Titanic in 1912.

Britain's campaign for moral or social purity first emerged in the USA in the late 19th century with the aim of imposing Christian teachings about sexuality upon society, particularly in suppressing prostitution and encouraging sex workers into other ways of life— rescue work as it was known. By 1914 the movement was wielding some serious muscle, not least with ministers and civil servants at the Home Office.

Anyone looking for a group to join was spoilt for choice. There was the Stead-inspired National Vigilance Association; the Association for Moral and Social Hygiene; The Public Morality Council; The Criminal Law Amendment Act Committee; the British National Committee for the Suppression of the White Slave Traffic; The Ladies' Association for the Care of Friendless Girls; The Travellers' Aid Society; The Girls' Friendly Society; the Metropolitan Association for Befriending Young Servants; and The Reformatory and Refuge Union, and in their wake marched a plethora of small faith-based local groups. In this world, "girls" was code for young prostitutes and "social" meant sexual.

Despite its censorious Victorian stance on public morality, the National Vigilance Association (NVA) did valuable work. In particular, they kept watch at the railway termini for vulnerable young women arriving from the Continental ports. London was the greatest market of human flesh in the whole world, according to Stead, where young women were regularly brought over from Europe for the purpose of being ruined. The woman that Damer Dawson encountered in 1914 was clearly a trafficker like the notorious Madame Charles, whose real identity was Isabella Gilchrist from Barking. Just weeks earlier, an NVA worker had tried to wrest some French girls from Gilchrist's clutches. The young women had arrived at Victoria Station on the train from Newhaven, a confused little group looking nervously around the great bustling hall. Mrs Sleeman was scurrying to the rescue when Gilchrist appeared, brandishing her umbrella and shouting "How dare you interfere, you nasty meddling old woman" and, pushing the girls into a taxi, she shot off.

Gilchrist ran what she liked to call an employment agency in London's Fitzrovia, where she was supplied with a steady stream of "goods" by a bureau in Paris. The victims were carefully chosen for their lack of relatives and friends—orphans were at the top of the wish list—so that nobody would come looking for them. Lured by the promise of a well-paid job, usually as a maid or a cook in a wealthy household, they arrived in London knowing no one, often with only a few words of English, and were immediately plunged into the capital's brutal uncharted underworld: robbed of their passports and money, held captive in a brothel, and beaten if they tried to escape. Damer Dawson would have heard NVA speakers spelling out the evils of the trade, but seeing it for herself that night at the station, in all its ruthlessness and cruelty, left her badly shaken.

It was only too clear that she and Sleeman were no match for the likes of Madame Charles and the viciously efficient operation that she represented. "I realised that it was very difficult to do that kind of refugee work if there were attempts at white slave traffic without having a body of uniformed, trained women," Damer Dawson would later tell a government inquiry. "I think that gave me the first idea of women police."

* * *

Damer Dawson was the eldest of four children of the physician Richard Damer Dawson and Agnes Hemming. Born in 1873, she had had a conventional late-Victorian, upper-middle-class upbringing in the decorous seaside town of Hove on the Sussex coast, and her early years were spent in a spacious, white-washed villa with a housekeeper and five servants. When the family then moved to an historic house near Burgess Hill, *Pigot's Directory* gave Dr Dawson pride of place on its roll-call of local gentry.

As a young woman, Damer Dawson had been a promising pianist, studying at the London Academy of Music and winning a gold medal, but she had gone on to devote her life not to music but to her vision of the public good. Despite an unassuming manner and a delicate appearance, she was far from ineffectual. When she was fired up by a cause, she could summon a ferocious energy, making up in courage and determination what she lacked in charisma.

She also had a kind heart and an instinctive urge to protect the vulnerable, which led her to set up a home for abandoned babies and to support the then fashionable cause of animal welfare, campaigning against vivisection and fighting for slaughterhouse reform. In order to be able to speak with authority about slaughterhouses, she put herself through the ordeal of witnessing the grisly business for herself, taking a camera with her. To distract herself during the killings, she ground the heel of one boot into the instep of the other foot. She didn't notice the pain at the time, but when she came to take her boot off she found it full of blood. She was awarded medals in Denmark and Finland for her international work on animal protection. A friend said of her: "She couldn't bear the sight of unnecessary suffering. It revolted her sense of the fitness of things."

When war broke out, forty-one-year-old Damer Dawson was already well connected and living comfortably, but she was about to receive a further leg up the social rankings. Her father had died back in 1900 and now, after fourteen years of widowhood, the sixty-two-year-old Agnes was preparing to marry again. Her choice of husband was Thomas de Grey, sixth Baron Walsingham. The de Greys, like the Boyles, traced their line back to the Normans, and Tommy, as he was known, had inherited the Norfolk family seat. The baron was characterised by his encyclopaedic knowledge of butterflies, his prowess on the cricket pitch and his feats on the grouse moor where he held the record for despatching 1,070 birds in one day. His rumoured predilection for housemaids was less widely discussed and, along with the mass slaughter of grouse, was unlikely to have found favour with Damer Dawson, but the family connection came at just the right time for what was to follow.

It began with a visitor to Cheyne Row. Constance Maud was a member of the Women's Social and Political Union and the Women Writers' Suffrage League, and the author of the much-admired 1911 suffrage novel *No Surrender*. She had come to warn Damer Dawson that she was behind the times with her big idea: someone had got there first. "And she told me of Miss Nina Boyle, the secretary of a women's suffrage society," Damer Dawson later explained to a Government inquiry. "She begged me not to cause confusion but to go and see this lady. I went to see her at her office."

That first meeting at Robert Street augured well. Despite their very different characters, the two women agreed about what was needed and decided that they could work together. "I found she was pretty much in the same position as myself," Damer Dawson recalled. "She had got the idea but done nothing about it. Between us we found we could raise about forty women."

.

PART II

YOU WILL GET YOURSELF KNOCKED ON THE HEAD

In Damer Dawson, Boyle and Watson had a powerful ally. Her social standing opened some heavy establishment doors, along with the fact that she had never appeared in the dock at Marlborough Street Magistrates Court, nor made fools of the Met by playing catch-me-if-you-can on the river. When she approached the Metropolitan Police Commissioner in the autumn of 1914, she was invited in for a meeting high up in his airy turret of an office overlooking the Thames.

Sir Edward Henry had settled into the Commissioner's chair in the imposing new red-brick palace known as New Scotland Yard in 1903. There were easier ways of earning a living. His predecessor, Sir Edward Bradford, had had a fairly good run, despite policing the largest city in the world at the hub of an empire that spanned a quarter of the globe. Before Bradford arrived, however, three Commissioners in a row had resigned in just four years, with one, Sir Charles Warren, driven out by the Met's hapless attempts to catch Jack the Ripper.

Trouble broke out on Henry's watch almost immediately, with persistent outbreaks of unrest on the streets. Some of it was fuelled by workers' protests, but much was played out under the banners of women's suffrage, with the demonstrations becoming steadily larger, more frequent and more violent. Here Henry's men found themselves in unknown territory, struggling to control large numbers of women using physical force. It didn't help that the protestors, unlike the officers themselves and the sorts of women they were used to arresting, were largely from the upper and middle classes—confident, articulate and well-connected. They were not only breaking the law, they were uppity with it and more than capable of causing a fuss.

The scandal that was waiting in the wings came on 18th November 1910, when the Metropolitan Police tried to break up a Pankhurst demonstration of around three hundred women in Parliament Square. The ensuing free-for-all ended with the police being accused not only of excessive violence, but also of sexual assault; some were said to have touched women's breasts and put their knees between women's legs as they grappled with them. The following day the front page of the *Daily Mirror* was splashed with a photograph of fifty-year-old Ada Wright lying crumpled on the ground, her hand pressed to her face, while a man in a top hat remonstrated with the officers looming over her. The picture would become an icon for what went down in suffrage history as Black Friday.

The testimony of a wheelchair-user, Rosa May Billinghurst, described in a government report as "a cripple lady", added to the national outrage. Billinghurst claimed that officers had thrown her out of what she called her "machine". The young Home Secretary, Winston Churchill, cleared Commissioner Henry of any blame and turned down the demands for a public inquiry, but ordered all one hundred and nineteen of those arrested that day to be released without charge.

A doctor's son, born in Shadwell in the East End of London to Irish parents, Henry had been educated at a Roman Catholic boarding school and began his career at the age of sixteen as a clerk at Lloyds of London before passing the Indian Civil Service entrance exam. When he arrived at Scotland Yard at the dawn of the 20th century, he was regarded as a moderniser. "He more than anyone else set the Metropolitan Police on the path away from the beloved Victorian institution of gentlemen amateur toffs commanding humble, loyal and rather comic policemen," according to one commentator. Henry was a natural diplomat, elegant in dress, dignified in bearing and emollient in manner, and he would fool the susceptible Margaret Damer Dawson into thinking that she had his unqualified support.

In 1914, Henry was sixty-five and about to retire, but the man lined up to succeed him was one of the most senior officers in the British army, the Adjutant-General, Sir Nevil Macready. As Macready was now needed at the War Office, Henry agreed to stay on for the duration of the war. It was probably not a prospect that he viewed with much enthusiasm, particularly since an assassination attempt two years earlier had left him in recurrent pain. One November night, on the doorstep of his Kensington flat, he had been shot by a man called Alfred Bowes whose application for a cab driver's licence had been turned down. The first two bullets missed, but the third went through Henry's stomach. At Bowes' trial, however, the Commissioner pleaded for leniency, saying that Bowes had become distraught when his efforts to earn a decent living to help his widowed mother had come to nothing.

As Nina Boyle had predicted, maintaining law and order on the home front was concentrating minds in Westminster and Whitehall by the autumn of 1914, so when Damer Dawson was escorted into the Commissioner's office, Home Secretary Reginald McKenna had already asked Henry for his thoughts on women police.

The Commissioner was not in favour of this plan. Only weeks earlier a Miss Beatrice McGregor had written to him about "the amount of temptation to immorality that haunts our evening streets", in Wimbledon of all places, and suggested that female police officers could be a wholesome check on many a young girl. Henry had brushed her off, saying: "It is improbable that any suitable and permanent sphere for her [the policewoman's] activities could be found." However, his real objection, he now told the Home Secretary, was "the strained relations between the sexes in connection with the agitation over the suffrage question".

He had a point. His officers might well resent having to work alongside women they had only days before been fighting in the streets and many of whom, like Boyle and Watson, had criminal records. And then there was the stress of having to deal day-to-day with extremists. The Prison Commissioners had had considerable difficulties with one employee, Henry said, who turned out to be a trouble-maker "in strong sympathy with the militant section of a suffrage organisation".

McKenna also asked for a legal opinion on whether the law would permit women to join the police, even if he were to sanction it. The lawyer could find nothing on the statute book to prevent it, but he thought that this was only because the idea had never crossed anyone's mind. If it were ever put to the test, it would surely be decided in the negative.

* * *

Henry received Damer Dawson with his customary grace and assured her that he was not at all averse to the idea of women police—not quite what he was telling the Home Office—but he said he was most definitely averse to Nina Boyle. She had been irritating him for some time now, not only through her suffrage protests.

During his time in India, Henry had served as inspector-general of police in Bengal, where he had devised a simple method of classifying fingerprints in order to solve crime. It would become a lifelong interest, and one of his first actions at Scotland Yard had been to set up a fingerprint bureau. Police officers across the country were told to take suspects' prints and send them to the Yard, where they were added to a fast-growing fingerprint bank. Launching his new initiative, Henry wrote a little instruction book with diagrams showing how to obtain the best results. However, not everyone shared his view that fingerprinting was an entirely innocuous practice and a boon to society.

A few months before the Damer Dawson meeting, Boyle had dashed off a batch of furious letters—discourteous was how the Home Office described them—to Commissioner Henry, Home Secretary McKenna, the governor of Holloway Prison and the Prison Commissioners, protesting about the fingerprinting of two Women's Freedom League members in Holloway. As the women were on remand and their status on the records was classified as unconvicted, Boyle said, it was quite irregular to take their prints, particularly when Henry knew perfectly well that the Women's Freedom League did not espouse militancy, unlike "a sister society that adopted sterner measures". Boyle did excoriating communications with some panache, and she singled out Henry for a particularly scathing attack, couched in the imperialist terms typical of the times. Referring to his time in India, she accused him of "encouraging the continual encroachment of oriental methods, absorbed by you in your long residence among a subject race, into the police work of this country". The exasperated Commissioner told the Home Secretary that Boyle was an intransigent in opposition to constituted authority. She would, of course, have relished the thought that she was so regarded at Scotland Yard.

Damer Dawson handled the Commissioner somewhat differently. Rather than haranguing him about human rights or police

brutality, she began as demurely as she intended to go on by showing him a sketch of the uniform she had designed and asking him
what he thought of it. Her friend from the Chelsea Refugee
Committee, the artist Annie St. John Partridge, had chosen the hat:
"It was a ladies' riding hat, slightly modified. We thought it would
stand the weather and might stand a fairly sharp knock on the head
if necessary." Perhaps Henry was reassured by St. John Partridge's
reinforced headgear or, more likely, by Damer Dawson's respectful
wide-eyed manner. While at one point he shook his head at the idea
of women pounding the streets, saying: "You will get yourself
knocked on the head and you surely don't expect me to look after
a lot of women?", she came away with his permission to go ahead,
albeit on a purely temporary wartime basis.

Henry even agreed to Boyle's involvement—Damer Dawson said
it would be unfair to drop her—on the strict condition that he himself wouldn't have to have anything to do with her and that Damer
Dawson would be in charge overall. It seemed that when the softly
spoken, elfin-faced Damer Dawson put her mind to it, she could
match Sir Edward for charm.

And so the Women Police Volunteers were born. An advertisement in *The Vote* invited capable respectable women of any age who
could spare two or three hours on two or more days a week to apply
by letter or personally to Miss Nina Boyle, between eleven and six
daily at No. 1 Robert Street, The Strand. A leading firm of West
End tailors who specialised in riding clothes was commissioned to
make the uniform: a blue serge Norfolk jacket and skirt and the
reinforced felt hat with a blue ribbon and a white armband bearing
the letters WPV. Edith Watson was photographed wearing it outside the Old Bailey, declaring herself to be the country's first policewoman. In the meantime, the applications flooded in.

TO FOLLOW A VISION

Mary Allen was outraged. She had put her considerable abilities and experience at the disposal of her country in its hour of need, only to be told to join a needlework guild. This was not what she had had in mind when she volunteered for war work. "To those of us who had been leaders and organisers in the tumultuous tide of the suffrage campaign, the ordinary channels of usefulness for the weaker sex in wartime—nursing, canteen work, sewing—made preciously little appeal," she announced.

Perhaps her reputation had gone before her and the recruitment officer had decided that the best plan for all concerned would be for Allen to spend the war at home, sewing quietly. This was never a possibility, however, for while Nina Boyle and Edith Watson were chaining themselves to courthouse doors, Mary Allen was breaking windows in Whitehall and fighting the police in the streets, shoulder to shoulder with Christabel Pankhurst. After several bouts of imprisonment, hunger strikes and force-feeding, Emmeline Pankhurst had banned her from any more militancy. The outbreak of war found her in the Women's Social and Political Union's Edinburgh office, in a desk job but plotting mayhem.

* * *

Like Boyle and Damer Dawson, Allen grew up in a comfortable, well-off, well-regulated family, although slightly lower down the social scale. She was born in 1878, her parents' third child, in a tall, narrow, grey-brick house in Roath, an affluent little community just outside Cardiff. The household consisted of Thomas and Margaret, their ten children—five boys and five girls—along with a nanny, a cook and a housemaid. Thomas was a Londoner who had joined the railway service as a fifteen-year-old junior clerk, and by the age of fifty had worked his way up to become chief superintendent of the Great Western Railway, a position that carried considerable status in that heyday of rail travel. He had also married well. Margaret was a vicar's daughter from a prominent Dumfries family, and she brought both cash and cachet to the union.

As Thomas continued his steady advance up the ranks, the family moved first to Ealing, then a small, pleasant town in Middlesex, northwest of London, and then to Bristol, each time to a bigger house with a larger domestic staff. When Queen Victoria died in 1901, Thomas accompanied the coffin on the Royal Train from Paddington to Windsor for the funeral; the following year, he was resplendent in a uniform specially designed for him in honour of the coronation of Edward VII. The family themselves travelled in style in a private carriage hitched to the back of the train, and they were welcomed with ceremony when they arrived at their holiday destinations in France and Switzerland.

Thomas was a well-built, fine-looking man with considerable presence. The stereotypical Victorian father, he held deeply conservative views and could be stern, but he appears to have been respected rather than feared by both his family and his employees. Mary particularly adored him, and he ruled his household with what she described as benevolent dictatorship, "a discipline firm but not harsh". She had encountered that same strong but just hand on the tiller in the nursery. That was how nanny had run things and it worked very well, she thought. She would never see any reason to change her mind. "It was a brave child who would dare defy nanny," she would recall. "She had been trained in the severest school as under-nurse and when the time came for her to assume the sceptre of authority she had imbibed the traditions of generations of experience."

Mary's earliest memories were of being cossetted and secure in nanny's idyllic little domain: "The nursery was our refuge … I can still see it at the end of day—the glowing fire behind the bars, the tea dishes and scattered toys cleared away, and Nanny, that benign stiffly-starched presence, the youngest nursling in her capacious lap, ready to beguile the early twilight with tales … of those other little ladies and gentlemen she had nursed before she came to us, who now shone in all the glory of naval or military grandeur, of political prominence or of sumptuous and beautiful maternity." Her memoirs are largely silent, however, about her own journey from Nanny's sanctuary to the road to Holloway Prison.

In one brief account, Mary claimed to have been a delicate child (without specifying any particular illness), educated at home by governesses and too sickly to play sport, while in another she described what sounded like a healthy, active childhood: "We invented games, made things, carpentered, jig-sawed, dug in the garden. There were outings to a pantomime at Christmas and three or four visits to the theatre." She never mentioned attending the girls' private school, Princess Helena College, when Thomas's job took the family to Ealing, but a pupil remembered her coming back to give a talk as a distinguished old girl who appeared large and important and "sort of marched about".

What led the carefully nurtured Allen to the stately Bristol Victoria Assembly Rooms, on what would turn out to be a momentous afternoon, remains a mystery. The subject of Annie Kenney's talk had never appealed to her in the slightest, but after a couple of hours of Kenney's wild firebrand rhetoric, Allen's life was changed forever. By then she was in her early thirties, a restless, energetic, purposeless woman, seemingly set on course for an easy unremarkable future and perhaps casting around for a cause before it was too late.

Allen's brothers and two of her sisters were married while she remained at home with her parents and the two youngest girls. It was unlikely that she would choose to marry for reasons that she perhaps didn't understand herself at the time. A family photo taken when she was in her late twenties shows an irregular-featured, square-jawed woman dressed conventionally in a high-necked ruffled blouse, her long, heavy brown hair parted in the middle and pulled up on each side of her face into two neat unflattering rolls.

By the time the Allens arrived in the city, Bristol, with its gracious Georgian architecture and slave-trading past, was a stronghold of the Women's Social and Political Union (WSPU). The former celebrity speakers at the Assembly Rooms, like Charles Dickens and Oscar Wilde, had been followed by Emmeline and Christabel Pankhurst and their fellow suffragette Annie Kenney. There were some lively scenes, and in 1905 the WSPU had resorted to hiring professional boxers to deal with the crowds of rowdy young men who had taken to turning up to disrupt their meetings. Back in 1831, however, there had been more trouble over the right to vote than the suffragists would ever come close to causing when a riot broke out over Parliament's failure to pass the Reform Bill, which would have widened the franchise for men. Fires raged across the city for three days, swiftly followed by hangings and transportations.

It wasn't hard to see why Allen was swept away by the flamboyant Kenney. The twenty-eight-year-old was a former mill hand from a proud, high-principled, poverty-stricken family in Oldham, Lancashire, who had started work at the age of ten, wearing a shawl and clogs, and had a finger ripped off by a spinning bobbin. It was a darkly romantic tale for someone from Allen's bland background. Fond of a melodramatic turn of phrase, in her memoirs Allen wrote that Kenney's belief in the "crusade" she preached gave her exceptional powers. Allen wasn't alone in finding herself dazzled—"the most irresistible blue-eyed beggar" was how another WSPU member described Kenney, and Christabel's sister Sylvia said of her: "She was eager in manner with a thin haggard face and restless knotted hands … Her abundant loosely dressed golden hair was the most youthful thing about her … The wild distraught expression … was found on better acquaintance to be less common than a bubbling merriment [during] which the crow's feet wrinkled quaintly." Christabel was one of several suffragettes who had a fascination and possibly also a physical relationship with Kenney.

Until then, Allen had been not merely disinterested in women's rights but positively opposed. "As a girl I had lived … in a home that was an ideal of security and peace," she would recall. "As was considered correct in my time and class, I had always dismissed with a delicate shudder the whole subject of women's suffrage." But now it was as though a throb of energy and frustration that had been festering over the years had finally erupted. She rushed home spoiling for a fight and burst into her father's study, demanding to know his views on votes for women, although she knew perfectly well what his answer would be.

"Second thoughts are not always best; had I waited perhaps I should never have dared to face him with such a request. He drew down his brows and looked more stern than I had ever seen him. 'I cannot discuss such folly', he answered. 'As for you, I wish you to think no more about it.' But I was my father's daughter. I gathered my courage together and said I would never give it up. There was a sinister silence for a moment, then: 'Either you give up this suffragette nonsense absolutely and for good or you leave this house!'." To a young woman in the early years of the 20th century, such an ultimatum was inconceivably dreadful. Allen recalled, "I was trained for no occupation. Where could I go? What could I do?"

If Thomas had assumed, as he almost certainly did, that this would be the end of the matter, he had seriously underestimated his daughter. He was no tyrant, but he was certainly not accustomed to being disobeyed, particularly under his own roof, and it was unthinkable that he should back down. Mary, however, was equally resolute. "Above the terror in my heart rose a strong determination not to be forced into an injustice. As steadily as I could I agreed to leave home. I never returned again in my father's lifetime. He was, I knew, unflinching in his decision. Yet he was extraordinarily generous. He continued and even increased my allowance." With comical irony, Thomas was now about to finance her new life as a militant suffragette. She packed her bags and set off in search of Emmeline Pankhurst and Annie Kenney in order to pledge herself to the cause. She would never see her beloved father again; he died on Christmas Day just two years later.

* * *

When Allen was summoned in to see Emmeline Pankhurst, the WSPU founder instantly joined Annie Kenney in Allen's hall of heroines: "She heard my story and became my leader. She understood why I had abandoned home, parents, friends and comfort to follow a vision." Pankhurst's quiet voice, her magnetic eyes and her deep sincerity were releasing forces in the world whose power has not yet been calculated, Allen remembered. "Some day Mrs Pankhurst will be recognised as one of the greatest figures of the 20th century." She urged Pankhurst to use her in whatever capacity she thought best.

Her new life began tamely enough, selling the WSPU newspaper on the streets of Bristol. A photograph shows her still convention-

ally dressed, with a wide-brimmed hat and a net veil crowning her
massy hair, but now a suffrage badge studs her lapel and a large
satchel of papers stencilled "Votes for Women 1d" is slung over her
shoulder. She is laughing into the camera, looking younger than her
years and supremely happy. Her first outing as a militant was in a
party of women handpicked by Pankhurst to try to force their way
through a police line into the Houses of Parliament. They escaped
injury in the struggle, but were held overnight in the cells and
appeared the following morning at Bow Street where the magistrate
polished his glasses and made a few witty remarks, Allen said, before
committing them to a month in Holloway in the second division,
which meant they were to be treated as common criminals rather
than as gentlewomen.

Mary Allen left no record of her transportation to jail, but when
Watson and Boyle were sent to Holloway, they travelled in a win-
dowless van, packed onto wooden seats in small compartments,
while the matron, the jailor and an overspill of prisoners were
squashed into the gangway. As the vehicle swerved and swayed,
they were left bruised and nauseated from the vibration. One girl
who was accused of stealing a work basket was faint with fear and
cried for water, but there was none to be had.

Holloway had been designed with terror in mind, a grim mid-
Victorian monument to the rule of law and the fearful consequences
of flouting it. It served its purpose well enough. When women
arrived at the ten miserable acres of wasteland on what were then
the fringes of north London, they were confronted by a faux medi-
eval fortress, complete with battlements and arrow-slits. From the
entrance gate that led up to the massive oak door, stone griffins with
keys clasped in their claws glared balefully down. It was enough to
put anyone in her place. Life within the walls came as something of
a shock to Allen, who declared in her memoirs with an air of origi-
nality that ordinary law-abiding people had no idea just what an
ordeal prison was.

She slept on a wooden plank with a pillow of coarse straw.
Wake-up was at five o'clock and meals consisted of rough brown
bread, water and a tasteless pale broth with lumps of what appeared
to be horse meat swilling around in it. She was particularly upset to
find herself without a toothbrush, a hairbrush or a mirror, but she

found a way of coping with her heavy mane. "Our duties included cleaning our cells. I soon realised that if I polished my dustpan till it shone and stood it on the stool, I could kneel down and get reflection enough to enable me to plait my hair and set my unbecoming prison cap at its least unbecoming angle." Watson, who unlike Allen, having grown up in the slums of Poplar, was familiar with disgusting conditions, described the place as vile; there were even bloodstains on the walls of Boyle's cell, she recorded in her memoirs. The message was clear: "You were being punished severely for wrongdoing. You were under no delusion."

Even so, Allen was undeterred. When her month in Holloway was up, she felt eager for her next mission. It proved a tougher call. "It was one thing to cause a minor riot with two score of supporters at one's back and quite another to act alone. Three times I rode round London on a horse-bus before I could force my feet to descend when passing Downing Street. I gripped my umbrella in my shaking hands and walked up to the door of the Home Office. The street was silent and deserted. Yet a moment after the crash and tinkle of falling glass had sounded it seemed to me that all London had turned out and gathered round, staring at me." She was sent back to Holloway for another month, and it was then that the WSPU came up with the idea that was to help define them. They would go on hunger strike in order to force the authorities to treat them as political prisoners. "They wouldn't dare kill us, surely?" Allen reasoned.

* * *

When she first began refusing food and water the warders laughed. Two days later they had stopped laughing and were starting to get twitchy. They made some tea and held it under her nose. "It almost drove me mad. My tongue was like leather with thirst and the hot fragrant smell started the saliva running at the back of my throat. I just shook my head and shut my eyes." On day four, they were back, this time with slices of chicken breast in a savoury-smelling gravy. Again though, she held firm. The following day, wasted and light-headed, she was released.

In Holloway some five years later, Boyle went down with an attack of malaria, and in an attempt to get some quinine Watson began shouting and banging her shoe on the bars. The other prisoners joined in, and through the clamour, Watson could just make out the brave, feeble, faltering cries of the hunger strikers.

When Allen was sent to prison for a third time in eight months—this time for breaking windows at the Bristol Liberal Club during a visit by Winston Churchill—she was put to work sewing men's shirts, and entertained herself by embroidering 'Votes for Women' on the tails. When she went on hunger strike this time, however, the authorities were ready with a plan. She was taken to the hospital wing and held down by six wardresses while doctors forced a pint and a half (.85 litres) of milk and raw eggs up her nose and down into her stomach. This was painful enough, but it would have been so much worse if, like many women, she had tried to resist. The following morning the medical officer William Cotton reported: "Rather restless night. Taking no food. Fed by oesophageal tube one and a quarter pints milk. Was rather sick and brought most of it up and a great deal of bile."

"Of course I was violently sick, getting rid of all the nourishment which had been so brutally shovelled into me," Allen said. "Finally, they made me so very ill, my digestion being permanently affected." Emmeline Pankhurst underwent the same ordeal several times and described more of the gory details: "My gums, when they prised them open, were always sore and bleeding, with bits of loose and jagged flesh … sometimes the tube was coughed up two or three times before they finally got it down. Sometimes, but not usually as I was generally too much agitated by then, I felt the tube go right down into the stomach; a sickening, terrifying sensation."

In his next medical report, Cotton was writing on Allen's notes: "Some sickness last night. Fed by oesophageal tube ¾ pint peptonised [fortified] milk and two teaspoonfuls of Valentine's [meat] extract. This patient may be thinner than when she came in [to the hospital wing from her prison cell] but she looks better." She was released the following day along with another hunger striker called Vera Wentworth. A reporter thought Wentworth seemed none the worse for her ordeal "but Miss Allen was far from well".

Annie Kenney refused food for eight days before she was released and a week later made a typically colourful appearance at a meeting at Knightsbridge Town Hall, arriving by horse-drawn ambulance on a stretcher which the bearers then placed on the platform across two chairs like a coffin on a bier. "She raised her right hand and fluttered a handkerchief and [then], covered with blankets, lay motionless," *The Times* reported. Miss Kenney, it was announced, was in a very weak state, and had asked that there should be no cheering.

After over thirty years of quiet compliance with Thomas and Margaret, Allen was intoxicated to find herself in the vanguard of this daring, dangerous movement alongside a line-up of extraordinary women. It came as a huge shock then when, at the outbreak of war, Pankhurst announced that the fight for suffrage was to be put on hold, and ordered her members to redirect their energies into working for the Empire and for victory. Christabel even stood on street corners handing out white feathers, the mark of the coward, to men of fighting age who were not in uniform.

Allen, now banned from militancy because of her health and running the WSPU office in Edinburgh, described the outbreak of war as a thunderclap, but the order to stand down astounded her even more and ruined her game plan. "I was—shall I admit it?—delightedly planning some further burnings of empty homes in which we had been successful of late." With the government's back to the wall, this was surely the time to step up the pressure rather than retreat, she reasoned. For her, disobeying an order was unthinkable, "But I can't pretend that I liked it." Frustrated and desperate for another cause, she was on a bus when she overheard two women laughing about the Women Police Volunteers; women in uniform patrolling the streets, what a ridiculous notion. It was all that Allen needed. Once again, she packed her bags and made for London, this time to join the WPV.

She found herself in a little group that was convening at No. 10 Cheyne Row in that fitful rainy late summer of 1914. Militant feminism meets radical Bohemia. Annie St John Partridge and Dora Meeson Coates were neighbours of Damer Dawson and members of the Artists' Suffrage League. The fifty-nine-year-old St John Partridge, a successful painter of flowers and country scenes, was on Damer Dawson's refugee committee and had designed the WPV's reinforced hat. Meeson Coates, forty-four, was an Australian married to a fellow artist, George Coates. The couple had met as students in Paris when Monet and Renoir were still painting. And then there were the activists. Olive Walton, the youngest at twenty-eight, was a former organiser in the Women's Social and Political Union like Allen, and had also been to prison, in her case for breaking the windows of the palatial new department stores on Oxford Street. (Selfridges, the grandest of them all, was a favourite target until Harry Selfridge refused to press charges, after which his huge glass showcase was spared.) Fifty-year-old Ellen Harburn, a school manager, had just changed her name from Haarbliecher because of the rampant anti-German feeling in Britain at the time. She had been close to Emmeline and Christabel Pankhurst in the early days, but had left them to join the Women's Freedom League. Another recruit was Mary Allen's older sister Margaret, now Mrs Hampton, known to everyone as Dolly.

Isobel Goldingham, aged forty, had read about the WPV in *The Vote* and, like Mary Allen, she found policing by far the most appealing of the war work on offer, but she was deterred by the involvement of Nina Boyle and the Women's Freedom League. Despite being a former Pankhurst activist, Goldingham believed that a women's police service should be independent, not hitched to a political cause, even one in which she believed so passionately. She was persuaded to change her mind, however, when Allen assured her that Boyle was not in charge and promised that the WPV would, in time, shake off any political connections. It would happen sooner than she thought.

Goldingham took an instant liking to Damer Dawson, as many people did, and decided that she would help her in any way that she could. For the impressionable Allen, however, meeting Damer Dawson went much further. Prosaic little Damer Dawson was a very different character from the fiery Kenney or the elegant Pankhurst, but Allen was once again entranced. "The meeting between Margaret Damer Dawson and myself struck an immediate spark and began a period of close association and intimate friendship," she said. Her description of Damer Dawson, in a memoir written eleven years after their first meeting, was fulsome and unquestioning, with a glint of the fanaticism that was later to claim her. Damer Dawson, said Allen, was of a fastidious, even scholarly turn of mind; but danger steeled her. "With her keen intelligence, her untiring energy, her lively wit, she made an instant impression upon those who came into personal contact with her." Others were also struck by Damer Dawson's fastidiousness and her tireless energy, but not everyone appeared to have noticed a lively wit.

Mary Allen would never again worry about the tilt of her hat or peer into a mirror trying to manage her hair. Soon after the founding of the WPV, she and Damer Dawson would have their hair cropped like military men and were putting their efforts into looking authoritative rather than becoming. In photographs at least, a laughing, carefree young Mary Allen was never seen again.

8

INFLUENCING AND, IF NEED BE, RESTRAINING

Sir Edward Henry's worst fears were realised. The applications coming in to Nina Boyle were virtually all from suffragettes, many of them militant Pankhurst supporters. In Mary Allen's view, the Commissioner had only himself to blame: it was women's experiences at the hands of his men that was prompting them to sign up, she wrote. Being forced into close, sometimes painful, touch with police officers had proved something of an epiphany, showing the often well-to-do suffragettes "how very unpleasant it is for an alleged woman culprit to be handled by men". Bessie Moncrieff could have told her that.

So there was joy in the morning, at both Scotland Yard and the Home Office, when in August 1914 a more acceptable face of womanhood came up with a separate plan of her own. Louise Creighton was the sixty-five-year-old widow of the former Bishop of London, and a grande dame of the moral purity movement.

It seemed that no petition, no letter to *The Times* from a roll call of the righteous, no deputation to Downing Street or the Home Office on the subject of sexual continence or alcohol, was complete without the gracious hand of Louise Creighton. As soon as war was declared in August 1914, she led the way in urging women to ensure that they were worthy of the cause for which the men were fighting: "They must be sober, and good and true, so that their men, returning, should find the homes and the homeland not only as good but, if anything, better than they left them."

Her husband's successor as Bishop of London, Arthur Foley Winnington-Ingram, reiterated the message, telling women it was their duty to send out the young men in the right spirit, free from

53

moral stain; he implored them to use all efforts to promote prayer, purity and temperance among young men in training. Like many moral purists, the bishop, who named his two lifelong foes as drink and lust, thought that Britain had gone soft. This was not the nation that had fought off the Armada and built the Empire, but this war would put people back on the right track. He called it a holy war for purity.

Since her husband's death in 1901, Louise Creighton had been living in a grace-and-favour apartment in Hampton Court Palace, courtesy of the Crown. Suite No. 6, on a lush green stretch of the river, had been designed in 1700 for the Duke of Albemarle. After she had assured herself that the place was large enough to accommodate her children, her staff and her books, Creighton was delighted to accept the royal offer and she moved in with four adult daughters, a cook, a housemaid, a parlourmaid and "a girl for the morning" to clean the boots and knives. "The drawing room and dining room are beautiful large rooms with dados and large windows, with splendid oak shutters opening onto the great terrace," Creighton reported. "From the dining room opens my sitting room … and it and my bedroom and the neighbouring large bedroom are all beautifully panelled."

It was all very pleasing and very suitable, as were Creighton's friends; Winnington-Ingram was one of her closest allies. A man of charisma and humour—his schoolboy nickname Chuckles followed him into adult life—he first came to the attention of the Church hierarchy through his success in running a mission house in the slums of Bethnal Green, where his easy manner had gone down well with the East Enders. Louise had noticed him and recommended him to her husband when the post of Bishop of Stepney became vacant. William Wand, a future Bishop of London himself, recalled how undergraduates would pack Oxford's St Mary's Church in the years before the war to hear Winnington-Ingram preach. They were entranced, Wand said, by the handsome, glamorous Bishop of London with his cockney accent, ready eloquence and exuberant friendliness. As Winnington-Ingram had been born and brought up in Worcestershire, educated at one of the most prestigious and expensive private schools in the country, and only arrived in Whitechapel when he was twenty-seven, he presumably had picked

Fig. 1: Suffragette Nina Boyle, editor-in-chief of *The Vote*, at her office. The Women's Freedom League newspaper highlighted many injustices faced by women in their interactions with law and order. Early 1910s.

Fig. 2: Nina Boyle (right) and her star reporter Edith Watson in their Women Police Volunteers uniforms, 1914 or 1915.

Fig. 3: A Women's Social and Political Union meeting, 1900s. Founder Emmeline Pankhurst is third from right. On her left is Charlotte Despard, doyenne of suffragism, who would break away with others to form the Women's Freedom League in 1907.

Fig. 4: Suffragettes in 1909 at their usual haunt for romantic entanglements and recovery from prison stints, the Blathwayts' house (daughter Mary standing). Mary Allen, an early Women Police Volunteer, joined the suffrage movement after being dazzled by Annie Kenney (centre) at a lecture.

Roll of Honour

Suffragette Prisoners

1905 - 1914

A
Abbey, Alfred
Abrahams, Dorothy
Adams, Eleanor
Adamson, Christine
Adamson, Kate
Ainsworth, Annie
Ainsworth, Laura
Aitken, Violet
Albert, Sophie
Aldis, Violet Mary
Alderman, Grace
Aldham, Mary Ann
Alexander, Isabelle
Allan, Janie
Allen, Doreen
Allen, Greta
Allen, Helen
Allen, Margaret
Allen, Mary
Andrews, Constance
Andrews, Edith Mary
Ansell, Gertrude Mary
Archdale, Helen
Archibald, Louise
Armitage, Lilian
Armstrong, Evelyn
Armstrong, Kathleen
Armstrong, Laura
Armstrong, Nora
Arnes, Helen
Arscott, Jessie
Arthur, Janet

Arton, Evelyn
Asquith, Lily
Atheling, Lelegarde
Atkinson, Helen
Atkinson, Jane
Atkinson, Robert
Auld, Constance
Auld, Winifred
Aves, Miss
Aylmer, Audrey
Ayrton, Barbara

B
Bacon, N.
Baines, Jennie
Baker, Annie
Baker, Frances
Baker, Lizzie
Baldock, Ethel
Baldock, Minnie
Bales, Agnes
Ball, Edith Warwick
Ball, Ethel
Ball, Gennie
Ball, Lilian
Ball, William

Fig. 5: A 'Roll of Honour' listing all suffragettes jailed for their activism in 1905–14—including Mary Allen, ordered by Mrs Pankhurst to retire from militancy after hunger strikes permanently damaged her health.

Fig. 6: Former social campaigner Margaret Damer Dawson (left), head of the Women Police Volunteers, with her subcommandant and probable lover Mary Allen.

Fig. 7: Louise Creighton—writer, researcher, 'moral purity' reformer, and resident of Hampton Court Palace. Her National Union of Women Workers would form rival police patrols.

Fig. 8: Arthur Winnington-Ingram, who succeeded Creighton's late husband as Bishop of London and remained her confidant. Here in his army chaplain uniform, Winnington-Ingram came out in support of votes for women at the start of the war.

up his cockney accent from his flock. Creighton had a great affection for him, and said that he was always ready to do anything for her.

The bishop would have a controversial war, however, due to his conviction that his country could do no wrong and that the British Empire was nothing but a wholly civilising influence across the world, from Bengal to Berlin. He did not start out quite so strident; a week into the conflict, in a sermon in St Paul's Cathedral, he said that the nation had a bitter cup before it but they must drink it calmly and, notably, with perfect charity. The German schoolboy choir who three weeks earlier had sung in English in his garden were the same boys now as then, and were no more responsible for the war than the congregation sitting before him now in the cathedral. A few months later, however, the bishop admitted that he was struggling to follow the commandment "Love your enemies" when it came to the Germans. Then in Westminster Abbey the following year, in an astounding volte-face, he described the killing of Germans as a great crusade, "… to kill them, not for the sake of killing, but to save the world; to kill the good as well as the bad, to kill the young as well as the old … and to kill them lest the civilisation of the world itself be killed."

Prime Minister Herbert Asquith would accuse him of preaching jingoism of the shallowest kind, but his views were shared by millions in Britain and far beyond, who regarded them as righteous and patriotic. The declaration of war had found the bishop on the south coast, in a military camp as the chaplain of the London Rifle Brigade, sleeping under canvas in a little bell tent, marching with the rank and file and joining in the fun in the evenings. He was good at that. When the brother of the Women's Freedom League co-founder and Sinn Fein supporter Lottie Despard, Field Marshall Sir John French, invited Winnington-Ingram to visit the Brigade in France, the commander's note read: "Dear Bishop, five minutes of you cheers me up. Come out for ten days."

The bishop was just one of Louise Creighton's friends in high places, but she was acceptable to the establishment as much for the people she didn't know as for those that she did. Like Damer Dawson, she not only had no links with the Pankhursts but, to Commissioner Henry's particular satisfaction, she had had no dealings with Nina Boyle either. Her credentials far outdid Damer

Dawson's on this score: she had once played a leading role in the women's anti-suffrage movement. Creighton was also invited in for a meeting, but unlike Damer Dawson, she met not only with Henry at Scotland Yard but also went to the Home Office in order to give a face-to-face briefing to the Home Secretary himself.

* * *

A fiercely intelligent, intellectual woman, Creighton was born Louise von Glehn, and grew up in a lively cosmopolitan household in Sydenham on the edge of south-east London. Peak Hill Lodge was a ramblingly comfortable jumble of rooms set in seven acres of meadows and woodland. Festooned with ivy, with chimneys towering from its pitched roof, its fairy tale charm set the pattern for Louise's love of spacious, characterful homes. She was the tenth of the twelve children born to Scottish-German businessman Robert von Glehn and Agnes Duncan, a Scotswoman who had been brought up in some luxury by her stepfather, Robert's business partner. Robert was a charming, attractive man and a star of the local social scene but, while he was good-natured and kind to his children, they found him a remote figure. "I don't think we were ever quite at ease with him," Creighton would recall in her autobiography.

She had a set-piece Victorian childhood, with tea in the nursery, lessons in the schoolroom, picnics in summer meadows and skating on winter ponds. The nursery governess, Miss Brunn, like Mary Allen's nanny, was a dominant figure in young Louise's life but Creighton's autobiography conversely betrays no trace of sentiment or romanticism towards the woman whom, she admitted, had given the best years of her life to the family. "I don't think that we either liked her or disliked her," Creighton said. "We accepted her; she was perfectly just and straight and aroused no resentment."

Peak Hill Lodge provided a stimulating environment for a lively child, with musicians, artists and writers constantly dropping in, but Creighton, like her mother and sisters, received no formal education, an omission that she passionately resented. Lottie Despard, who was from the same generation, had grown up with a bitter anger over missed opportunities: "There were moments in my hot youth when I would rail against Heaven for having made me a woman. What might I not have been; what might I not have done had I the freedom and intellectual advantages so largely accorded to men?" Creighton fared better than Despard, however. Home-schooled in French, German, literature and music according to a strict daily timetable, she went on to attend the new Crystal Palace enrichment classes for young women, and then sat the first London University General Examination for Women. Its syllabus included the subjects normally taught only to boys, such as Chemistry and Greek. "I crammed it all up," she said. "The examination ... lasted several days. Eight young women went in for it and, of these, six, of which I was one, passed with honours." Even so, they were still barred from being awarded degrees.

A portrait painted when Creighton was twenty-seven depicts her sweet-faced, wide-eyed and girlish, staring directly and slightly wistfully out at the world. But the portrait which hangs in the guard room at Lambeth Palace, of Creighton in her late sixties, shows an imposing woman in part profile, with a fine bone structure and a stern expression.

* * *

Creighton promised that her women patrols would operate discreetly, staying in the background, keeping a quiet eye on girls and steering them away from temptation. They would wear no uniforms, just plain dark coats with armbands, and they would operate through her charity, the National Union of Women Workers, whose patroness was Her Majesty the Queen. Even more importantly for the Home Secretary and the Commissioner, Creighton's patrols were not to be seen as policewomen.

The National Union of Women Workers (NUWW) offered something akin to social services before the modern professional social worker existed. From a network of branches across the country, volunteers dispensed advice and practical support on matters such as child welfare, healthy living and managing money to working women struggling to manage their homes and their families. The service was much needed, even if it did come with the inevitable smack of moral guidance and middle-class control. Creighton had played a leading role in its founding in 1885, at a meeting of the

Ladies' Association for the Care of Friendless Girls, where the delegates decided to set up a new body, bringing together the many women's groups working in the same field. Creighton knew none of the participants but felt "great joy and surprise to find amongst this collection of rather ordinary looking middle-aged women so much intelligence, capacity and zeal".

As the day went on and they thrashed out a constitution, Creighton discovered to her surprise that she had a latent talent for planning and administration. Her contribution was such that she was offered the role of president on the spot. Her friend, the socialist economist Beatrice Webb, was another early member, but she quickly became irritated with the ordinary-looking middle-aged women. "Louise Creighton has distinctly a statesmanlike mind … and the women who now control policy are a good sort: large minded and pleasant mannered," Webb wrote. "The screeching sisterhood [the suffragettes] are trying to invade them but Louise's battalions of hardworking, religious and somewhat stupid women will, I think, resist the attack." Resist it they did. Webb finally lost patience with them, the last straw being their insistence on opening their meetings with prayers.

Creighton's reputation for brusqueness and arrogance did not bode well for her meeting with the Home Secretary. The spare, ascetic, meticulous Reginald McKenna had his own line in social awkwardness. Under the heading "McKenna, Reginald", the index to his biography includes the entries: "Dislike of big social events: p40, 157, 180; Dislike of small social events: p94, 253, 309; Dislike of any social events: p272". Before he entered politics, McKenna had been a successful banker and was now an extremely wealthy man. His four-storey neo-Georgian townhouse in Smith Square had been designed for him by Sir Edwin Lutyens, and it was here that his young wife Pamela, who had all of the dash and animation so lacking in her husband, would entertain the dinner party guests from their political circle.

Despite any possible awkwardness, however, Creighton's meeting went well and as soon as his visitor had left, McKenna directed his Permanent Under-Secretary Sir Edward Troup to write to the country's chief constables. The police chiefs were told that the NUWW was an organisation such as to command confidence, and the Secretary of State hoped that they would instruct their officers to do all in their power to assist the patrols. Enclosed was one of the identity cards that the Commissioner of the Metropolitan Police was issuing to them, and Mr McKenna would be glad if the constabulary chiefs would follow Sir Edward Henry's example.

If Troup had set out to irritate chief constables across the nation, he appeared to have achieved his objective. He was addressing a breed of men who were ferocious in defending their territory, particularly from any suggestion of superiority on the part of the Commissioner, and several of their replies dripped with offence taken. The Chief Constable of Bradford clambered up onto his high horse: "Although I have already expressed my disapproval of the employment of women in such a capacity, as I am of the opinion that they run great danger of being insulted by indecent loafers, if not outraged, at the same time I shall be glad to acquiesce in the wishes of His Majesty's Secretary of State." The chief constable of Cheshire was only prepared to recognise a member of the NUWW if a reputable person from the county could vouch for her, while Nottinghamshire's chief said he had no large military training camps in his area and there had been no bad behaviour by women and girls around the small ones. If anything changed, he would do as McKenna suggested, but not before.

Typically, Creighton announced her initiative in a letter to *The Times*, co-signed by the prison reformer Adeline, Duchess of Bedford, and Lady Alice Chichester of the Mothers' Union. Creighton was, she said, recruiting women of common sense and experience, who would "render such quiet service as in influencing and, if need be, restraining, the women and girls who congregate in the neighbourhood of the camps now scattered across the country."

The outbreak of war would bring forward quite a few people with a predilection for restraining women in one way or another.

I COULD EASILY GET A MAN DOWN
AND SIT ON HIM

As Louise Creighton was rallying the troops in *The Times*, Nina Boyle was in the Women's Freedom League office on Robert Street sifting happily through the pile of applications, adding capable, respectable names to the little clique of artists and militants at Cheyne Row. She also put an appeal in *The Vote* for donations to buy uniforms for women whom the war had tipped into hardship.

Commissioner Henry issued both groups with identity cards, and recommended some textbooks. *The Police Code* claimed to cover all of the offences that are punishable by law, from card-sharping to murder. Written by Howard Vincent, the first head of the Criminal Investigation Department, soon after he took up his post in 1878, it was described as "a little book [that] can be fitted into any ordinary pocket as easily as its contents can be fitted into any fairly intelligent head". *The Metropolitan Police Guide*, on the other hand, was a muscular volume, hefty with authority, that "placed in the hands of the Metropolitan Police a compilation of those statutes to which they have constantly to refer". And so it did, all 1,734 pages of it, starting with "A" for Abduction, taking in Hay and Straw, Lotteries, Poison and Sweeps along the way, and ending with "W" for Women. A third essential read, entitled simply *The Instruction Book*, not only covered the law but included guidance on the character and behaviour expected of an officer in the Metropolitan Police, including the stricture to live a sober life.

The Commissioner also arranged training on how to wear a uniform, walk a beat and perform first aid, along with lectures on court procedure and the law as it related to women and children. And then there was Japanese wrestling.

Ju-jitsu had arrived in Britain in the 1890s and immediately seized the nation's imagination. It was seen as particularly suitable for women, being both a graceful sport and an ideal form of self-defence, relying as it did on balance and speed rather than strength. Soon Ju-jitsu parties were all the rage among fashionable upper-class women. Invitation cards went out with the word "wrestling" embossed in elegant script, wrestling mats were thrown down on smart salon floors, and celebrity instructors presided over the fun. Among the first to take it up was the adventurous Mary, Duchess of Bedford (not Louise Creighton's supporter but her sister-in-law, Mary Du Caurroy Russell)—aviator, ornithologist, radiographer and hospital founder; one of a breed of aristocratic dare-devil ladies with a hefty dose of noblesse oblige—was among the first to take it up. By 1906, *Vanity Fair* magazine was announcing that the singer and tennis ace Toupie Lowther was having lessons, and that the Baroness de Meyer also intended to take instruction "in the gentle art of twisting an adversary's neck with a dexterous turn of the wrist".

Behind the glitz, though, lay the acknowledgement that what were known as sheltered women—those from the middle- and upper-classes—were steadily gaining the freedom and confidence to venture out unaccompanied. Working-class women, on the other hand, had of course never had a choice but to take their chances out alone on the blackest of streets. Marie Studholme, one of the celebrated Gaiety Girls from the West End's Gaiety musical theatre, told women that with Ju-jitsu at their command, any hooligan demanding money was easy prey. If he struck out with his right hand, "grip his wrist with your right hand and then bring the left arm across his biceps. His forearm would then be resting against your elbow joint and on applying the slightest downward pressure his arm can be broken with the greatest ease". She added: "Hitherto it seems to have been a man's privilege to act as a defender of women. But why should this be so?"

The point was not lost on the suffragists. The Women's Freedom League had first taken up Ju-jitsu in order to deal with the men who turned up at their meetings in order to shout them down. In 1909, the League announced that it had trained twenty-five members who had, to quote their instructress, "already punished rude men". But as the suffrage struggle hotted up, Ju-jitsu proved very useful for another purpose.

At the Japanese School of Self-Defence in Soho's Golden Square, the 4ft 10in Edith Garrud had trained the Pankhurst bodyguards, an all-woman protection squad known as the Amazons. *The Sketch* published a series of photographs showing the diminutive Garrud, wearing a full-length coat and a superbly unsuitable hat, bringing down a thirteen-stone constable in under ten seconds. The headline ran: "If You Want to Earn Some Time Throw a Policeman". The Amazons had been set up in the wake of 1910's Black Friday clashes, but they stepped up their action in 1913 with the introduction of Home Secretary McKenna's Prisoners' Temporary Discharge for Ill-Health Act, or Cat and Mouse Act as it was universally known.

When Mary Allen embarked on her first hunger strike in Holloway Prison, the Home Office, the prison service and the Women's Social and Political Union itself were in unknown territory. When Allen had comforted herself with the thought that, whatever happened, "They wouldn't dare kill us, surely?" she had been right; the first hunger strikers were routinely released when they were became seriously malnourished. Allen had not foreseen the Home Secretary's next move, however, but much to McKenna's frustration, force-feeding was not an option for all prisoners.

Holloway's governor thought Ella Stevenson looked much older than her fifty-four years. She was suffering from thickened arteries, a high pulse and rotting teeth, one of which crumbled when she tried to bite the doctor as he was ramming the feeding tube down her throat. Now with the medical officer warning against any repeat performances, McKenna had little choice but to let her go. "If she is allowed to starve herself to death, it will give the suffragettes the martyr they want and probably lead to an outbreak of public feeling against the government," a Home Office official predicted. "The only course, in spite of the outcry which will follow, is to release her".

Just weeks after they freed Stevenson, the Cat and Mouse Act received Royal Assent. Described by *The Times* as a modest little Bill, it still allowed a prisoner to be released early on health grounds, but now there was a catch. As soon as she had recovered, the woman was to be re-arrested and sent back to prison, where the whole

ghastly cycle of starvation and—if sanctioned by the medical officer—force-feeding would begin again. It was the Amazons' job to
enable these women to stay on the run. Just in case something more
than a perfectly executed body drop was required, and as befitting
the organisation that Nina Boyle had described as "one which adopts
sterner measures", Ju-jitsu was not the Amazons' only weapon.
They also carried clubs beneath their skirts.

When Emmeline Pankhurst and Annie Kenney turned up at a
meeting at the London Pavilion one afternoon in the summer of
1913, after their medical furlough had expired, Scotland Yard
received word that their two most high-profile "mice" were on the
loose. By the time the pair came to leave, detectives were guarding
the entrances and exits, and two cabs waited outside the stage door
to take them to Holloway. When the officers moved in to make the
arrests, however, they were met by a wall of women, and within
seconds a heaving bundle of policemen and militants was rolling
across the pavement and into the Piccadilly gutters, clubs and
umbrellas flailing. Kenney was finally dragged into a cab, leaving her
defenders bruised and breathless, coats torn, hats crushed, hair
hanging loose down their backs. Pankhurst, however, assuming her
familiar stance of dignified martyr, strolled quietly out of the hall
and, skirting the melee, hailed a taxi back to her flat.

That fight was not a scenario to trouble Allen and her friends in
the slightest, but neither Damer Dawson nor Boyle, let alone Henry
of course, would have sanctioned women with weapons. For the
Women Police Volunteers, then, Ju-jitsu was the perfect answer.
Garrud's Japanese School of Self-Defence gave them a fifty per cent
discount: twelve sessions for two shillings and sixpence. One WPV
member was to boast to an MP:

"I could easily get a man down and sit on him."

"If nobody came along for a considerable time you might have to
sit there a long time?"

"Yes, I think one could do so and still keep him in agony."

Another described how she had dealt with a nuisance on the
streets of Edinburgh: "A man who was very drunk was molesting a
woman. I could not imagine why she did not get rid of him.
However, in the end he got his arm round her and she threw him
off. I said: 'Is that your husband?' She said: 'No.' I said: 'You are

behaving rather foolishly in not trying to get away.' She said: 'I have got a very bad heart and I cannot walk fast.' So we Ju-jitsu-ed him and got him to a constable." The man was arrested and convicted of being drunk and disorderly.

* * *

Like Louise Creighton, the Bishop of London had been mulling over the question of women's suffrage for a while, and in 1914 he too came out in favour, describing himself as a late convert to a limited franchise. His conversion, however, was fired not so much by support for women's rights but by a cause close to both Creighton's and Damer Dawson's hearts: the fight against sexual exploitation and trafficking. After years of calling unsuccessfully for more legal protection for women, the bishop decided that once armed with the power of the vote, women would be able to force the politicians into doing what he had failed to do despite his standing, his oratory and his seat in the House of Lords. Like Creighton, however, Winnington-Ingram saw militancy as irresponsible and counter-productive, calling it the Devil's work and describing the planting of a bomb in Westminster Abbey in June 1914, which damaged the Coronation Chair, as madness and insolence.

By now, the bishop was doing sturdy work as a recruitment officer. When many of the men in the London Rifle Brigade, who were reserves rather than full-time soldiers, failed to volunteer for overseas service, their commanding officer asked him to put a little ginger into a sermon. Winnington-Ingram obliged, delivering a homily of such rousing oratory that by nightfall the whole brigade had signed up, as did all the men he addressed the following day when he preached from the back of a covered wagon. The men of Agincourt, Crécy, Alma and Waterloo were with them, he assured them, and Christian love should be manifested through obedience. In all, ten thousand men responded to the call. Lord Kitchener thanked him, and *The Sketch* published a photo of him in field-kit with the headline "Leader of the Church Militant, The Bishop of London in War Paint."

When the bishop then sailed into the force-feeding furore, however, he managed to infuriate both Mrs Pankhurst and the Home

Secretary at the same time. The trouble began when the Women's Social and Political Union (WSPU) started targeting senior clerics, trying to persuade them to speak out against force feeding, which they said was being used as torture rather out of concern for women's welfare. Typically, Annie Kenney went straight to the top, stalking the Archbishop of Canterbury and camping out in the grounds of Lambeth Palace, but the Union also had a job for Winnington-Ingram. They asked him to look into the stories coming out of Holloway of "heart-breaking shrieks of pain, uncontrollable, terrible pain" followed by loud moans emanating from the cell of Rachel Peace.

The thirty-two-year-old Peace was a seamstress from south-east London who was on the Home Office's dangerous suffragettes list. When McKenna gave permission for the bishop to visit her, Winnington-Ingram duly arrived at the prison gates one morning after deliberately giving the governor only half an hour's notice in a quick phone call from Fulham Palace. He found the prisoner lying on a comfortable bed, fully dressed, in a well-warmed cell, he said, "much larger than those I have been accustomed to seeing in the prisons I have visited". He conceded that her face was a little pale, but she wasn't emaciated and showed no signs of distress. She complained of indigestion but denied ever shrieking. "Though everyone must deplore the necessity of imprisoning any such poor woman or of forcibly feeding anyone at all … the fears which you expressed … are not borne out," the bishop told the WSPU.

They were not done with him yet, however, and asked him to visit two other prisoners. Again he presented himself at the gates, this time without any warning phone call flourishing another permit from McKenna. Kitty Marion, like Peace, was warm and comfortable, he reported. She looked pale but not ill and she told him she was very well, considering. He then went to see Phyllis Brady. Brady and the woman arrested with her would be the first to be released under the Cat and Mouse Act. Brady's face, like Peace's, was pale but not gaunt, the bishop said, and she told him that the wardresses had been exceedingly kind to her.

The bishop now informed the WSPU that he considered his mission done: "I have paid two surprise visits to the prison and have described as fairly as I could the conditions of your three friends, and I am convinced that I saw things exactly as they are." Whatever the morality of force feeding, he said, the officials carrying it out were doing so in the kindest possible spirit. Brady later claimed that she had been drugged when he spoke to her and a WSPU doctor who examined her on her release said she appeared to have ingested large doses of the sedative bromide. When the WSPU's Norah Dacre Fox read his letter out at a meeting in Knightsbridge, it was received with hoots of laughter and shouts of "What a farce". Winnington-Ingram was clearly in league with the Home Office, Dacre Fox said. She also accused him of breaking his promise to see force feeding for himself. In fact, his chaplain had phoned the Home Office to ask if his permit allowed it, and was told that it did not.

The bishop had been naïve and ready to believe the best of the authorities, but he had been acting in good faith, for he had privately told the Home Secretary that force feeding had to stop; it was incompatible with a Christian civilisation. An irritated McKenna replied: "I fail to understand what course you recommend instead of forcible feeding. Do you wish that the women who burned Lady Carlisle's house, the hotel at Felixstowe and other buildings, who attempted to destroy pictures in the National Gallery and the Academy, and who carried explosives to Nottingham on the occasion of the King's visit should be released with the practical certainty that they will burn more houses, destroy more pictures and use more explosives? Or do you agree with those who think they should be allowed to die in prison?" The bishop countered: "Since you are good enough to ask my advice I can only repeat that forcible feeding is in my opinion objectionable in itself and also that it very largely fails in its object." McKenna snapped back: "I did not intend to put you to the trouble of giving me advice but merely wanted to understand your position."

* * *

Mary Allen thought that the militants were particularly suited to police work because they were used to operating under strict discipline. She was deeply unimpressed with Creighton's National Union of Women Workers, seeing them as a bunch of amateurs, strolling about with their armbands as and when they had a gap in their social diaries, in search of girls in need of an improving chat. The Women Police Volunteers (WPV), on the other hand, "were conceived of as a trained body of professional women who were to give their whole time to their job, to be ready to answer a call day or night or to go to any part of the UK". It was a very different vision from that of Boyle and Watson and certainly not how Boyle had described the role in her recruitment ad.

Despite the scuffles with the police that had landed Boyle and Watson in Holloway, the pair had no plans to grapple with miscreants on the streets any time soon. For them, the WPV was part of the wider struggle for equality and justice, not a full-time day job. Boyle carried on editing *The Vote*, albeit a slimmed-down war-time edition in order to save paper, while Watson was fast becoming a familiar figure around the Old Bailey. The men on the doors had not only given up trying to keep her out, they were also sending her messages if one of her cases was about to begin in another courtroom. On one occasion when she failed to turn up, the leading prosecution counsel, Archibald Bodkin, remarked facetiously, "We can't start yet, our lady isn't here".

In fact, the nearest that Boyle and Watson would come to police work seems to have been when they posed for photographs in their uniforms. Despite their suffrage protests, they were first and foremost writers, speakers and thinkers, and now that their groundbreaking initiative was up and running they were more than happy to leave the dull routine to Damer Dawson and Allen. It turned out to be a very bad call.

10

THEY ARE NOT ALL SUFFRAGETTES

London, in that first sobering autumn of the war. Recruits present arms at Marble Arch, requisitioned buses, vans and carts are lined up in Hyde Park, searchlights scour the night skies, and an anti-aircraft gun stands ready on the Foreign Office roof. In St James's Park, they have drained the lake for fear that the moonlight glancing off its surface will present the enemy with a glittering bull's eye. Down the road at the Reform Club in Pall Mall, where the members include the Prime Minister Herbert Asquith and the Home Secretary Reginald McKenna, they are pondering whether to insure their stately Italianate temple against Zeppelins. Soldiers in uniforms from across the Empire are piling into the capital, and streets familiar in daylight are now alien territory by night, the shop signs switched off and the lamps dimmed. And all the while, the man with the jabbing finger and the thicket of a moustache is making his call to arms from a thousand billboards. Fifty-four million posters of Lord Kitchener will be issued before this is over.

Against this bewildering backdrop, the Women Police Volunteers (WPV) ventured out in search of a role. As Commissioner Henry had made clear to Margaret Damer Dawson, they were on their own, left to write their own job descriptions from scratch in a setting where nothing was ordinary, nothing certain, and for which there was no blueprint. They were only too aware of the pressure. "The lines on which it could most usefully be run had to be searched for and found," Nina Boyle would later explain. "No precedents existed, no authority was available." And they had only one chance. With the Home Secretary and the Commissioner watching warily from the sidelines, one slip was all it would take for them to be finished. "It was self-understood," Mary Allen wrote in her memoirs, "that everything we hoped to attain in the future depended on our immediate success in grappling with each situation as it presented itself. We could not afford mistakes."

Before the women were allowed anywhere near the public, Henry made them sign a pledge to keep their politics to themselves and, in particular, to avoid any suffragette propaganda, as he called it. This would have presented no difficulty for Damer Dawson, who had never been a suffragette, while for Allen and her militant friends it was almost certainly a compromise worth making, especially now that the struggle was on hold. The relentlessly principled Boyle was another matter, but if she did refuse to sign then perhaps Henry decided to turn a blind eye. He had, after all, a city in turmoil to police and 1,000 fewer men with which to do it. This was probably not the time for another tussle with a subversive.

The Derby Daily Telegraph tried to put its readers' minds at rest: "We are assured that, though this organisation may serve as a conduit for pent-up suffragette feeling, they are not all suffragettes." The prevailing view in the press was that if the volunteers could look out for women and children on the streets and give friendly advice to the troops, refugees and other newcomers filling the city, then they were to be welcomed. There was certainly no harm in letting them try and, besides, they would only be needed for a short while. When the war was won and life reverted to normal, the returning men would need no help in policing London. They had, after all, managed perfectly well before.

Not everyone was happy, however. Some people were discomfited at the sight of women wearing masculine-style uniforms, blatantly signalling that they were in a position of authority. Damer Dawson had been warned about that when she first showed her design around. It looked so severe, and no one liked a severe woman, she was told. "They seemed to expect us to police the streets wearing 'pneumonia' blouses and velvet shoes," she complained. And then there were those who thought policing unseemly. A Canadian army officer stopped one volunteer and told her to stay home and concentrate on bringing up her family "instead of walking the streets in a way no decent woman should". Often, though, the hostility came from other women. It was, after all, two women on an Edinburgh bus ridiculing the WPV that had prompted Mary Allen to join, while another volunteer said that women would make loud comments in her hearing, such as: "How unwomanly" and "Not quite nice, do you think?".

Aside from the debate over uniform, the WPV was full of momentum. Head down in her bustling hub in Cheyne Row, Damer Dawson was immersed in the day-to-day running of her service. Like Louise Creighton at the inauguration of the National Union of Women Workers, Damer Dawson discovered she had a talent for administration. She set up a council of three—herself, Mary Allen and Isobel Goldingham—at the top of the hierarchy. Allen was in her element. In the seven years since Emmeline Pankhurst had wrenched power from her members and the democrats had broken away to form the Women's Freedom League, the Women's Social and Political Union had been run under the strict autocratic control that Lilian Ball had witnessed when she was summoned to The Gardenia and issued with her orders. Allen had spent the past six or more years under that regime, and at the WPV she added a military spin. Damer Dawson was the chief officer commanding, while she, Allen, was responsible for directing the action on the field of battle, and Goldingham for the welfare of the troops.

It was at that point in October 1914 that a letter from an unremarkable provincial town in the back of beyond dropped through the door at Cheyne Row. Grantham in Lincolnshire, population 20,000, was a market town where nothing of much excitement had happened since the installation of gas lighting in 1833. That is, until the outbreak of war, when the third Earl of Brownlow, Adelbert Wellington Brownlow Cust, placed his entire estate at the disposal of the Government. It would make a good military training camp, he thought; his only stipulation was that the camp stopped at his doorstep. The War Office agreed, and work began immediately on transforming Brownlow's seven hundred acres of thick woods and rolling grassland into a massive regimental base.

In six months, Belton Park, just three miles down the road from Grantham, had become a small town in its own right, home to 18,000 men, with lines of barracks, latrines, wash houses, mess huts, a hospital, a cinema, four churches and a railway line. The War Office was in a hurry, so while construction was underway a temporary tent city went up into which thousands of fit young men were steadily dumped, many of them straight from school or college, with nothing to do in their spare time but wander into Grantham and upset the locals, whom they would eventually outnumber. It was a predictably dreadful fit. Along with pop-up brothels and illicit drinking clubs came soliciting and drunken brawls in the streets, and in their wake came a tsunami of outrage from the town.

The camp commandant, Major-General Frederick Hammersley, had been removed from a previous command suffering from shell shock. An entire career spent fighting wars had left his nerves in shreds, and for a brief time he was given the soft option of running Belton. Even so, tasked with turning thousands of raw recruits into soldiers before shipping them off to face God knows what, Hammersley had more than enough on his damaged mind without having to fend off complaints from furious aldermen and the Mothers' Union. In October 1914, Captain, later Colonel Kensington was in training at Belton, and when he came forward with a plan for restoring order to the streets of Grantham, the beleaguered Hammersley was ready to listen. The upshot was that Kensington received permission to write to his sister-in-law, Margaret Damer Dawson, asking for her help.

So, on a dismal foggy November day, a jittery but resolute Damer Dawson and Mary Allen, along with Mrs Pankhurst's friend Ellen Harburn from Cheyne Row, shrugged on their immaculate new jackets, the bulky pockets like parcels on their hips, and made their way across town to King's Cross station where a little gathering of friends and relatives had assembled to wave them off. Allen and Harburn were wearing Annie St John Partridge's round hard hats, but Damer Dawson had acquired a naval-style peaked cap befitting her status.

Mary Allen had left the sheltered young woman of her father's house far behind, but when she stepped out of Grantham station, her spirits sank at the sea of sludge and squalor that confronted her. She quickly pulled herself together, however. It was vital that they proved themselves able to handle whatever was about to be thrown at them, so they straightened their backs and, as Sir Edward Henry's drill sergeant had taught them, marched stolidly to their lodgings through the sheeting rain, past the run-down shops and the dispiriting pubs, skirting the puddles of mud and last night's vomit. Grantham, for its part, was fascinated by this outlandish little trio and as the Chelsea three strode on, a growing cavalcade of small boys and random local eccentrics came tagging along behind them.

Allen had a feel for publicity—after all, the suffragette game plan relied on drawing attention to themselves—and, unlike Creighton's patrols, going quietly about her business was not what she did, so as soon as the women were settled in, they posed for pictures in the local paper. Damer Dawson sat in the foreground wearing her cap, her chair flanked on each side by the solemn, rod-straight Allen and Harburn. The women were in town, the *Grantham Journal* said, "because trained women could effect more good in keeping girls and young women from evil influences than inexperienced persons". Damer Dawson told the paper that the WPV had been set up in a spirit of earnest and responsible endeavour, and not with a view to sensational effect or amateur effort.

Throughout their time together, Allen would acknowledge Damer Dawson as her leader, just as she had with Emmeline Pankhurst. Yet as their relationship took hold, another element crept steadily into play as Allen began to exert a powerful influence over the chief, as she now called her. Before they met, Damer Dawson was often described as lady-like and fastidious—feminine was also frequently used. A photograph of her on election day in 1910, campaigning against one of the candidates, a surgeon who supported vivisection, showed a graceful little person in a long, draped coat and a tricorn hat, perched up on the driving seat of a two-horse van, her slender pianist's fingers clasping reins that looked too heavy for her hands. She would always be gentle and softly spoken, but now she began to assume those outward trappings of macho power and the appetite for control to which Mary Allen had become so attached. The cap was just the start.

* * *

In London, meanwhile, Edith Watson was busy pursuing the leading Old Bailey lawyer Archibald Bodkin, whom she accused of not putting enough effort into a case when he was prosecuting a man charged with attacking a woman. One column, under the headline

"Why is Mr Bodkin Employed?", began: "It is difficult to understand how any affair of importance can be trusted to the slack hands of the gentleman who most frequently acts as prosecuting counsel for the Crown." But the injustices facing the capital's women were too great for a lone campaigner. Watson was planning to use the Women Police Volunteers to train a team of crime correspondents to build upon her work. She believed that she could already discern a glimmer of improvement in how children were treated: "The first time I entered Clerkenwell Court a little girl of twelve was standing alone in a court of men being questioned by a counsel. In the case of Moore last week, however, a police matron brought the child into court and when she cried, stood in the witness box beside her". That was just the start. Her reporters, she believed, were capable of transforming the criminal justice system.

* * *

With the first-night nerves over, Annie St John Partridge, Dora Meeson Coates, Isobel Goldingham and their new-found colleagues at the Women's Freedom League were settling into a routine, patrolling the streets in pairs and sitting in at the magistrates' courts. Their most notable intervention in their first few outings had been to perform first-aid on a woman who fainted, but it was very early days and, besides, Nina Boyle soon found a job for them that was, like Watson's reporters, exactly in keeping with the pair's vision when they had put together their plan and sent Damer Dawson off to sell it to Commissioner Henry. It was also exactly what the Home Office and the Metropolitan Police had been worried about.

PART III

.

11

THESE DRINKING WOMEN

14th October 1914, *Birmingham Daily Post*

At the Thames Police Court during the past two days several women whose husbands are fighting in France have been charged with drunkenness. It was stated in evidence that the women, as soon as they got their husband's money, spent it on drink. Mr. Wilberforce commented severely on this state of affairs.

15th October 1914, *Yorkshire Post and Leeds Intelligencer*

Sir Thomas Hughes, chairman of the Licensing Bench, expressed the opinion that a great deal of money received by soldiers' wives from the Relief Committee was spent on drink. He suggested that the allowance was, in many cases, too generous.

23rd October 1914, *Dundee Courier*

The Dundee Public Morals Committee, having considered the amount of excessive drinking that prevails, especially amongst women of the city, resolved … to petition the Sheriff to diminish the sale of liquor. Staff-Captain Alvey, Salvation Army, said that a great many women, after receiving their allowances at the Post Office, streamed off to the public houses.

30th October 1914, *Chelsea News*

Mr. H. C. Biron, sitting at the Westminster Police Court, suggested that a very drastic course should be adopted to deal with the increase in drunkenness amongst women since the outbreak of the war. The case before him was that of Elsie Howell of Medway Street, Westminster, who was charged with being drunk and incapable of taking care of herself. A salutary course to adopt would be to prohibit women from going into public houses [Biron said].

* * *

The working women of Britain were a disgrace. Margaret Taylor, opining from a Georgian mansion in Pimlico, wrote to *The Times* to express her disgust: "When we see the increasing numbers of our poorer sisters in and out of gin palaces we realise the immediate possibility of the degeneration of the homes our men have left behind them." Women were going into the charity office where she was a volunteer, claiming that their children were starving and their boots were falling apart, while all the time "puffing into our faces fumes of whisky, gin and the like".

An activist in the Women's Social and Political Union called Helen Fraser saw it differently. She said that Taylor and her friends were simply in shock at their first encounter with life as it was lived at the bottom of the heap. Some working women had always taken a drink. It was just that with a little extra money in their purses and their husbands out of the way, some of them were drinking a little more.

The government was also worried about alcohol consumption, and not only among women. David Lloyd George, then a senior cabinet minister, would tell the country: "We are fighting Germany, Austria and drink, and so far as I can see the greatest of these deadly foes is drink". When he came up with the idea of nationalising every pub in the land in order to close them down, his Cabinet colleagues thought he had taken leave of his senses. He did, however, manage to dupe the King into giving up alcohol for the duration of the war. It was not a mission that the First Lord of the Admiralty, Winston Churchill, would have taken upon himself.

Lloyd George assured His Majesty that judges, Cabinet Ministers, clergymen, doctors, leaders of industry, and possibly also trade union leaders, were about to sign up to abstention in order to set a good example. After the king had gone public with his pledge, however, he was not best pleased to discover that hardly anyone else of note was planning to join him. Prime Minister Asquith certainly had no intention of doing so and, with some chutzpah, Lloyd George also failed to commit himself. Brought up by an austere abstemious uncle but having been close to his English bon viveur of a law tutor, when it came to drink the minister was somewhat conflicted. Some prominent figures were annoyed at the mere suggestion that they should give up alcohol. The hard-drinking Tory MP Frederick Smith told the minister: "My dear George, next time you see His Majesty I hope you will tell him with all respect that he isn't going to put a key on my wine cellar."

While the rich and powerful were bickering over claret and Napoleon brandy, soldiers' wives were under increasing scrutiny in the pubs, and there was plenty of well-meaning advice on offer about how to get the erring women back on track. The Bishop of London urged ladies to "go among the wives of men at the Front, make friends with them and encourage them to save against coming times of difficulty". The Bishop of Worcester agreed, urging the middle-classes "to make real friends of their sisters, protecting them from themselves". Emily Juson Kerr, a member of the Women's Freedom League, proposed hiring rooms where the women could meet and drink tea and coffee. With cheery fires and simple amuse-ments, she predicted that they would soon give up the doubtful joys of the gin palaces.

The assertion that the women were awash with taxpayers' cash, whatever they might be doing with it, was open to question. Some were certainly better off than they had ever been now that they were receiving the allowance paid to wives to compensate for the loss of their husbands' wages. But the huge numbers of men who had queued at the recruiting offices that summer—half a million by mid-September—had left the War Office inundated with applica-tions. While civil servants struggled with the paperwork, families were left destitute, and mothers were forced to apply for parish assistance under the Poor Laws in order to feed their children. Charity workers like Margaret Taylor of Pimlico, who as a breed did not come out of this too well, advised them to sell their furni-ture or move their families into one room to save on rent.

At the height of the outcry in late October 1914, Louise Creighton arrived at the Bishop's Palace in Lichfield to give a talk on the role of women in war. She was late, having been delayed by a troop train, but she was a class act and her audience found her speech worth waiting for. She had obviously been reading the papers, for she told the packed hall that, while it was impossible to feel anything other than immense pity for the women, they were failing both their country and their homes at a time when their support was most needed. With their husbands at the Front, "they fly to that refuge of the ignorant, the bewildered and the excited—the public house," she said.

Now, clearly, what the country most needed was another high-level deputation to the seat of power. The Duchess of Marlborough, described by her mother-in-law (Churchill's grandmother) as stupid, pious and dull, led the charge, trooping into the grandiose Home Office building on Whitehall to demand that the Government tighten the restrictions on the sale of alcohol, particularly to women. Louise Creighton was represented by her deputy. Also in the party was the vivacious young Pamela McKenna, who was petitioning her husband on behalf of the Liberal Party's women's section. Mrs McKenna would later distinguish herself on a grants committee—the *Daily Mirror* wondered what on earth made anyone think she was qualified to be there—by announcing that there was one type of unmarried mother who under no circumstances should receive a pension: "I mean the mentally deficient woman … who drifts from one workhouse to another, burdening the community with a succession of feebler-minded children. It would be better for her to be exterminated than endowed."

McKenna received them with Sir Edward Henry at his side. He looked unusually relaxed, according to one reporter, showing no signs of the defensive steeliness that he usually adopted when confronted by women. He told the duchess that he would like nothing more than to clamp down on the sale of alcohol to both men and women, soldiers and civilians, and in peacetime as well as war, but Parliament would never stand for it. MPs had, after all, only just given local authorities emergency powers to regulate pub opening hours. Until then, it had required an impending riot to close the bars.

Nina Boyle was becoming increasingly irritated by what she saw as an out-of-touch, self-important clique indulged by both the Home Secretary and the Commissioner of the Metropolitan Police because they had money, a sprinkling of titles and a virtuous air. "Among the 'influential societies' who approached Mr McKenna, not a single one represented the women themselves," she pointed out. "Charitable bodies, reform bodies, temperance bodies, church workers, workers among soldiers' and sailors' wives, and a duchess … [were in] this deputation that is in such haste to spread a shameful slander."

Not that there was any fondness for alcohol at the Women's Freedom League headquarters. Lottie Despard was a member of the temperance movement, which had sprung up in the 1840s and spread fast among the working and lower middle-classes. In the past, Despard had put herself in the Margaret Taylor camp, referring to feckless female drunkards in the Battersea slums, but she now wrote to *The Times* to challenge Taylor, saying that not one of the women who used her soup kitchen smelled of gin. One mother of a large family had spent too much of her first month's allowance, it was true—but on children's boots rather than alcohol.

Boyle decided to ask Asquith if he too would receive a deputation. This one, though, would be to discuss the legality of refusing to serve reputable persons in licensed premises, because London landlords were taking it upon themselves to ban women without waiting for the law to catch up. The group would consist of Boyle; Sylvia Pankhurst, the Marxist daughter of Emmeline, who had split with her mother and Christabel over their support for the war; and four soldiers' wives. The reply came from Asquith's private secretary and soon to be son-in-law, a thirty-year-old cricket blue called Maurice Bonham-Carter (known as Bongie). Regretfully, the Prime Minister's heavy engagements did not permit him to receive her, but he wanted to point out that the licensees of London had decided of their own accord not to serve women before 11.30am. Boyle retorted that this was because Sir Edward Henry had threatened not to renew their licences if they didn't.

Meanwhile, officials in Whitehall had come up with a way to control women's drinking that bypassed any irritating interference from Parliament. The War Office was already drawing up plans to take the allowance away from wives who were deemed unworthy, which they defined as those who were engaged in immoral behaviour, had been convicted of a crime or were neglecting their children. The police and the now all-pervasive charity workers were instructed to put army wives under surveillance and report those who fell from grace. It was a simple matter, then, to add drunkenness to the sin list.

Behind the refined portals of No. 1 Robert Street, the alarm about the direction that events were taking was growing fast, and it went way beyond a woman's right to a glass of beer in a pub. If this story wasn't killed off fast, Boyle and Despard could see an existential threat to the entire suffrage movement down the line, as soon as the war was over. "'What!', we can hear them say," Boyle predicted. "'Enfranchise those irresponsible creatures whom we had to keep from wholesale drunkenness by coercion?'".

It was at that point that she came up with a perfect job for the Women Police Volunteers (WPV). They had been set up to provide practical assistance to women; what could be more appropriate, then, than for them to look into these shameful allegations and expose the truth behind the hysteria? Commissioner Henry and Isobel Goldingham, from the Cheyne Row circle, would both have taken issue with her definition of practical assistance, while using the WPV to fight a political battle was exactly what both had feared that Boyle would do given the chance.

The first premises that Boyle chose to investigate was not a pub at all, but Henry Chartres Biron's courtroom on a Monday morning as the magistrate tut-tutted his way through the weekend's line-up of miscreants. "Of more than forty people charged with being drunk and disorderly, just nine were women," the WPV detectives reported, and as more reports trickled in there was some satisfaction in Robert Street:

- Saturday afternoon in a pub in Whitehall, chosen because women were constantly in and out of the nearby War Office. One hundred and forty-seven men present, and two women.
- Eight o'clock on a Saturday night in Stockwell Road, Clapham. "A number of licensed houses overflowing with men, a large number of those in uniform being the worse for drink, and not more than a dozen women".
- Closing time on a Monday night at the Windsor Castle, Victoria. Fifty-four men and four women came out.

- Harrow Road, West London, during school hours, when the pubs were said to be packed with women on war benefits. All premises crowded with men, with a few women being served on the doorstep.

Boyle published her findings in *The Vote* and sent a copy to Bongie at No. 10 along with a warning: "Repeated attacks on our liberties … are producing a strong feeling that the truce voluntarily called by women suffragists has been gravely abused by the Government." This time, though, there was no response. The government was determined to press ahead. McKenna even introduced a card index system to make it easier for the police to check the names of the women they took into custody. When the Home Secretary's cards arrived at Scotland Yard, however, Henry refused to take them. He couldn't imagine why anyone should think that soldiers' wives needed the police to look after them, and he told Louise Creighton: "They are respectable women and we do not as a rule know much about the affairs of respectable families because it is not our business." He also instructed his men that if a soldier's wife were to be arrested for drunkenness and it was her first offence, she should be allowed to sober up, given a warning and sent home. Creighton thought such leniency regrettable: "If anything a higher standard should have been demanded from them … They should have been made to realise that they too, like their husbands and sons, were under discipline."

The following year, the Government set up an all-woman committee to investigate women's drinking and asked Louise Creighton, everyone's committee woman of choice, to chair it. The Duchess of Marlborough wrote from Mayfair to recommend that the members be chosen largely from the representatives of the working class or those in close touch with them. Perhaps Boyle's criticism of her deputation had struck home.

Of Creighton's eleven committee members, just one had her roots among working people—the socialist Eleanor Barton was the daughter of a prison warder—but, unlike Margaret Taylor and her sheltered friends, they all had first-hand knowledge of the living conditions of the poor. Florence Booth, the daughter-in-law of the founder of the Salvation Army, for example, had worked for years with street women in the slums of Whitechapel. As for the witnesses heard by the committee, as well as the stalwarts from the usual line-up—the British Women's Temperance Association and the inescapable Mothers' Union were in there—those who shared their experiences included Mrs Deal, Mrs Palmer and Mrs Rowse from Rotherhithe, described as working women, while interviewers across the country took testimony not only from clergymen, magistrates and mayors, but from barmaids, shopkeepers and rent collectors.

It was a thorough and thoughtful investigation, but the results were a stew of anecdote and speculation so confusing that no one knew what to do with them. The committee was at a loss, for example, when faced with the chief constable of Chester, who was adamant that drinking among women had increased since the start of the war, and the chief constable of Birkenhead, who was equally convinced that it had not. Creighton had the resources and the authority of the state behind her, but while her report certainly weighed more than Nina Boyle's quick rundown of a few London pubs, it turned out to not be much more reliable. Sir Edward Henry was one of the few people to provide any hard facts. Over a four-week period in London, 2,745 men were convicted of drunkenness, compared with 1,227 women—at a time when there were far more women than men in the capital, he told Creighton, which caused him to wonder after all if women weren't quite the offenders that some people thought.

Despite the shortcomings of her inquiry, Creighton had the confidence to reach some conclusions. Drinking among women had gone up during the war, she said, but only among those who were already drinking. The increase was across all social classes but, because those women higher up the ladder drank behind closed doors, working-class women were being scrutinised in a way that their betters were not. And women's drinking should not be treated separately from that of men: "The man who spends his wages on drink instead of maintaining his family is as great a danger to society … as the woman who … neglects her home and children." It was also clear that many women were spending their allowance on their homes and children, she added.

Creighton then went on to look at why some working women drank: "… worn out by a constant struggle with poverty, many of them trying to keep their children on the small and uncertain portion of wages made over to them by their husbands, have sought relief from their troubles in drink," she wrote. "The crowded and insanitary slums of our great cities, by their lack of air and light, encourage depression, which leads the struggling women who inhabit them to gain at least a momentary feeling of exhilaration by the use of stimulants … When we consider the conditions under which so many of the poorer working women live, we can only wonder that so many of them have been able to lead sober and self-respecting lives under circumstances full of difficulty and temptation." It is only possible to speculate how much the voices of the barmaids and rent collectors, the working wives of Rotherhithe and committee members like Flo Booth, echoed through Creighton's words.

This was absolutely not in the Government's script. Its shiny new Central Control Board (Liquor Traffic), which had commissioned the report, seemed to have assumed that they had entrusted their inquiry to someone who could be relied upon to come up with the right answers. Creighton was, after all, on record accusing women who drank of failing their country and their homes, and calling them ignorant and bewildered. But what the men from the Board had failed to understand was that Creighton was a complex woman, despite the rigidity of some of her purity pronouncements, and not always easy to predict. They responded by picking their way through her report line by line, like an exasperated tutor marking an essay: "In what sense are the words 'seen to be worse in certain towns' used?"; "It is difficult to attach a meaning to this sentence"; "Nowhere is any definition given of 'drinking', 'drinking amongst women' and 'these drinking women' etc". They did have a point.

In a courteous phone call, the chairman of the Board, Lord d'Abernon, invited Creighton in to discuss matters. d'Abernon was a diplomat and a politician whose main claim to fame thus far had been to preside over a run on the Ottoman Bank, which left many investors ruined while at the same time making him a fortune. The episode seemed to have done little to impede his career.

Creighton duly arrived at the Board's offices with her committee in tow, ready for a meaningful dialogue with the men at the top. She was outraged, then, to be received not by d'Abernon, nor by any members of the Board, but by a single official, the unfortunate Mr Sykes, to whom the job of breaking bad news had been delegated. Creighton could be formidable even when she wasn't furious, and it took an apparently nervous Sykes some time to get to the point. He finally managed to explain that the Board refused to accept that there was no significant increase in drinking among women who were not already doing so, and that they would not publish Creighton's report unless she agreed to change its entire premise.

Creighton was incredulous as well as angry. When she agreed to lead the inquiry, she had taken it for granted that publication of its findings was assured. Refusing to discuss the matter with a mere messenger, she swept out with her committee behind her. However, back home within the soothing wood-panelled walls of Hampton Court Palace, when she had calmed down a little, she began to ponder how she might salvage something from all those months of work and at the same time prevent what she believed to be important information from being buried. She decided that she would take back the report and work with the Board to rewrite it in a way that was acceptable to both sides. Her offer was refused.

The Board eventually agreed to publish a short statement, memorialising that Creighton believed that drinking had increased only among those women who were already doing so before the war. They followed it, however, with a statement of their own: the Creighton report was receiving careful attention, but it was just one of a wide range of opinions that they were considering, as it was their duty to do. They had, after all, been set up with just one purpose in mind: namely, the successful prosecution of the war.

* * *

Fortunately for the fledgling Women Police Volunteers, Nina Boyle's survey went unremarked, and perhaps also unnoticed, by both McKenna and Henry. She would certainly have tried to force it to their attention, but it turned out to be unnecessary in the end.

Elsie Howell, who had prompted Biron to recommend his "very drastic course" when she stood before him in the dock, turned out to be a sixty-year-old woman living in precisely the misery and squalor that Creighton had described. Her husband had been wounded at the Front and was now a prisoner of war. Inspector Ashton, who had been doing his best to keep an eye on her, told the magistrate that she had been constantly drunk since her husband's departure and was now a very sick woman, recently hospitalised with delirium tremors. "She is alone, there being nobody there to look after her," the policeman explained.

The narrative of widespread wartime profligacy and drinking among soldiers' wives, whatever the truth behind it, somehow passed into history as proven fact. No reliable evidence was ever produced to show that women's overall consumption of alcohol went up by any significant degree during the war years.

12

LOITERING AND SOLICITING

Sunday, 29th November 1914. *The People* carries a small paragraph tucked away on page nine. Competing as it does with headlines like "French Inflict Severe Losses on Enemy's Artillery" and "We Can Afford to Lose a Dreadnought a Month—Mr Churchill", many readers might fail to spot it, but it's worth a glance: "Yesterday a novel court-martial was held in Cardiff when five women of a certain class were tried under the Defence of the Realm Act for being out of doors between the hours of 7pm and 8am."

The Defence of the Realm Act, DORA, was rushed through Parliament four days after the declaration of war. Over the next four years it would go through six revisions, each time grabbing more powers until it was a bloated ragbag of disparate measures, from the seriously hefty, such as press censorship and imprisonment without trial, to the seemingly fatuous, like the ban on flying kites and whistling in the street. (In fact, the latter wasn't as absurd as it sounded: policemen on bikes would blast out Zeppelin warnings on their whistles.) As public irritation grew, so the cartoonists began to depict DORA as a bossy, interfering old harridan, which was ironic given some of the uses to which it would be put.

This first version was simple enough, just two hundred and twenty-five words, but it allowed the authorities to control communications, secure the ports and commandeer any land, buildings and property essential to the military. Most people viewed these as reasonable measures in a time of war. One short phrase in one clause, however, was to prove troublesome: "Any person who breaks any of the regulations given in the Order may be tried ... by court-martial."

The Cardiff women had contravened an order from Colonel East, Commander of the Severn Defences, banning any woman that the military or civilian authorities decided was disreputable from being out on the streets at night. East was not concerned with anyone's morals, he said, but only with protecting his troops from sexually transmitted diseases. Some of the accused were illiterate—the police had to read the order to them—and they had no lawyer to advise them. They were led out before a panel of grave legal men where they stood baffled and helpless. One tried to explain herself, saying "Seven o'clock seemed so early—it seemed like a dream to me", but no one was listening and they were sent to prison for sixty-two days.

"Women of a certain class" was yet another euphemism for prostitute, or at least for a woman a police officer had decided was a prostitute, for this was a judgement call and a capricious one at that. Any working-class woman out alone at night, particularly if she were ragged or homeless or smelt of alcohol, could find herself accused of being what the law dubbed a common prostitute and under arrest for soliciting. And while full-time sex workers might have qualified for the label in many people's view, including their own, the definition wasn't as clear-cut as it might seem. What about the women who existed in the shadowlands of destitution, resorting to the occasional fumble down an alleyway to buy food or pay the rent?

What about the women scraping what passed for a living in the sweated trades, where the pitiful pay often fell below the breadline? The washerwomen, the sack-makers, the fur-pullers, the matchbox-makers? The needlewomen like Edith Watson's mother Martha, biting off their cotton thread in the race to finish their quota of shirts for the day? Martha might well have married the man who beat her daughter, Alfred Willet, in the hope that as a docker he would bring in a steady wage. What then of the women running away from men like Willet or deserted by a wage-earner, desperate to keep themselves and their children out of the workhouse?

Then, as now, prostitution wasn't an offence but soliciting was, and for this the police relied on The Vagrancy Act (1824), which made any prostitute "behaving in a riotous or indecent manner in a public place" liable to a fine or imprisonment, while in London the Metropolitan Police Act (1839) also prescribed a fine for any prostitute "loitering or soliciting for the purposes of prostitution to the annoyance of passengers or residents". What passed for the evidence usually involved no more than a constable telling a Vagrancy magistrate that he had seen the woman approaching men in a public place, just as PC Lee had done with Bessie Moncrieff. There was no requirement to produce a witness to say that he had been solicited.

The physician, writer and national inspector of prisons, Mary Gordon, held cutting-edge views on the causes of female criminality, blaming factors such as exploitation, lack of education and a deprived childhood. One of her key themes, however, was that the law manufactured prostitutes by branding young women with a label which then defined their lives. "The common prostitute, by being something which it is not an offence to be, can commit offences which other women cannot commit", Gordon wrote. "But how does a woman become a common prostitute? She becomes one by the simple process of the policeman moving her on, probably telling her she is one, warning her he will arrest her, and finally arresting her, swearing in court she is one, and that she has loitered with the intention of soliciting or that he has seen her soliciting. After that she is eligible for punishment and takes her place in the ranks of common prostitutes." This was the culture of assumed guilt and essential criminality in place when the press and the police began to turn their attention to wartime prostitution.

It seemed that Louise Creighton had been right when she warned about the dangers of the army camps, for the furore about women drinking had no sooner subsided than another of the great moral panics to which the British are prone seized the nation. Overnight crowds of seemingly respectable young women and girls—some of them, unthinkably, from the middle-classes—were found hanging around the gates of the army bases, accosting soldiers. The trainloads of professional prostitutes flooding into the military towns were bad enough; the brothels in parts of London were said to be virtually empty, but these so-called enthusiastic amateurs were much more disturbing. They presented a threat to the moral fabric of the Empire.

The age-old idea that women had to be put in check to stop men behaving badly was on a roll in the early years of the war. In Victorian times, women had been seen as the guardians of the nation's virtue, holding the fragile line between an upstanding Christian country and a 19th-century Sodom and Gomorrah. In sexual matters in particular, the responsibility and the power lay with them, they were told, because no one could expect a man to resist temptation. As for the question of "professional" temptation, British law and order had long seen women as the sole targets of any crackdown.

* * *

Back in 1887, the then Metropolitan Police Commissioner Charles Warren had decided to publish guidance on who was and who wasn't a prostitute, after a seamstress called Elizabeth Cass went out one June evening to buy a pair of gloves in Regent Street and found herself in the dock. As she pushed her way through the crowds celebrating Queen Victoria's Golden Jubilee, Cass felt the heavy hand of the law upon her in the person of PC Bowen Endacott, who arrested her and marched her to Tottenham Court Road Police Station where she was charged with soliciting and held in a cell overnight. The following morning, Endacott told the magistrate, Robert Newton, that he had seen Cass on three previous occasions soliciting in Regent Street. However, when Cass's employer, a dressmaker with an impeccable reputation, testified to her good character, Newton had little choice but to find her not guilty. Even so, he couldn't resist giving her a piece of advice: "If you are a respectable girl, as you say you are, don't walk in Regent Street at night, for if you do you will either be fined or sent to prison after the caution I have given you."

After PC Endacott had stood trial for perjury—he was found not guilty; the jury accepted that he had made a genuine mistake—and the magistrate had been reprimanded by the Attorney General, Commissioner Warren decided that a little clarity was in order. He told his men not to call any woman a common prostitute "unless she so described herself or had been convicted as such", and that a police officer "should not assume that any particular woman is a common prostitute, though he may be perfectly convinced in his own mind that she is". He added that there could be no offence of soliciting "without the presence of [an individual who was] annoyed, who is capable of proving the annoyance".

Twenty years after Cass, however, little had changed. One night in 1907 in Glasgow, a boarding-house keeper called Jessie Brown was arrested by two plain clothes constables on her way home from a friend's house. Charged with loitering about and importuning five men for the purpose of prostitution, she was held in a cell for two nights and then brought before a magistrate, who found her guilty on the word of the two officers. Not one of the five men who had supposedly been importuned was produced.

Brown got off with a warning. Like Elizabeth Cass, though, she was what the law classed as a person of good standing. She also had money and she set about trying to clear her name, first by putting herself through the indignity of being examined by two doctors and producing certificates to confirm that she was a virgin. When this failed to quash her conviction, she tried to sue the police officers for wrongful arrest but lost on a technicality. The Justiciary Appeal Court in Edinburgh finally overturned the verdict but her fight for compensation went on for years, eventually forcing a statement from the Lord Advocate but still, ultimately, getting nowhere.

In the meantime, the Court of Sessions ordered the same two constables who had arrested Brown to pay £40 in damages to a coppersmith called Duncan Harvey for false arrest. Harvey, who was taking his mother's alarm clock to be repaired when he was stopped, had faced the somewhat less defamatory accusation of refusing to unwrap his parcel when ordered to do so.

In an attempt to explain the frightening new phenomenon of camp followers, a novel idea was gaining traction. Could it be that the sight of large numbers of men in uniform marching to the strains of military bands was driving women insane? Their sex was, after all, famously weak-minded and prone to hysteria. The condition was even given a name: Khaki Fever or War Nymphomania. While the spotlight was on Grantham, fathers and husbands living near camps across the country began petitioning Whitehall, demanding that something be done. No one, however, seemed too sure what. An exasperated civil servant in the Home Office scribbled across one letter: "If he can't control his daughters, I don't know what he expects me to do about it."

The purity movement was fond of a bracing pamphlet, and Louise Creighton put out a little publication called *A Word to the Girls* which warned of the consequences of being found wanting: "Often girls sink so low in their sin that they can never rise again". As well as issuing Old Testament-style portents of doom, however, Creighton was also putting her academic, analytical eye to good use. Along with the Khaki Fever stories came the rumours of the consequences, and the Church of England decided to look into an alleged hike in births to single mothers, setting up a competent commission of ladies to investigate the nature and extent of the danger. It was to be convened by Creighton with Adeline, Duchess of Bedford, on the team.

At this point, Nina Boyle stepped in. Like Creighton, she assumed her customary, but very different role, tearing into the Archbishop of York for saying that the responsibility for men giving way to temptation lay with those who pestered them with their attentions. Boyle asked him: "Are you aware that a large number of the girls [found with soldiers] are of ages from twelve to sixteen, and that the men are in no case under eighteen? Are you aware that intercourse with girls of that age is a criminal offence? Are we to understand that you regard 'temptation' by mere children as a valid excuse for grown men who commit criminal offences? Do you hold that to shelter men from the consequences of their evil actions and lay the blame entirely on the shoulders of young girls and children is according to the tenets preached by the founder of the Church?"

When the Archbishop's secretary replied that no excuse could be made for men who assaulted children, Boyle sent another long angry missive demanding that the archbishop publicly repudiated his speech, "which has given grave offence to a number of … women who consider his attitude far more damaging to public morality than the sin which he so heavily condemned in irresponsible girls?" The Archbishop had had enough: "His Grace regrets that you are not satisfied with his utterance, but it is impossible for him to continue correspondence with you."

In the summer of 1915, Creighton told her sixty-odd National Union of Women Workers' branches to look into the allegations, while her patrols were to investigate the areas around the military camps. Their reports read with some monotony: "nothing abnormal"; "no increase expected"; "no appreciable increase". "People had spread abroad the war babies scare, but never had a bubble exploded as that one did," Creighton remarked. "There was absolutely no foundation for the sensational outcry."

* * *

As Colonel East was proclaiming his women's curfew in Wales, the Commander of the South West Defences in Plymouth, General Arthur Pole-Penton, was banning all women, whether they were of a certain class or not, from being served alcohol after 6pm. This meant, Boyle pointed out, that a woman having dinner with her husband in a hotel couldn't have a glass of wine. Men could carry on drinking until nine o'clock. Pole-Penton batted away all criticism, saying that DORA allowed him to deal with any situation in a drastic manner as he saw fit. The situation requiring a drastic manner here was drunken men fighting in the streets, sprawling senseless across the cobbles and harassing women on public transport.

Boyle came across Pole-Penton while she was trying to see off another plan to regulate the women of Plymouth. She just had sent a telegram to the council: "Women's Freedom League hears with amazement and indignation of suggestion of Plymouth Watch Committee to revive the Contagious Diseases Acts. Hopes that commanding officers will place all possible restraint on men rather than encourage this wholesale insult to womanhood of country". The following morning, she and Lottie Despard set off for Downing Street to seek an interview with the Prime Minister.

The first Contagious Diseases Act had come into law in 1864 with the aim of stopping the spread of syphilis and gonorrhoea in the armed forces. It allowed the police in naval ports and army towns to arrest any woman they decided was a prostitute and force her to undergo an internal examination. Surgical rape, the critics called it. If the doctor declared her to be infected, she was incarcerated in a special hospital for forcible treatment. The law had been extended in 1866 and again in 1869, taking in more towns and lengthening the time that the woman could be held from three months to a year. By 1870 there was talk of extending it to the entire country. The MP Josiah Wedgwood, descendant of the famous potter, remarked: "There is great danger, no doubt, from gonorrhoea and syphilis and all these loathsome diseases, but there is a better remedy than passing Acts of Parliament, and that is not to go with prostitutes".

The evidence appeared to show that the measure didn't work. Florence Nightingale certainly thought so, and in the 1870s she challenged England's first woman doctor, Elizabeth Garrett Anderson, over the issue. Nightingale had a fiercely analytical brain and, while her name is forever linked with nursing, she was also a brilliant mathematician. After her return from the Crimea, she campaigned for healthcare reforms using statistics to make her case. Anderson had backed up her support for the Acts by quoting leading members of the medical profession, but Nightingale said that their views were worthless. They might be highly regarded, but they knew nothing about this subject. Similar laws in countries like France had proved useless, and there had been no drop in cases of syphilis among the military in British ports and garrison towns after the legislation was brought in.

The Acts were finally repealed in 1886 due to the powerful arguments over the years of opponents like Nightingale, but the immediate catalyst for change had been public anger over young Elizabeth Burley. Burley was not a prostitute, although that might have been only a matter of time, given her situation. The eighteen-year-old was described as having fallen on hard times, but being born into them was probably more accurate. She had been in the workhouse at some point but then found work as a domestic servant, almost certainly not as a member of a large, well-ordered staff in a smart household but as a maid-of-all-work. This was the kind of job that Edith Watson had been forced to take, and that had led her to question what virtue had to offer a woman who was on the poverty line.

When two police constables spotted Burley on the streets of Dover, she had just been sacked and was homeless and dishevelled. Confusing her with a woman they had seen earlier with group of soldiers, the officers approached her, whereupon she panicked and ran away. A chase then ensued through the town and down to the quayside where, cornered and terrified, the girl flung herself headlong into the dock. She was fished out only to be charged with attempted suicide.

In 1913, the government set up a Royal Commission to look into the prevalence of sexually transmitted diseases, their effect on the health of the nation and at how those effects might be mitigated. Naturally, Louise Creighton sat on the Commission. She said that she had agreed to take part with immense reluctance, adding: "And many trying and wearisome hours I spent on it." Like most feminists, Creighton believed that sexually transmitted diseases and prostitution were key issues for the women's movement but for her, as always, there was a religious and moral dimension. "Those who want to work for purity must be careful about the purity of their own souls," she warned. As with her drink committee, the Commission failed to produce any reliable data, but it estimated that at least ten per cent of people living in big cities had syphilis, while the percentage for gonorrhoea was far higher. Before the committee started work, they were ordered not to recommend a return to the Contagious Diseases Acts, which were gone for good.

Boyle and Despard were received cordially enough by Bongie at No. 10, who promised to let them know if the Prime Minister was able to see them. They returned to Robert Street and Bongie phoned later, sending apologies and explaining that the Cabinet meeting had overrun and Asquith was unable to fit them in. Boyle bashed out another of her apocalyptic warnings, this time prophesying that the recrudescence of these infamous Acts would cause women to feel so insecure that the consequences would be incalculable.

The reply came the following day. No one could reintroduce the regulations without the approval of Parliament, and as the Government had no intention of putting forward any such legislation, that was an end to the matter. Boyle was not entirely reassured but it was the best that she could hope for. In fact, in March 1918, Regulation 40d under the ubiquitous DORA would make it a criminal offence for any woman with a sexually transmitted disease to have sex with, or to solicit, a member of the armed forces.

The next morning saw a now hyperactive Nina Boyle boarding the train for Plymouth, where she had secured a meeting with the mayor, a local businessman called Thomas Baker. He was friendly, polite and also embarrassed, she thought, keen to hush the matter up. Baker admitted that a revival of the Contagious Diseases Act had been considered, but assured her that the plan was now dead. Promising to warn her if there were any attempts to resuscitate it, he sent her on her way. It was then that she heard about Pole-Penton's curfew and was thrown into another fury. Up in Grantham, however, General Hammersley was rather taken with the idea.

THE KEEPING OF A PURE TONE

Louise Creighton's connections and years in public service made her patrols an altogether slicker, more professional operation than the Women Police Volunteers. As well as the backing of the Duchess of Bedford and Lady Alice, Creighton had the entire moral purity movement behind her. After her appeal in *The Times* in October 1914, the cash began flowing in and the volunteers were signing up at National Union of Women Workers' branches across the country. A full-time patrol secretary, Mary Carden, a sixty-five-year-old widow with eleven children, was installed in the head office in Victoria Street, a stroll away from Westminster Abbey and the Church of England's head office, and from here Carden proceeded to send out a stream of encouraging reports to the Home Secretary.

Things were going well, she told McKenna, and many parents of girls who at first saw the patrols as interfering toads soon felt it "rather wonderful that they should leave their homes and go about so quiet and ladylike". *The Times* also liked their style: "They have no uniform and they act quietly and without parade". McKenna responded to Carden's missives with a two-sentence acknowledgement. Given that he was running a key department of state in a country at war, it was possible that he didn't always pay her the attention for which she might have hoped.

Among the early recruits was a clever, driven, quietly alluring woman in Hampshire called Sofia Stanley, who had a disabled husband and a mysterious past. Sophia Croll Dalgairns was born in Palermo, Sicily, the eldest of the five children of a Scottish engineer. (The reason for the change of the spelling of her first name is unclear). For the next forty years, however, Stanley shows up only occasionally in the flickering spotlight of the official records. There was a move from Sicily back to the London suburb of Penge when she was five, followed by her father's bankruptcy; a marriage in Brighton in 1899 to Henry Stanley, a deputy superintendent with the Madras railways in British India, and the birth of her only child, Theodora, in Madras in 1902.

The Stanleys came back to England in 1914, this time to Southsea on the southern edge of Portsmouth. By then, Henry was forty-one and paralysed from an unspecified accident. Like Boyle, Stanley wrote no memoir and no private letters have survived. One story has it that she ran away from home in her teens, and at some point was the headmistress of St Mary's School for the Daughters of British Army Officers in Pune, India, but this remains unauthenticated. Stanley joined the National Union of Women Workers' patrols after a family friend, a senior police officer, told her about Creighton's new venture. She thought it sounded interesting and, of course, it would only take up a couple of hours a week.

Another Creighton recruit was the twenty-eight-year-old writer Dorothy Peto in Somerset, who was from a wealthy, high-profile West Country family. Peto's father was the builder and landscape artist Morton Kelsall Peto, while her grandfather was the engineer and MP, Sir Morton Peto. The latter had made a fortune building some of London's most iconic landmarks, including Nelson's Column and the Houses of Parliament. Dorothy had found a prestigious home for her first novel, with a publisher called Smith, Elder & Co., which counted Charlotte Brontë, William Thackeray, Robert Browning and Thomas Hardy among their authors. Peto's *A Pilgrimage of Truth*, however, appeared on the publisher's "popular" list, which was aimed at the mass market. It was a tale of men with square jaws and honourable principles and a woman torn by conflicting emotions, set on a remote beach in Morocco.

When the book failed to become an instant bestseller, Peto decided that she was done with literature and looked for another way of spending her time. She completed her first stint on patrol with an umbrella hooked over one arm, holding up her full-length skirts behind her as she negotiated the steep streets of Bath in the pitch-dark, looking for adventure. She clearly had a novelist's imagination: "I felt—nay I hoped—that each group of persons we passed might turn out to be plotting some nefarious deed."

* * *

But who was the woman Stanley and Peto were working for? Besides moral purity, what cause did she support? What were her politics, and how had she ended up on a separate, parallel track to the Women Police Volunteers of Nina Boyle and Margaret Damer Dawson?

Louise Creighton's suffrage views had only crystalised after years of analysis, argument and equivocation. After passing the University of London exam, she had continued to educate herself, reading widely in the Bodleian Library in Oxford and writing a series of history books, while at the same time following the traditional Victorian route of making a good marriage to a man of high social position and having a large family. The twenty-seven-year-old Anglican priest Mandell Creighton, Fellow of Merton College, Oxford, had been intrigued when he glimpsed Louise von Glehn at a lecture given by the writer and critic John Ruskin. Max, as he was known, picked the twenty-year-old out of the crowd because she was wearing a yellow scarf which he thought rather daring, and he asked to be introduced. Louise wrote to her mother: "Mr Creighton is by far the nicest man I have met up here. He is so bright and intelligent and delightful to talk to." Within a month the couple were engaged. They married the following year and went on to have seven children.

Unlike Winnington-Ingram and Robert von Glehn, there was nothing handsome or glamorous about Mandell. His narrow face was bisected by a large, curved nose on which were jammed a pair of gold-rimmed spectacles. His legs were spindly, his gait awkward, his auburn hair thinning and the soft ends of a large bushy beard curled onto his collar. Yet for all that, he had an imposing, confident stance and a flair for dress that attracted attention. Louise adored him. She had a reputation for being demanding and argumentative—the Prime Minister's wife Margot Asquith would say of her: "Uncomfortable woman, always expecting people to be what they are not", while Beatrice Webb said she was sometimes ugly in her brusque directness—but a friend who knew the couple well noted that "Only

Mandell seemed to be able to handle her and her submission to his will was striking to those who saw them together. He literally became the centre of her life and he could do nothing wrong, say nothing unwise." It was a loving and supremely happy relationship.

Soon after their marriage in 1872, the couple signed a pro-suffrage petition after hearing Lydia Becker speak. Becker was a self-taught scientist who corresponded with Charles Darwin about botany for years. In 1867, with extraordinary prescience, she had warned against depleting wild holly and mistletoe by using it for Christmas decorations. Artificial greenery was not only more sustainable, but making the garlands would create more jobs for women, she said. But Becker was also far ahead of her time in another sphere. She helped to thrust women's suffrage onto the political agenda and prepared the ground for the celebrities who would come after her, long before anyone had heard of Emmeline or Christabel Pankhurst or Annie Kenney.

With her large, flat, sensible face and plait of hair coiled like a dozing adder on the crown of her head, Becker resembled a mid-Victorian woman of good works who had stepped out of a Dickens' novel. Eclipsed by the glitter of the leaders of the Women's Social and Political Union, and lacking their flair for publicity, she has been passed over by history. In 1913, however, twenty-three years after she died, the Women's Freedom League would publish an appreciation, saying that she stood alongside Florence Nightingale and Elizabeth Garrett Anderson as one of the leading women pioneers of her time.

When Becker first took on the suffrage cause in the late 1860s, she wrote to her brother about a young lawyer who was campaigning alongside her: "I like Dr Pankhurst—he is a clever little man with plenty to say—and some strange ideas …". Richard Pankhurst would go on to marry Emmeline Goulden, a woman from a politically active Manchester family twenty-four years younger than himself. Emmeline had been fourteen when she first heard "the great Miss Lydia Becker … a splendid character and truly eloquent speaker … I left the meeting a conscious and confirmed suffragist." Becker failed to make such an impression on the Creightons, however. The couple signed her petition "not because we were carried away by Miss Becker herself", Louise said. "We thought she had a grin like a

Cheshire cat; that is all I remember of her." It was clearly not the life-changing event that it had been for Emmeline Pankhurst, or that the encounter with Annie Kenney had proved for Mary Allen.

In 1884, Max was appointed professor of ecclesiastical history at Cambridge University and the couple left the wildly beautiful village on the North Sea coast that had been their home for ten years. Here, Max had combined his ministry as vicar with writing acclaimed church history, and Louise, despite her refined air and academic bent, had made a success of the humdrum role of the wife of a rural clergyman, trudging for miles down muddy tracks in winter to visit the parishioners in their remote cottages. The sophisticated pair even found themselves providing a hands-on folksy medical service, with Max dispensing his own home-made remedies and Louise mixing up ointments and dressing old women's leg ulcers.

Max's new job meant exchanging the weird and wonderful Northumbrian vicarage, with its 14th-century keep, for a conventional house in a conventional Cambridge avenue. Unsurprisingly, Creighton hated it: "It was cramped and the hideous common appearance always weighed upon me." She was reconciled to the underwhelming drawing room once her blue carpet was down and the custom-built overmantel was in place, but there was nothing to be done about the meanly proportioned dining room, which she complained could accommodate no more than ten dinner guests.

Despite having been extremely happy down among the leg ulcers, Creighton was pleased to find herself back in an intellectual, literary scene. She chose a small group of women as her inner circle of friends; all of them, like her, were married to senior academics, and one of the clique, Mary Ward, persuaded her to help with an anti-suffrage petition. Ward would go on to set up the Women's National Anti-Suffrage League and she also published a stream of best-selling novels under the name Mrs Humphry Ward.

Together, Ward and Creighton persuaded over one hundred prominent women across the country to sign a letter which described giving women the vote as a measure distasteful to the great majority of women in the country—unnecessary and mischievous both to themselves and to the State. The signatories included a countess, four duchesses, twelve women from Girton College, the poet Christina Rossetti and the actress Ellen Terry.

Having signed Lydia Becker's petition for the vote a decade before, Creighton's decision to put her name to the opposite view was carefully thought through. Unlike Ward, she didn't see women as intellectually inferior to men. On the contrary, she would be a lifelong advocate of a woman's right to enjoy the same education, pay and working conditions as a man, to enter the professions and to hold influential positions in society. Her anti-suffrage views were grounded in the Victorian context of marriage, children and, increasingly as a bishop's wife, religion. A woman should stand above the grubby trade-offs of party politics, she believed: "In her hands rest the keeping of a pure tone in society, of a high standard of lofty devotion to political life." Women would lose that moral high ground if they followed men into the political rough and tumble.

Max's death from stomach cancer in 1901, at the age of fifty-seven, left Creighton devastated. She chronicled the gradual breakdown of his health as his impressive energy leaked steadily away before her eyes. At the end, she wrote: "And then came another morning … 'Louise come to me. I need to say that I leave everything to you; you are me and I am you. You will know what to do.'

'God's will be done. They will pray for you in all the churches.'

'Let them pray, whether I live or die'."

He died after sending a message of love and loyalty to the Queen, who died the next week. The following Sunday, Creighton collapsed on her way back from a service at St Paul's Cathedral. She sat by the fire unable to eat and was soon forced to take to her bed; it would be three months before she left it. Her sickness was due to appendicitis, which required surgery, but losing Max was a major factor in her lengthy recovery. When she was finally able to face the world again, her first project was to start work on his biography, a task that she found more demanding than she had imagined. She also threw herself back into public service and continued with it for the rest of her life.

Five years later, in 1906, Creighton stood up at the National Union of Women Workers' conference and, with her characteristic confidence and intellectual honesty, announced that she had changed her mind once again. She accepted that women were now deeply involved in party politics, in which case they had better have the vote. The "wild performances" of the suffragettes had also influenced her, she said. They needed to be steadied by responsibility.

14

NO ORDER, HOWEVER DISTASTEFUL

Grantham, five months into the war. Mary Allen quickly recovered from her shock at the state of the town and threw herself into her duties. The women's days were spent in plain clothes, visiting homes, reassuring parents and warning girls about the dangers of Belton Camp, much as Creighton's patrols would have done. At night, however, they were in uniform down among the drunks in the back alleys, sometimes for twelve hours at a stretch, plodding wearily home at midnight over the sodden fields. Damer Dawson admitted that they were a mere drop in the bucket, but it wasn't about numbers. "We were able quite by ourselves to deal with places which no military picket ever thought of attempting to clear," she would later tell a government inquiry. "We simply got in among them and called for a non-commissioned officer to take them home. We got large quantities of them home at night quite easily."

It was hard to imagine. Damer Dawson was petite, even fragile-looking, and Allen's health had been damaged by force-feeding. However, their Ju-jitsu-for-beginners' skills were never called for, nor were Annie St. John Partridge's reinforced hats ever put to the test, for the women had some advantages that Henry had not antici-pated. The uniform not only unnerved the offender, Allen said, but showed the world "that the power and majesty of the law is behind the figure in official blue". That thought must have delighted her soul. And there was something else. Class deference would take a considerable battering as the war went on, but in 1914 a clipped officer-class accent could still work wonders.

Ellen Harburn was then given a terrifying task. She was ordered to carry out spot-checks on the town's pubs to ensure the landlords were complying with the war-time regulations. Like most refined middle-class women, she had never been into a public house in her life and the prospect of that Hogarthian world was the stuff of nightmares. As it happened, though, fear gave her a severe, authoritarian air, described by Allen as very different from her usual easy-going manner, and when she entered her first bar, steeled for debauchery, she was astounded to be met with seemly behaviour and respect. So it continued; the landlords and customers were as unnerved as she was.

The women's next duty was to accompany the military police on their raids in search of missing soldiers. Again, this was unknown territory, but again they showed themselves entirely capable. There was even an amusing side. "Women, answering the sharp military knock on their doors, could assume an air of shocked indignation at the mere suggestion that they received visits from soldiers", Allen said, "while dimly discernible in some corner would be overcoats, unmistakably masculine and military. Myriads of nephews or first cousins were claimed by women with angelic faces of injured innocence. Mothers confronted with erring daughters would rend the air with lamentations, to be repeated a few days later on a second complaint with no less vehemence."

In the backstreets, however, they stumbled upon something dark. Young children, hanging around fruit and cake stalls in a lane at night, were being assaulted. The Women Police Volunteers rounded them up, took them home and ordered their parents to keep them there.

Protecting young children was uncontroversial, but when it came to older girls and vulnerable women, safeguarding invariably meant locking them up, and Grantham began opening shelters to receive them. The Bishop of Southwell, who seemed slightly confused about who was at risk from whom, said shelters were essential to defend the camps from any evil that might be caused through the careless behaviour of girls and women. When Damer Dawson rescued two teenaged sisters whose father had turned the family home into a brothel, the girls were put under what amounted to house arrest. It might have been worse. The original plan had been to send them to prison for their own protection, but the police were unable to find anything with which to charge them. No action was taken against their father, nor the men who had been frequenting the house.

Taking his lead from events in Portsmouth and Cardiff, in December General Hammersley announced that the women of Grantham were to be confined to their homes from eight at night until seven in the morning. Damer Dawson wasn't unduly concerned. "If we found it a mistake we could quite easily point it out and the restriction could be removed," she said. After just a month in the town the women were pronounced a resounding success by the military and civil authorities and the residents alike. So much so that General Hammersley then went further and invested in Damer Dawson the most extraordinary, unprecedented authority. The WPV would no longer be accompanying the military police on their raids. They would be carrying them out on their own.

> By virtue of the powers conferred on me under Regulation 3 [of DORA], I, Frederick Hammersley, being a competent military authority under the said regulation, do hereby authorise (name) to have the right of access to any land or building within a six-mile radius of the Post Office, Belton Park Camp, in the execution of her duty.

In her evidence to a government inquiry into women policing in 1920, Damer Dawson sounded like a house mistress checking the dorm at lights out: "It gave us power to go into women's houses to see if the girls were in bed and who was in the house." Her rationale for bursting into private homes in the middle of the night was that if the WPV were to be taken seriously then they had to show that they were capable of obeying orders. "No order, however distasteful, could be shirked," was Mary Allen's view.

* * *

Predictably, the events in Grantham were causing ructions in Robert Street. Boyle and Watson were aghast to find that the organisation they had set up specifically to support women was, on its very first outing, acting as an arm of the state to oppress them. When Constance Maud had brought Boyle and Damer Dawson together, it was clear that they not only had very different personalities but their motivations were not entirely aligned. Boyle was fighting a battle on several fronts against the institutional discrimination—

legal, financial and political—faced by women. It was about freedom, as the Women's Freedom League's name made clear. Damer Dawson, on the other hand, was driven by the wish to protect the vulnerable by stamping out sexual exploitation, albeit without Louise Creighton's faith-based conviction.

Trafficking was also an important cause for Boyle and Watson, but was only one element in a weightier, multi-faceted agenda. The three might have been united in their determination to see women in uniform and on patrol, but Boyle's world of protest, civil disobedience and radical politics, along with her anarchic streak, was alien to Damer Dawson's conventional, law-abiding mindset. And into this mix had now come the increasing influence of the authoritarian Mary Allen.

When Damer Dawson left Robert Street that day, she and Boyle believed that they could work together. Damer Dawson's conciliatory attitude towards Scotland Yard and the Home Office must have discomforted Boyle, but she needed the well-behaved Damer Dawson, first to sweet-talk Sir Edward Henry and then to act as an intermediary, for Boyle could no more contemplate working with the Commissioner than he could with her. She saw now, however, that her judgement had been monumentally skewed and that the mistake would cost her dearly. There was no way back; any further association with Damer Dawson was unthinkable.

* * *

"Nina was furious," Watson would later recall in her memoir. "Nothing in her eyes could excuse women being differentiated under law from men, nothing excused officials and police from safeguarding men and victimising women." Boyle described Hammersley's extraordinary order as terrorism and accused Damer Dawson of holding candle to official iniquity. The Women's Freedom League could not be associated with anything that involved the coercion of women and girls to make life easier for the police and the army, "for that was what it amounted to in the end". She and Watson announced their intention to take their movement back under the control of the WFL, and they demanded Damer Dawson's resignation.

The chief, however, had been emboldened. The trepidation that she'd felt as she boarded the train bound for gloomy Grantham had given way to elation. They had inspected the pubs, confronted the drunks and searched the homes, just as they had been ordered to do, and they had passed all the tests. In just one month, they had shown Grantham what women were capable of, and the town was delighted with them. Doubtless urged on by Mary Allen, Damer Dawson was not about to go without a fight. Trading insults was not her style, so she ignored Boyle's intemperate blasts and decided instead to put the question of the future direction of the Women Police Volunteers to the membership. Boyle and Watson were both big on democracy and could hardly object and, indeed, there is nothing to suggest that they did.

Back in London, in February 1915, Damer Dawson called the WPV together and asked them for a vote of confidence in her leadership. The results were extraordinary. She won by forty-eight votes to two; only Edith Watson and a riding instructor called Eva Christie voted against her. Overnight, Boyle and Watson had lost control of the organisation that only weeks earlier, against all odds, they had conceived and steered into life.

It seemed that Damer Dawson's hands-on approach, along with the quiet kindness that marked her one-to-one dealings with people, had sparked loyalty, not only from the devoted Allen and her friends in the Chelsea circle, but from those women Nina Boyle had personally recruited at Robert Street. Boyle might have been the more outgoing and immediately attractive character, but to the volunteers she was a distant figure, issuing feisty statements in *The Vote* and firing off combative letters to the likes of Bongie in Downing Street, but showing little interest in the volunteers personally or in the routine business of pounding the streets.

Allen would later reflect that, with hindsight, the split had been inevitable. They had tried to work together, but ultimately their views were just too divergent. She and Damer Dawson believed that men and women in public service should work together, not spend their time fighting each other. The vote, she said, proved transformative: "Before ... the WPV had been simply a nucleus of women loosely held together. After they became a closely knit organisation, clear as to their aim."

Damer Dawson was canny in victory. Rather than trying to oust Boyle and Watson, she abandoned the WPV to found a new organisation, setting up shop in three cramped rooms in a gracious redbrick block in Little George Street at the north end of Parliament Square. She was confident that the forty-eight would follow her and that she had the support of the Met Commissioner. Indeed, how could Henry be anything other than delighted to see the back of Nina Boyle? He even allowed Damer Dawson's new body to adopt the more official-sounding title of the Women's Police Service. At the same time, Damer Dawson and Allen replaced their own uniforms with dark blue army officer-style tunics with epaulettes, Sam Brown belts, breeches under their skirts, gleaming riding boots and greatcoats festooned with flashes and badges. And along with the regalia came a new regime, with Damer Dawson assuming the title of commandant and the lower ranks addressing their superiors as "Sir".

Boyle and Watson were now back in full control of the WPV, but there was little left to control beyond a few papers and textbooks that Damer Dawson had handed over. They did their best to put a gloss on it, announcing a new direction, parts of which bordered on the delusional. Watson would head a criminal investigation bureau while Christie would lead a mounted section and concentrate on animal welfare. The Men's League for Women's Suffrage offered them rooms opposite the British Museum in Bloomsbury, a bohemian, intellectual part of town, well away from the taint of Scotland Yard and Whitehall, and from here they set about trying to breathe life back into their decimated organisation. There was no denying though that it was an utter disaster. Despite the rhetoric, trying to rebuild from scratch was a task that no one, not even Edith Watson, had the energy to take on. Besides, while it was liberating to make defiant statements about breaking all ties with the agents of state control, the truth was that some form of official recognition was essential if they were to put their plans into effect. It was unimaginable that Sir Edward Henry, having once got shot of Boyle, would ever have allowed her back—or that she would agree to go.

Boyle was characteristically stoic once she had calmed down. It was a shame, she remarked, that suffragists, especially Women's Freedom

Leaguers, should be so ready to drop their principles for the sake of a little official favour, but from the start it had been clear that "a certain section" craved recognition and wanted to work hand-in-hand with the police rather than "cultivate an honest independence". Watson took it harder. The chance to deliver some justice for the victims of the violence and abuse whose plight she had worked so hard to expose had slipped through her fingers in a matter of weeks.

"It was a sad ending to a project that had started out with such high hopes," Watson wrote in her memoirs, "and I do feel that Nina and I were not treated very generously. It was our idea, based entirely on my work, and neither of us has been given the credit due." Yet Boyle, she added, "never sought recognition but let the whole question go by default." The WPV then proceeded to slide slowly and quietly into oblivion.

* * *

London, 8th December 1916:

Dear Friends and Colleagues,

I want to send you a word of greeting before leaving for the uncertain fortunes of hospital work in the near East … I am not taking up war work of this sort because I believe it to be my duty or because I am fired with feelings of patriotism developed by the exigencies of the European crisis. My patriotism has never needed that sort of spur, and is quite as well served and displayed in working for the welfare of my fellow women as in any other way. That is my real work; I am only leaving it for a time because I believe I shall come back to it fresher, fitter and more competent. After five and a half years I have felt myself getting into a groove, and lacking in initiative and in fresh ideas. A change of work as well as scene is the best tonic. Also, this great war is the biggest thing the world has yet known; and I think it becomes me, who talks politics and finds fault with politicians, to see something of it for myself at first hand, and not to be dependent on other people's impressions.

Ever sincerely yours, C. Nina Boyle

By the time Boyle published this letter of farewell in *The Vote*, there were established routes for women medical volunteers on the

Eastern front. Hundreds of British women went out as doctors, nurses, medical aides and ambulance drivers, and their stories of courage and endurance are extraordinary. Shortly before Boyle arrived, one team had set up field hospitals, dressing stations, fever hospitals and clinics in a matter of months. Boyle's friend, Vera "Jack" Holme, the cross-dresser, music hall star, chauffeur to Emmeline Pankhurst and regular guest at Eagle House, was driving an ambulance.

Boyle presented her venture as a fact-finding expedition, but it was more complicated than that. She was clearly also motivated by altruism, as she had been in South Africa, but there might have been another reason for the change of scene. It was a bizarre story that left Watson baffled. In the spring of 1915, just after the split with Damer Dawson, Watson dropped in on her friend in her apartment by Chelsea Bridge one afternoon and found her with a handsome, suntanned cavalry officer called Harry whom Boyle introduced as an old friend from South Africa. A few weeks later she told Watson that the pair had become engaged.

Watson was astounded: "She was older than he was and I had always thought of her as a dedicated spinster." As had everyone else. The more Watson saw of Boyle and Harry together, the more bewildered she became. "They didn't appear to want to be alone together and they seemed only to talk of the past, never of any future plans." Several times Boyle even suggested that Harry should take Watson out for tea, as though trying to throw them into each other's arms, Watson thought. She always declined to go but she started to like Harry more and more, so much so that she didn't care to think about him marrying her friend. She even forgot about Eustace and the fact that she was still married to him.

At the time the couple were living apart once again. They had moved out of the Camden bedsitter and into two rooms on the third floor of a Victorian house near Primrose Hill in northwest London. Out on a walk one day and in high spirits, Eustace picked up his wife and ran across the grass with her. When he then tripped and fell, Watson smashed her hip on a rock. Eustace seemed concerned at first but he quickly lost patience when, instead of jumping up after what he considered to be a reasonable amount of time, Watson continued to lie on the ground waiting for the nausea and shock to wear off. Over the following days the pain grew steadily worse, and Watson struggled to climb the stairs to their rooms. Eustace told her to pull herself together. Eventually, in agony, she staggered into the Royal Free Hospital where the damage was discovered to be considerable. While her husband had been berating her for her self-indulgence, a huge bulk of fibrous tissue had been building up around her hip bone, damaging her spine. She would probably end up in a wheelchair, she was told. Eustace, now livid, announced that he was leaving her: "I faced a crippled, painful future, no money, no work, no home, no husband".

She spent four months in hospital, where some wealthy supporters of the Women's Freedom League paid her fees in those pre-NHS days. Then miraculously, after a course of experimental injections, she began to recover. Eustace walked out a few days after she was discharged, but she was too delighted at being able to walk again to care: "Now that I was better I could easily get along without him". Nina Boyle found her a room, coincidentally near Hampton Court Palace where Louise Creighton was living, and paid her rent until she was able to work again. It seemed extraordinary that the spirited, confident Edith Watson, who argued with judges, bullied lawyers and fought with police officers, should have tolerated a man like Eustace for one moment.

Harry was equally attracted to Watson, and when his regiment was sent to Dublin to quell the republican Easter Rising of 1916, he sent her what amounted to a love letter. "I wrote back a cheerful, bantering letter, ignoring his expressions of endearment," Watson said. "Back came another letter, even more decidedly a love letter … The worst of it was that … in other circumstances I would have welcomed his headlong courtship."

On Easter Sunday, she arrived at Boyle's flat for dinner to find her friend badly shaken. A large picture had crashed down in the middle of the night, which foreshadowed death according to superstition. "Nina tried hard to pretend she didn't believe in such rubbish but she was not very successful."

A week later she received a note:

Dear Wattie, I was so sorry all those people were here when you came—there seems to have been people here all the time and I wanted to see you so much. Harry was shot storming a barricade after having been wounded several times. He is buried in Dublin Castle.

Love from your affectionate pal, CNB.

"If I had to lose a lover in war it would be storming a barricade," Watson reflected. "Nothing so mundane as dying of trench fever. Poor dashing Harry. I couldn't let anyone see what a blow it was to me. Nina could mourn openly. I could not."

Before long, she had taken Eustace back and was now losing Boyle. The League gave Boyle an affectionate send-off at The Despard Arms, tickets two shillings. It was a sell-out affair.

Watson couldn't afford to join Boyle on a war-time adventure in the Serbian mountains. She took a job in an army records office, where a shock awaited her: "The number of soldiers incapacitated through venereal disease was an eye-opener." Watson wondered whether, after all, there was something to be said for some of the Defence of the Realm Act measures. She did not, however, share her thoughts with Nina Boyle, knowing exactly what her friend's reaction would have been.

* * *

When Damer Dawson, Allen and Harburn returned to London after two months patrolling Grantham, they sent two women up to replace them: Edith Smith, a qualified nurse, and one Miss Teed. Ten months later, in December 1915, the chief constable John Casburn signed a warrant card giving Smith powers of arrest, thus making a thirty-six-year-old widow with four children the first woman in the country to be sworn in as a constable and paid a salary out of the police budget. Smith was by all accounts a highly intelligent woman, devoted to her job. Dorothy Peto, who had come across her on a short-lived joint training course for the National Union of Women Workers and Women's Police Service, described her as of outstanding personality; fearless, motherly and adaptable.

Casburn announced that any women sworn in must be carefully selected, because the female temperament was different from that of a man, although he found the Grantham women level-headed, sensible and capable. "They do sometimes jump to conclusions which are beyond me," he admitted, "but [they] are quick to grasp that a prosecution ... requires something more than a mere supposition to satisfy a magistrate." Now that they were over the shock of finding that there was not a law to deal with every little thing, they were doing really useful work with women and children which men could not possibly do so well, he told a government inquiry.

Smith was not raiding houses for long—ironically, given all the fury and heartbreak that the policy had caused, it was quickly abandoned as ineffective—but Boyle and Watson would have found some of Smith's other activities in Grantham just as outrageous. She kept a blacklist of women who had been banned from theatres and cinemas because of their "unseemly conduct" and kept an eye on wives who were suspected of being unfaithful, reporting back to their absent husbands. At the same time, however, she befriended many vulnerable girls, keeping them off the streets and out of the courts, while the professional prostitutes were said to be giving up on Grantham because the policewoman was such a nuisance.

The Home Office was not so happy. Their lawyers argued that Smith's swearing-in was invalid in law. Casburn was the only chief constable in the entire country to attach any importance to it, according to Sir Edward Troup, adding "but I am inclined to think he is in the hands of some strong ladies and that his senior policewoman is perhaps a better man than he is".

When the MP Frank Perkins asked the new Home Secretary Herbert Samuel if the women could be sworn in, Samuel said that naturally the women wanted the prestige but "the main source of the authority exercised by a police constable is not any privileges with which the law has vested him but the fact that he is as a rule above the average man in physique, is armed with a handy weapon and is likely to come off best if force is used". In fact, all social order rested upon physical force, the Home Secretary said.

This distinction between women volunteers and male professionals had real consequences, and certainly did not save the policewomen from physical attack. One of Margaret Damer Dawson's women, known as Buckie, would campaign to be sworn in after she was posted to a munitions factory. She was doing what they called proper policing, she said, not merely searching and patrolling, but investigating crimes such as theft. They should be able to issue a summons and see a case through rather than having to pass it over to the regular police. What's more, knocking off a policeman's helmet was punishable by six months with hard labour, but because a policewoman was, in the eyes of the law, a private citizen, the maximum sentence for knocking the woman herself to the ground was just one month in prison.

Edith Smith's swearing-in should have been a breakthrough, marking the start of women's steady progress as fully attested constables into the police force. However, that narrative still had some way to go, while Smith's own story ended in tragedy. She was badly exploited, given accommodation over the shop in a room above the police station and forced to work all hours in order to cope with a massive load. She staggered on for more than two years before resigning, defeated, in 1918, citing chest trouble which became steadily worse in winter due to spending long late hours in the fog and the damp, and returned to nursing. Three years later she committed suicide, aged forty-six, by taking an overdose of morphine.

15

THOSE SMILING KHAKI-CLAD GIRLS

July 1915, eleven months into the war.

Accompanied by ninety brass bands playing patriotic songs, and escorted by hundreds of officers from the Metropolitan Police on foot and on horseback, the procession shivered its way along the Embankment under lowering summer skies in the bitter driving rain. Wave after wave of women—said to comprise some 60,000— in close ranks two miles long, were led by a girl in a white Grecian robe fringed with gold. Behind her came a cavalcade of floats and players in costumes, symbolising the Allied nations. The slender imposing figure of Belgium dressed in mourning, a dark purple veil streaming out behind her, typified the soul of "that martyred but unconquerable land", *The Times* thought. She held her national flag aloft, "torn and tattered, but still beautiful" as she stepped barefoot through the slush, "on her delicate face … a moving expression of pride and sorrow".

The emotions were real enough, but the finely choreographed piece of theatre that was the Women's War Pageant had been put together by two most unlikely collaborators with a very cool-headed goal in mind. David Lloyd George, who had just moved from the Treasury to the new post of Minister for Munitions, was not known as the Welsh Wizard for nothing. He had given Emmeline Pankhurst £3,000 to organise the event, and when the drenched procession arrived back on Victoria Embankment after circling the West End, he was on a platform in the gardens of Munitions House waiting to greet them with his colleague Winston Churchill at his side. He then ushered Emmeline and Christabel Pankhurst and Annie Kenney into his office.

One clue to this startling show of unity was to be found on the swaying banners of the women who trooped behind the patriotic set pieces. There were one hundred and twenty-five contingents according to the man from the *Daily Chronicle*, who counted them in. Their slogans proclaimed: "Women are prepared to pay any price to defeat the enemy"; "We demand war work and service for all"; and "Women's battle cry is Work, Work, Work". Prominent among them were the munition workers, wearing the mob caps that prevented them from being dragged into the machinery by their hair and the masks that protected them from TNT (tri-nitro-toluene) poisoning; they were known as canaries because of the sickly yellow tinge of their skin. Their banners urged: "Drop every mortal thing and send them plenty of munitions" and "Shells made by a wife may save her husband's life". By the end of the war, over 700,000 women were working in munitions.

The suffragettes in the procession were following Pankhurst's lead in supporting the Empire. At the same time, like the thousands of women marching alongside them who were by no means all Pankhurst fans, the Women's Social and Political Union saw the war as their chance to move in on jobs that had been strictly male territory, just as Boyle, Watson and Mary Allen had done. The first roles to fall had been in the soft areas of hospitality and retailing, including, unthinkably, the pampered, ultra-conservative otherworld of the gentlemen's clubs of St James's. "Of all places in London, it was begun in the Atheneum," recalled the journalist Michael MacDonagh. "I called there for confirmation and was told by the secretary that seventeen of the male servants had joined the army and, as there were no suitable men over military age, women had been taken on as an experiment."

At Sainsbury's grocery stores, women in white overalls, who were—unlike the men—allowed to work sitting down, weighed sugar, cut butter and sliced bacon. At the Army and Navy Stores, girls in smart liveries operated the lifts. At the Bank of England, the female clerks were no longer hunched over their ledgers in the back office but out on the counters, dealing with the public. As the war went on, women would be delivering the post, collecting tickets at the railway stations, lighting street lamps, installing gas meters, boiling sugar, driving delivery vans and emptying dustbins. Many

Fig. 9: Crowds waiting for Mrs Pankhurst outside Bow Street Magistrates' Court. Nina Boyle, Edith Watson and Mary Allen were all sent to HMP Holloway after being tried at Bow Street for militant action.

Fig. 10: Mrs Pankhurst lifted right off her feet during an arrest outside Buckingham Palace, 1914. Confrontations between militant suffragettes of the WSPU and the Metropolitan Police were often physical.

Fig. 11: The arrest of Yorkshire mill worker Dora Thewlis, aged 16, was front-page news in 1908. She was dubbed Baby Suffragette for her role in the Rush on the House of Commons, the same action that landed Mary Allen in Holloway.

Fig. 12: Dora Marsden, another working-class Yorkshirewoman, was arrested in 1909 for storming her alma mater, Manchester University, in protest at the force-feeding of suffragettes on hunger strike.

Fig. 13: The Prisoners' Pageant at the Women's Coronation Procession, 17 June 1911, in which tens of thousands of suffragettes marched for the vote—including hundreds in white, representing '690 Imprisonments to Win Freedom for Women'.

Fig. 14: Arrested suffragettes being marched through St James's Park, gripped at the arm by police, following an attempt to petition the King at Buckingham Palace, 21 May 1914. More than 2,000 police were deployed and dozens arrested.

Figs 15–17: Women from all walks of life were arrested during the hours' long clashes between the Met and suffragettes outside Parliament on Black Friday, 18 November 1910.

SUFFRAGETTES BATONED BY POLICE

Evening News 6.30

Figs 18–20: The police man-handled hundreds of women, who complained of both physical and sexual assault. All charges against the women arrested were dropped the next day amid public outcry, with images of the violence making the front pages.

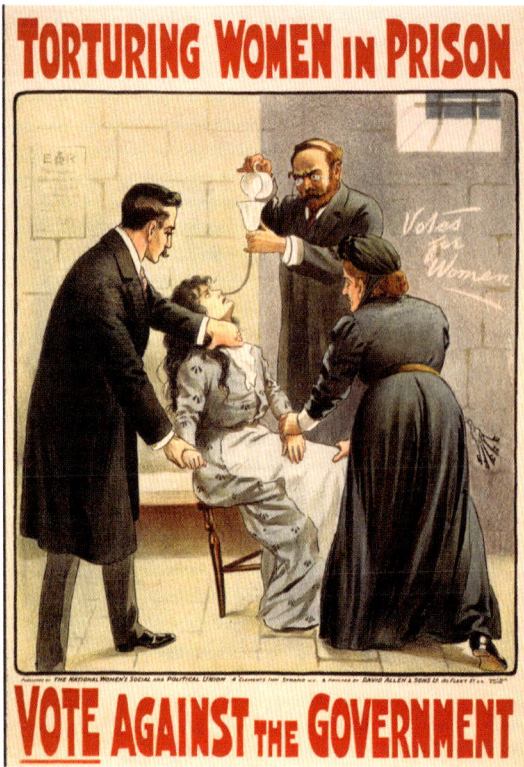

Fig. 21: The WSPU fought hard in the court of public opinion, including with posters exposing the force-feeding of suffragettes on hunger strike. Mary Allen endured milk and raw egg poured through her nose into her stomach.

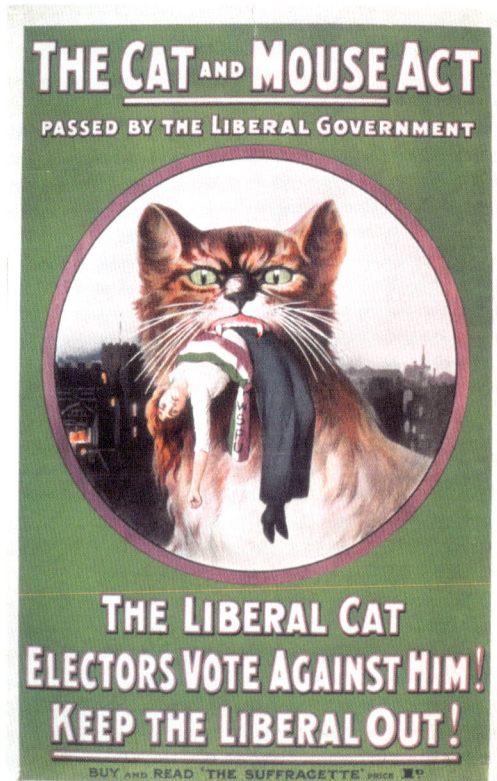

Fig. 22: A WSPU poster condemning the 1913 law allowing temporary release of prisoners weakened by hunger strike—known as the Cat and Mouse Act, for the brutality of freeing women only until they were well enough to be force-fed again.

Fig. 23: The suffragettes also suffered internal battles, caricatured here. Disputes arose over the Pankhursts' dictatorial leadership of the WSPU and its increasingly violent tactics.

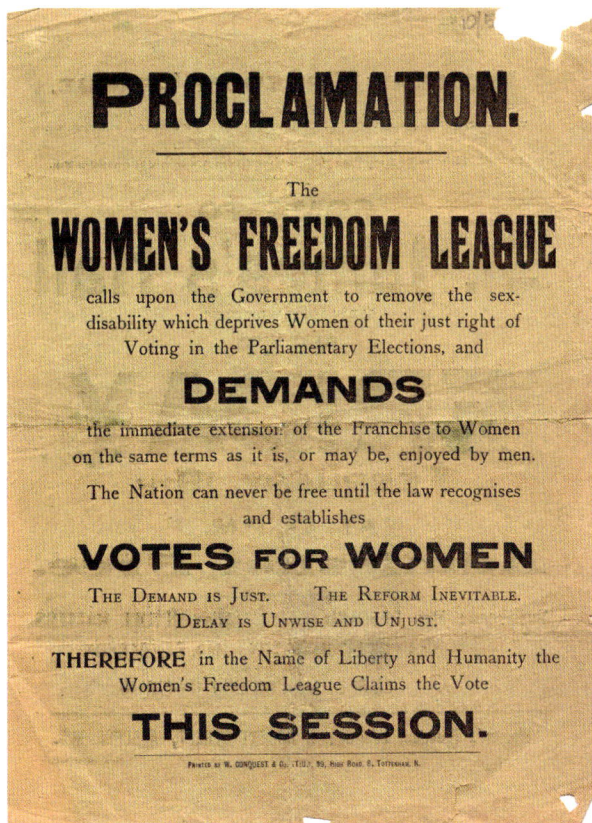

Fig. 24: Proclamation from the non-violent Women's Freedom League, founded by discontented WSPU members in 1907. Nina Boyle became head of the political and militant department in 1913.

Fig. 25: The formidable Lottie Despard, flanked by two colleagues from the new Women's Freedom League, faces off against a rather large policeman.

Fig. 26: Sir Edward Henry, Commissioner of the Metropolitan Police and a great enemy of Nina Boyle. In 1914 he was charmed by Margaret Damer Dawson into letting the pair start up a force of Women Police Volunteers, many of them WFL members.

had come from domestic service so, as well as the satisfaction of "doing their bit", they were earning more money. Sainsbury's paid one pound a week, compared with around eighteen pounds a year that a girl in service could hope to earn—and they were also enjoying some status and independence. "Not a parlourmaid to be had," Virginia Woolf noted.

The greatest need by far, however, was in the munitions industry, where the origins of the pageant and Lloyd George's cheque to Emmeline Pankhurst lay. Three months earlier, in the spring of 1915, a scandal over a shortage of shells that threatened to lose Britain the war had brought down Asquith's government. It had also set Lloyd George off on a frantic mission to turn the country into a vast armaments machine, opening weapons factories across the land. One of the first sites was a desolate six-thousand-acre strip of bog on the western fringes of the English-Scottish border. Gretna lay just above sea level, under heavy scotch mists with mounds of drifting sea wrack marking its shoreline. When George Duckworth from the Department of Munitions and Supply came up to check on construction, he found the experience a depressing one. The township was at that point nothing more than a cluster of weatherboard huts, resting gently in a sea of mud. It would be known locally as Timber Town.

A welfare officer called Mabel Cotterell met the first workers off the train at the little country station—fifty fisherwomen from the herring production lines of Aberdeen—and walked them over the fields. "It was well they came first in the summer days —it was warm and sunny, and there were flowers and the birds sang—for there were no proper roads, no lights, no shops, no halls or clubrooms, while at the factory the canteens were not ready for use," Cotterell said. There was a reason to be cheerful, however. The new jobs might have been considerably more dangerous than gutting and salting fish, but they were much better paid.

* * *

As Gretna was gearing up, Lloyd George found himself in need of another type of recruit, and for that he turned to Sir Edward Henry. The Commissioner was probably more than happy to assist, and not only because it involved supporting the war effort. It also gave him the chance to get the increasingly tiresome Damer Dawson and Allen off his back. With three sets of women now striding the streets, the public weren't alone in feeling confused. Even the police and the Home Office were hard put to work out who was who and, more importantly now that the complaints had started to come in, who was to blame for what.

Damer Dawson's booted and suited Women's Police Service were the obvious culprits, but Creighton's morality-fuelled patrols were also in the frame. In their eagerness to protect young women, both groups were following couples down dark alleys and patrolling the parks at night, flashing torches into the faces of what the Home Office described as "respectable citizens sitting on benches". They were also accosting women in the street—usually young working-class women—telling them to stop smoking, wear less make-up and straighten their hats.

One mother complained that her fourteen-year-old daughter had been accused of dressing herself up and walking about in order to attract the attention of men. Another woman was outraged to be confronted outside the Crystal Palace, now a naval training camp, where she was meeting her officer husband, and asked if she was waiting for a sailor, which of course she was. Nina Boyle wrote to the *Daily Mirror* to assure its angry readers that none of this had anything to do with the Women Police Volunteers.

His Majesty's Inspector of Constabulary, Sir Leonard Dunning, who, as a former chief constable of Liverpool, had a somewhat more varied and colourful life experience than most of the women involved in this moral policing, said that they didn't understand that the decorum that governed relations between the sexes in their own social sphere did not apply to all of society. *Punch* magazine satirised the culture clash in January 1918 with a cartoon of a woman at one of the clubs that Creighton's National Union of Women Workers had opened to keep girls off the streets, saying: "Of course you know, dear girls, ladies never talk to gentlemen until they have been properly introduced". A girl replies, "We knows it Mum and we feels sorry for yer."

Nor did the women realise, Dunning said, that failing to live up to their standards was not necessarily immoral and, even if it was, that still didn't make it any business of the police. When Sir Edward Troup had allowed Damer Dawson and Mary Allen into the Home Office to make their case for women to be sworn in, he said that Damer Dawson had displayed extraordinary ideas, hugely overestimating a constable's powers. He then whisked through the women's arguments, dismissing them one by one, and later recorded that he had seen a Miss Damer Dawson and also a Miss Allen, "the latter of whom is the stronger".

When the National Union of Women Workers (NUWW) turned up on the streets of Manchester in January 1915, its Miss Ashton was taken aback by the rage that greeted them. The chair of the Watch Committee described their presence in the city as an insult to the King's uniform—the men who wore it did not require a bunch of women to spy on them—while Councillor Fox, bellowing in order to make himself heard above the roars of approval in the town hall, said that first it had been soldiers' and sailors' wives who needed protection and must be instructed in how to spend their own money, and now it was young girls. He envisaged the patrols peering around corners, finding a soldier and his sweetheart kissing and reporting the girl to the authorities, damning her character for ever. The idea of amateurs roving the streets, carrying torches for the purpose of going down dark alleys, was preposterous.

Ashton did her best to calm everyone down, saying that the patrols only wanted to protect those girls who got out of hand, but no one in the council chamber that night appeared won over. One chief constable told Mary Carden that he didn't like the idea of a lot of women flaunting about with armlets on. When Carden assured him that the NUWW didn't recruit the flaunting sort, however, he said: "Well if you put it like that, you may try."

As public anger grew, Sir Edward Henry wasted no time in passing on Lloyd George's request for munitions factory supervisors to Damer Dawson. The minister needed one hundred and forty women immediately, with more to follow. They would search the workers for matches, metal hair pins and anything else that could cause a spark and blow them all to pieces, and they would also put a stop to any of what Lloyd Gorge described as "larking about" on the factory floor. Damer Dawson was so delighted that she offered to pay for the women's training and uniforms herself for the first six months. She and Allen then threw themselves into the task.

* * *

Frederick Mead, the rancorous chief magistrate at the Marlborough Street court and target of the protest that landed Nina Boyle and Edith Watson in Holloway, was a throwback to an era on the retreat. Even before the war changed everything, the seemingly immutable ground upon which Mead had planted his confident feet for nearly seventy years was starting to slide beneath him. In 1940, at the age of ninety-three, he would give a talk on the BBC Home Service as part of a series called "I Was There". The historic event that Mead had witnessed was the funeral of the Duke of Wellington in 1852.

When Emmeline Pankhurst and Lottie Despard had put their campaigns on hold, Mead lost one of his favourite sources of outrage; but even without any suffragists in the dock, women were still managing to plague him.

Like the Bessie Moncrieff affair, the trouble began in Hyde Park, three hundred and fifty dubious unlit acres in the heart of the capital, heavy with shrubbery that offered cover for a whole range of criminal activity, particularly what the law defined as indecency. The Met had long seen it as demeaning for an attested member of the Sovereign's constabulary to go poking around in the undergrowth in order to catch people in sexual activity. When the situation began to get out of hand, therefore, Henry decided to pay a small number of NUWW patrols six shillings a day for a short period to investigate and deal with "certain evils at present prevailing in the metropolis", by which he meant checking the Royal Parks for what he called unseemly conduct.

Catharine Bagster and Kate Summerton, described as mature women, were duly patrolling Hyde Park late one night when they came across two men under the bushes committing what the law called an act of gross indecency. The women had a constable with them—Henry's critics said it was ludicrous for him to pay the women while still having to send an officer with them to carry out the arrests—and the men were taken into custody. The Hyde Park police frequently arrested men for gross indecency but the cases usually ended in acquittal because, according to Superintendent Short, juries found it hard to believe that such acts took place in the open spaces of the metropolis.

Mead listened to the constable's testimony, but when he was told there were two more witnesses, Creighton's patrolwomen, waiting to give evidence, he refused to hear them; they weren't needed, he said. The accused had declined to enter a plea, which was tantamount to pleading guilty. This was nonsense, as Mead knew perfectly well. The case was headed for the Old Bailey where the men might well plead not guilty. A few days later a group of NUWW trainees were in the public gallery when a constable recounted how a prostitute had shouted "You fuck off" at him. Mead sentenced the woman to a month's hard labour and then hauled the trainees' leader up before him, telling her: "I should have thought your natural instinct would have revolted against a matter of this kind."

The NUWW asked Henry if Mead was in order. The Commissioner had no idea and asked some of his senior officers for their views. Some of the answers were surprising. The inspector at Hyde Park thought that the women's evidence would have a powerful effect on a jury, while Inspector Jackson at Richmond—who faced similar problems in Richmond Park—said he was sure that the women wouldn't shrink from doing their duty, even if it did mean standing up in public and describing filthy conduct. His superintendent added, with a touch of puzzlement: "It is a sign of the times that work properly falling to men is being performed by women, often with satisfactory results."

Henry decided that Bagster and Summerton would give evidence when the case reached the Bailey, and that in future a solicitor would be on hand to support the patrols. Mead was both offended and confounded. He wasn't concerned, he said, about the effect on the women because, after all, "They have already, in taking up this peculiar work, sterilised any maiden modesty they may have had". His objection was that it was embarrassing for men to hear such details being discussed in front of women. In this he was undoubtedly correct. Edith Watson's memoirs record that the first time she had stayed for an indecency case it had been "to the great embarrassment of everyone, not least my own". Henry did his diplomatic best to pacify Mead, saying that these were not normal times and perhaps it was better not to be too hasty.

Another few days later, and the Marlborough Street court was once again dealing with indecency in the park. A constable told Mead how he had found a man and woman in a suggestive position, their clothes in disarray. He was followed into the witness box by a patrol member. After his run-in with Henry, the magistrate didn't dare to refuse to hear her, so the expressive Mrs Frazer was free to play her five minutes of fame for all it was worth, painting the jury a graphic scene of the couple's movements. Mead was apoplectic. He threw the case out despite the evidence of three eyewitnesses, calling Frazer "one of these abnormal women who seem to suffer from some sort of moral obliquity".

* * *

Margaret Damer Dawson was on slightly less controversial ground when she set about advertising for munitions policewomen. Applicants should be between twenty-five and forty-five, well-educated and able to work out-of-doors in all weathers. Those of strong physique were preferred. One of the recruits was twenty-three-year-old Gabrielle West, a vicar's daughter from Christchurch in Hampshire. She and her friend Buckie had been looking for war work, wading listlessly through an uninspiring batch of vacancies that included canteen workers in Darlington, a cook at Bristol Infirmary and a housekeeper at a girls' school in Warwickshire.

"Then we heard that women police were badly needed so we went to their offices to see what that was like," West said. "All the WPS we saw were very smart in a very dapper uniform of navy blue." They were interviewed at Little George Street by a "very nice" inspector. "Nice" and "very nice" were West's favourite terms of approval. "They have taken up our references and if we are accepted I think we shall go … it sounds nice."

The Government had no idea how many women would be needed as the programme rolled out so Damer Dawson, worried about war-time shortages of cloth and leather, bought in bulk. Soon the jackets, boots and badges were piling up, and the bills were flooding in. Her reckless offer to fund the operation was draining both the coffers of the Women's Police Service and her own bank account, especially when she ran out of recruits with private means and had to start paying salaries to women like West and Buckie. Just as the situation was becoming desperate, however, the Government stepped in with a grant and she also received a large donation from a woman whose two sons had been killed in action. The WPS were not only solvent once more, but they were able to move out of Little St George Street across Parliament Square into a larger office in St Stephen's House, an elaborately hideous Victorian pile even closer to Scotland Yard. From here, Damer Dawson and Allen would recruit nearly 1,000 munitions police before the war was over.

West and Buckie were accepted and they travelled back to London to stay with West's friend Joan for their two weeks' training: attending lectures and the courts and drilling, followed by patrolling in the evenings around Victoria station and other lively neighbourhoods. There were about twenty of them, mostly ladies, West observed, although: "… some were middle-class … [and] all a better class than the average policeman".

After they finished their training, West and Buckie were sent to an explosives plant at Queensbury near Chester: "Very nice rooms, very nice landlady, very nice place and very nice work". They worked three gruelling shifts: 5.30 am—2 pm, 2 pm—11 pm and 10 pm—6 am. The factory was about five miles outside the town, which for the early shift meant getting up to catch the train at four, which was not very nice at all; in fact it was "horrid!".

After just a month, West was promoted to sergeant and she and Buckie were transferred to Pembrey in South Wales where they found the workers a fascinating if difficult bunch. "They are so full of life and cheerful and there are so many characters … Some of them are from lonely little sheep farms in the mountains who speak only Welsh or a very little broken English … very good sorts, though rough," West said. Their language, though, was sometimes "too terrible" and their temperaments unpredictable: "friendly one minute and shrieking with rage, almost ready to tear one to pieces the next". When West and Buckie first tried to get their volatile workers out of the dining rooms and back to their sheds, they were put to the test. The girls declared a strike and, climbing up to the top of a sand hill, they stood jeering, a menacing mob, threatening to "down" the first policewoman who dared approach them. "However, Buckie and I marched boldly amongst them, much to their amazement, and [we] commenced to hold forth," West recalled. "By and by one or two shouted to the others to shut up [saying,] 'They've got a bit of pluck anyhow'." After a ninety-minute stand-off, work resumed.

Conditions at Pembrey were bad. The site was below sea level, which meant that there were no drains. "The result is a horrid smelly swamp," West's diary records. "There were until recently no lights in the lavatories and as these lavatories are generally full of rats and very dirty the girls are afraid to go in … Buckie has at last persuaded the manager to put in lights …. This has made us very popular." Every night, around twenty people were found staggering around like drunks, poisoned by wafting acid fumes, but the medical room had only four beds. The cramped changing rooms had cattle troughs instead of wash basins, and soap and towels were in short supply. The protective clothing, "danger clothes", were often no more than filthy rags, and many of the outdoor workers lacked the prescribed boots, oilskins and sou'westers. The peripatetic West and Buckie would encounter plenty of dangerously poor conditions during their postings, including one to a shell-filling factory in Hereford where the acid made Buckie ill.

The recruitment drive continued apace, with help from a familiar figure. When Sir Edward Henry warned Reginald McKenna against allowing militant women to patrol the streets, pointing to the difficulties that the Prison Commissioners had had with one of their employees—"a trouble-maker in strong sympathy with a militant suffrage organisation"—he had Mary Gordon in mind. Gordon, a member of the Royal College of Physicians of Edinburgh, the Royal College of Surgeons of Edinburgh, the Faculty of Physical Surgery in Glasgow and a qualified midwife, had taken up her post in 1908, the first female national inspector of women's prisons. When the Commissioners had described her appointment as a new departure, they underestimated just how much of a departure the fifty-eight-year-old would prove to be, for over the course of the next six years Gordon leaked information to the Women's Social and Political Union, sending them confidential reports on the condition of suffragettes in prison, including on Emmeline Pankhurst during her hunger strikes. The game came to an end in 1914, when the Met raided the WSPU headquarters in Clement's Inn and stumbled across her letters.

Nevertheless, Gordon had managed to hang onto her job as inspector of women's prisons, arguing, correctly, that the WSPU was a perfectly legal organisation and that she hadn't done anything damaging to the State, and she continued her work trying to rehabilitate young sex workers in prison. Gordon was untouched by the heavy hand of moral purity. There was no talk of sin or of falling, and God didn't get a look in. She spoke harsh practical truths that the women could relate to, and she tried to empower them: "The men who call you little darlings and buy and sell you and joke about you behind your backs despise you. They give you diseases but they don't marry you. They inform against you and make laws to send you to prison. They take care not to send themselves. You have all seen the old women in this prison who began as you began and have been coming here ever since. Is that life?"

She was now attempting to rehabilitate women prisoners by encouraging them into munitions work on their release and she invited Damer Dawson and Allen to accompany her on a prison visit. About a dozen of what she described as the most incorrigible girls were seated around a long table, and Gordon told them that they were free to say exactly what they liked. When one young woman complained that they wouldn't be able to find work when they came out, Damer Dawson stepped in. "There is work for every one of you if you go to it and stick to it honourably. I'll get it for you," she promised.

The girl then asked if Damer Dawson would meet them when they came out. She replied, "No I won't. You know where to find me. You can make your own free choice." That was a masterstroke, Gordon believed: "They were feeling thoroughly inferior [but] at this point their feelings of power and independence woke up". When they were released, some went straight to the Women's Police Service to find munitions work.

* * *

When the first 100 policewomen moved into the rough makeshift huts at Gretna that Mr Duckworth had found so forbidding, the drains were still going in and the roads were torn up in all directions as the trolley lines went down. After tramping through leagues of mud, Damer Dawson's inspectors came off duty looking like plough boys after a hard day in the fields for, as well as patrolling the factory floors on the look-out for hair clips and frivolity, they also paced the huge, blacked-out industrial site in the pitch-dark and all weathers. Clad in shooting boots and leggings, carrying heavy-duty lanterns, they were armed with truncheons in case of encounters with burglars or prowlers lurking around the women's accommodation or, a constant worry, German spies. Ju-jitsu was definitely not up to the job.

In the early days, when the labourers were still on site, the women also stood outside the canteen at night when it was serving beer, holding up their lanterns to light the way across the uneven ground for the men stumbling out, which was definitely not part of their duties. By the time the labourers finally left, months after the first munitions workers moved in, Gretna comprised four factories and two townships with a railway line, a power station and its own water supply. The laundry washed 6,000 items a day and the kitchens cooked 14,000 meals.

Arthur Conan Doyle, the creator of Sherlock Holmes, was a war reporter at the time and was fascinated by the production of cordite: "The nitroglycerin on the one side and the gun-cotton on the other are kneaded into a sort of a devil's porridge, which is the next stage of manufacture," he wrote; "… those smiling khaki-clad girls who are swirling the stuff round in their hands would be blown to atoms in an instant if certain small changes occurred." At its peak, Gretna was producing eight hundred tonnes of devil's porridge a week, more than all the other munitions plants in Britain put together, and by the time Conan Doyle saw it, it was employing over 11,500 of the khaki-clad girls. The Women's Police Service found it almost impossible to stop cigarettes and matches being smuggled in, and hair clips—dangerous because of the risk of the metal reacting with the chemicals—proved the worst challenge. When the workers spotted a policewoman approaching, the shout would go up: "Look out girls, 'air raid!". One policewoman snipped the metal buttons off a worker's blouse.

And then there were the risks that went with operating heavy machinery. Hearing a strange noise coming from the engine in one of the workshops, a policewoman dashed in to find a girl with her long hair caught in a contraption that was dragging her steadily into its metal innards. Grabbing the hair with both hands, the police-woman held on with all her strength while the foreman ran to switch off the power.

Many of Conan Doyle's smiling girls were indeed girls. Sixty per cent of the female workforce at Gretna was under eigh-teen, which saw the WPS taking on a role that Lloyd George and Henry had probably not foreseen, advising very young workers who were often far from home about how to behave, particularly when it came to boyfriends, as they thought any good parent would do. While some of the girls came to them with their problems, how-ever, the more worldly and independent among them resented what they saw as patronising, stuck-up ladies bossing them about. These were not the kind of parents that they recognised.

Meanwhile, the Gretna authorities were desperately trying to steer them away from the lights and the fun on offer in the pubs and cinemas of Carlisle. The policewomen at Gretna had their own distinctly middle-class amusements: singing, playing in an orchestra, playing cricket and tennis and having quiet evenings by the fire in the recreation room. But for the workers, the town offered a tempting escape from the wooden huts and the weari-some hours among the explosives. The factory's social and recre-ation department countered with dances, films judged to be suit-able for girls, an "improvement" club, a music society, sports clubs and a gymnasium.

It was the familiar theme of care versus control, for alongside the knowing town dwellers signing on at the nation's factories were the naïve child-like girls from the country. Seventeen-year-old Olive Taylor, from the isolated marshes near the River Humber, was working as a cook for a doctor when she decided to apply for a job in munitions. Like Edith Watson, she was desperate to escape her situation in a house where she was treated like a slave. The English factory she joined, near Morecambe Bay, proved a revelation. "It was there to my disgust that I was told how babies were made. I refused to believe it and told the women in no uncertain terms what I thought of them, remarking that my mum and dad would never do that … Women in the country had no idea of what was to happen to them when they married." Her colleagues nicknamed her "Molly-Never-Had-It".

Peggy Hamilton came from a wealthy Berkshire family. With no need to earn a living, she had taken up munitions work in the belief that she was helping to win the war that would end all wars. While not as innocent as Taylor, Hamilton was shocked at the sexual banter at her Birmingham factory. Her puritanical upbringing hadn't prepared her for anything like it, she said, adding: "My innocence drove them to greater and greater lengths until they burst out laughing, screaming 'Oooo, she's a novice'." In 1917, the Bishop of London paid a visit to Gretna. He praised the girls for taking on such dangerous work, but warned them that the greatest peril they faced lay not in the factory, but in the moral pitfalls awaiting them outside.

16

CLOSE ASSOCIATION AND INTIMATE FRIENDSHIP

A photograph of Margaret Damer Dawson and Mary Allen shows them cruising around town in a state-of-the art motorcycle combination. The pair are splendid in their greatcoats and peaked caps, Allen driving the bike and Damer Dawson in the sidecar, a drunken man they had apparently just hauled off the streets slumped beside her. It later emerged that the picture was a mock-up for publicity purposes—the "drunk" was Isobel Goldingham—but the bike was real enough. Meanwhile, Sir Edward Henry's superintendents were still visiting their stations by pony and trap.

Only Damer Dawson and Allen knew the exact nature of their relationship. They had both grown up in traditional Victorian middle-class families where sexuality, much less same-sex relationships, was not up for discussion. Nor were emotions, although Allen said that on first acquaintance the pair had struck up what she described as a close association and intimate friendship. For Allen, that meeting had been an epiphany, as formative and impactful as her first encounters with Annie Kenney and Emmeline Pankhurst, and over the years that followed she would gradually edge closer and closer to revealing her sexuality.

In a studio portrait probably taken at some point after the spring of 1915, Allen and Damer Dawson are standing shoulder to shoulder against a soft-focus country backdrop, wearing greatcoats, collars and ties, long boots and peaked, braided navy-style caps starred with a metal badge. Damer Dawson is holding a cane. Their expressions are purposeful rather than severe. It is a conventional shot of two professional, if somewhat ludicrously dressed, women—except for one thing. They appear to be holding hands. The incongruity and the pair's oblivion to it makes the picture instantly ridiculous. On second look, however, there is also something touching there. They are clearly, in some sense, a couple, and they appear to have reached out instinctively for each other.

In the early 20th century, sex between women was regarded with revulsion, prurience and denial in equal measures. In public life, and in private too for the most part, what were known as inverts, or sapphists after the Greek poetess Sappho, weren't mentioned: if they weren't acknowledged, then they didn't exist. Some minds also baulked at the mechanics. Was it anatomically possible? What did they actually do? Queen Victoria was rumoured to be among the doubters and the myth persists to this day that she was the reason that sex between women was never made a criminal offence. A little enlightenment was available for anyone who troubled to look, however. *School Life in Paris*, published in 1899 by the Erotica Biblion Society of London and New York, was typical of the material that was changing hands in the small but lively undercover trade in lesbian pornography. In telling the story of a young woman's awakening at a Parisian finishing school, the anonymous author spared no detail about who did what to whom and the rapture that followed.

In 1918 would come the court case that blasted the subject into the public consciousness and, while the proceedings resembled a comic opera—or a madhouse, thought *The Daily Telegraph*—Mary Allen would be among the many women who would find its reverberations liberating. Damer Dawson, sadly, was to be a different story. The Maud Allan scandal had everything: same-sex relationships, female sexuality, a secret book of shame, blackmail, German perfidy and a wicked woman. There were also walk-on parts for Herbert and Margot Asquith, the former Prime Minister and his wife; Lord Alfred Douglas, Oscar Wilde's lover and nemesis; and, the lover of King Edward VII and great-grandmother of Queen Camilla, Alice Keppel, along with a defendant who appeared to be teetering on the brink of insanity. The prospect of sapphism being discussed in open court had the establishment shuddering. Quite apart from the revolting evidence that was bound to emerge, there was the fear that airing the subject might entice previously unsullied women to give lesbianism a try. The Reverend Francis Knight wrote to the Home Office begging that the case be thrown out before it was too late.

Allan was a Canadian dancer, celebrated across Europe for her seductive Dance of the Seven Veils. She had a pouting sultry beauty and a habit of draping herself in little but wisps of gauze and webs of beads. When she announced that she would be performing in a new production of Oscar Wilde's *Salomé* in London's West End, *The Morning Post* spoke for many when it declared "These perversions of sexual passion have no home in the healthy mind of England." The right-wing anti-Semite MP Noel Pemberton Billing was moved to write an article in his newspaper *The Vigilante*— "founded in the interests of purity in public life"—under the extraordinary headline "The Cult of the Clitoris", a phrase that *The Times* decided was unprintable.

Allan sued and Billing was charged with criminal libel, which meant that the case would be heard not in a civil court but at the Old Bailey. The MP was accused of maliciously publishing a false and defamatory libel "meaning that the said Maud Allan was a lewd, unchaste and immoral woman and was about to give private performances of an obscene and indecent character, so designed as to foster and encourage unnatural practices among women, and that the said Maud Allan associated herself with persons addicted to unnatural practices." The judge announced that he would not soil his tongue by describing what the words meant, but it was impossible to conceive of anything more filthy. So much for hushing the matter up.

The trial lasted six days. The public gallery was packed with spectators, many of them women, and the newspapers devoted pages to the proceedings. It proved a spectacularly entertaining show, as thrilling and fantastical as any performance of *Salomé*. Billing claimed that Allan would attract some of the 47,000 high-profile gay men and women who were named in a Black Book. He described them as a catholic miscellany, which included Privy Councillors, chorus boys, Cabinet Ministers and their wives, dancing girls, diplomats, poets, bankers, editors, newspaper proprietors and members of His Majesty's Household, all of them implicated in disgusting sexual perversions. He had been unable to track down a copy of the book he admitted, but it had been seen by no less a figure than Prince William of Wied in Albania. Mr Justice Darling remarked that that none of this had anything to do with libel before going on to give

Billing full rein, appearing more concerned with how the play had made it onto the stage in the first place.

The witnesses included a twenty-five-year-old officer discharged from the military for what was described as paranoid delusional insanity. The court heard testimonies that included the claim that the King's mistress, Alice Keppel, was working undercover for the German government—or perhaps it was the British government, Billing was a little hazy about the matter—and an account of a clandestine meeting over afternoon tea in the Hut Hotel in Ripley. When the judge ordered one woman to leave the witness box, Billing pointed at him and shouted, "Is Mr Justice Darling's name in that book?" and the witness replied, "It is". Lord Alfred Douglas, whom the police would later throw out of the court, described *Salomé* as an abominable piece of work. Wilde, he said, had been the greatest force for evil in Europe for the last thirty-five years from whose clutches his father, the Marquess of Queensberry, had saved him.

Struggling to stay in the real world but not appearing confident that he was succeeding, Allan's lawyer said that while the play might be tragic and unpleasant, it contained nothing suggestive of any of those horrible vices referred to in the libel charge. "Everyone concerned appeared to have been either insane or to have behaved as if he were," Sir Basil Thomson, head of Special Branch at Scotland Yard, wrote in his diary.

Billing was found not guilty. When the verdict was announced, it was clear that he had become something of a national hero. The crowds in the gallery sprang to their feet cheering, with women waving their handkerchiefs and men their hats. The MP left the court arm-in-arm with his wife to be greeted by another ovation from the crowds waiting outside. It later emerged that Margot Asquith was paying the rent on Maud Allan's apartment in Regent's Park, where the dancer lived with her secretary and lover, Verna Aldrich.

The closest that Britain would come to criminalising sexual acts between women would be in 1921, and it had nothing to do with Her Majesty but more with Arthur Foley Winnington-Ingram. The bishop had been calling on the Government for years to do more to protect young girls from exploitation by older men. In the House of Lords, he had tried to tighten the Criminal Law Amendment Act of 1912, which had cracked down on brothels and sex trafficking but did nothing about sexual assault. The government promised to deal with the omission with follow-up legislation, but in 1914 the bishop ran out of patience and introduced a Bill of his own. It proposed raising from thirteen to sixteen the age at which an accused could claim that the victim had consented to sexual contact; raising the age at which a girl could consent to unlawful intercourse from sixteen to eighteen; and removing the defence that the accused had reasonable cause to believe that a victim was over sixteen for sexual assault and over eighteen for abduction.

These measures met with huge resistance, including from the Lord Chancellor. The lawyer Lord Parmoor opined that any changes to the law "should not be influenced by outside resolutions got up by various bodies who may very well be carried away by sentimental notions", by which he meant the over seventy organisations, including Nina Boyle's WFL and Louise Creighton's NUWW, who were backing the bishop. The Bill finally emerged so mutilated that Winnington-Ingram feared that it would do more harm than good—The National Society for the Prevention of Cruelty to Children warned that it could put a complete end to their work— and he withdrew it.

In 1921, however, the bishop was back and MPs again raised concerns that decent, respectable men—men like themselves— might become the unwitting target of wicked accusations by scheming little girls. This time, though, they tried a different tactic. They proposed an amendment to the Bishop's Bill, as it was known, which read: "Any act of gross indecency between female persons shall be a misdemeanour and punishable in the same manner as any such act committed by male persons under Section 11 of the Criminal Law Amendment Act 1885". In 1895, Section 11 had sent Oscar Wilde to Reading jail for two years with hard labour. The amendment was in fact a wrecking device. The MPs calculated that the outrage and hand-wringing that discussing lesbians would spark in Westminster would dominate the debate and cause the Bishop's Bill to run out of time.

On the floor of the House, all the old fears about putting the unspeakable into the public domain resurfaced. One MP warned that the institution of marriage could be undermined by husbands losing their wives to the wiles of a lesbian. Josiah Wedgwood said that the clause would advertise "this beastly subject", while Lieutenant-Colonel Moore-Brabazon set out three ways of dealing with perverts. Executing them or locking them away in asylums would rid society of them, but the best method was simply to refuse to acknowledge their existence, which had worked in Britain for hundreds of years. The proposed clause, he said, would only introduce into the minds of perfectly innocent people the most "revolting" thoughts.

The plan worked and the Bill fell. "There existed in the House of Commons a number of men who were absolutely determined to protect their sex in their assaults on young girls," Louise Creighton observed. A form of legislation was finally enacted in 1922 without the contentious clause, but in the last half of the 20th century, it would ironically come under fire for curtailing young women's freedom to express their sexuality.

* * *

Despite Edith Watson's best efforts to discredit Archibald Bodkin, in 1920 the now Sir Archibald was appointed Director of Public Prosecutions. Bodkin was a tall, rod-thin, austere figure who travelled miles between London courtrooms on foot and had no interests outside of the law, his only recreation being the occasional game of billiards. *The Times* said he possessed a bubbling, if somewhat heavy sense of humour, which, the paper said damningly, he never allowed to get out of hand. His colleagues tended to believe the story of him being seen leaving his chambers one Christmas night carrying a stash of papers.

As Director of Public Prosecutions, Bodkin was accused of exceeding his powers by bringing cases that offended against his personal morality, especially where books were concerned, and in 1922 he famously banned James Joyce's *Ulysses*, telling the Home Office: "I have not had the time, nor may I add the inclination to read through this book. I have however read pages 690-732 …". *The Times* thought that he needed to get out more, saying that he should have taken up "rather wider intellectual interests outside his profession".

It was inevitable, then, that the publication of Marguerite Radclyffe Hall's semi-autobiographical novel *The Well of Loneliness* in 1928 would prompt Bodkin to bring a charge of obscenity against the publisher. The case, in common with that of Maud Allan although lacking the fun, would splash lesbianism across the news pages. The book tells the story of Stephen Gordon, an upper-class woman with what Radclyffe Hall described as a congenital sexual inversion. The term was coined by proponents of the new science of sexology, who saw same-sex attraction as an inversion of heterosexuality. Radclyffe Hall's heroine falls in love with a woman she meets while serving as an ambulance driver in Serbia during the war, but the story of their relationship doesn't prove an uplifting experience.

A month after the book came out, the publisher Jonathan Cape issued a statement: "We have received a request from the Home Secretary asking us to discontinue publication of Miss Radclyffe Hall's novel. We have already expressed our readiness to fall in with the wishes of the Home Office in the matter." Cape had deliberately over-priced the book at fifteen shillings, they explained, in order to put off the general novel-reading public—so this was not then a book for salacious ill-educated members of the hoi poloi—but Cape felt it was time that the subject was discussed in a wider forum than the science text books. George Bernard Shaw and H. G. Wells berated them for caving in.

Two months later, a publishing house in Paris reissued the book at the even higher price of twenty-five shillings with a view to importing it, but the first consignment was seized at Dover. Bodkin then put out a call for expert witnesses who were prepared to testify that "those wicked women (as I deem them) who voluntarily indulge in these practices" were risking destruction morally, physically and perhaps even mentally.

The magistrate Henry Chartres Biron, last seen under Nina Boyle's critical gaze while sentencing the drunk and disorderly during the war, ordered all copies to be destroyed and threatened to throw Radclyffe Hall out of his courtroom after she challenged him for saying that the women volunteers who drove the ambulances in Serbia were known to have been addicted to certain practices. The author told him: "Those women were the finest, the most courageous, the most sacrificing, and above all, the purest members of the British Empire." Among them was Nina Boyle's young friend Vera Holme. *The Times Literary Supplement* described the book as sincere, courageous and high-minded, while protests against censorship poured into the left-leaning newspaper the *Daily Herald*. Radclyffe Hall was brave to put herself in the firing line but her wealth and status, together with the bohemian circles in which she moved, allowed her to float above the commotion. Women from the middle- and, particularly, the working classes enjoyed no such protection.

* * *

As always when women demand equal rights with men, the suffragettes were derided as extremists and man-haters, the butt of cartoons and music hall jokes, and from there it was a short step to insinuating that the movement was, literally, a hotbed of perversion. Some of the speculation about scandalous goings-on in suffrage circles centred on Eagle House, a villa dating back to the late 17th century, set in four acres in Batheaston, Somerset, the home of Emily Blathwayt and her husband Linley, a retired Indian army colonel. Emily and her daughter Mary were members of the Women's Social and Political Union, and the colonel was a firm supporter.

With his meditative face and long, white, Bernard Shaw-like beard, Linley was not everyone's idea of a high-ranking army officer in the Jewel in the Crown of the British Empire. Back home in the West Country, he built a summerhouse in the gardens of Eagle House as a refuge for recovering hunger strikers, and the guest list was a roll-call of suffragist fame. Emmeline, Christabel and Adela Pankhurst and Annie Kenney were among those seeking respite there. Linley also lent them his beloved motor car for trips out and created a memorial garden where the women were invited to plant a tree in their names. It was known as Annie's Arboretum after Kenney. Lottie Despard planted a holly tree in 1911. There is no record of Mary Allen ever staying at Eagle House, but Emily Blathwayt's diary entry for 12th November 1909 notes: "This morning we went down to the police court. Vera Wentworth, Miss Pitman and Mary Allen were all tried. Vera W. and Mary Allen each have fourteen days in the second division."

Nina Boyle's friend Vera Holme, known as Jack or Jacko, was a frequent visitor. The daughter of a Lancashire timber merchant, Holme was sixteen years younger than Boyle, a snub-nosed, round-faced irreverent woman. Sylvia Pankhurst described her as a noisy and explosive young person, frequently rebuked by her elders for lack of dignity. Holme had begun her career on the stage, singing and dancing at the Savoy Theatre where she frequently took on cross-dressing roles. After joining the WSPU, however, she became Emmeline Pankhurst's chauffeur, driving the elegant matriarch around town in the Union's magnificent Austin Landaulette, wearing a uniform in the Union colours of green, white and violet, her peaked cap starred with the Royal Automobile Club's badge of efficiency. *The Chauffeur* magazine described her as Britain's first lady chauffeur.

When Holme, who had been educated in a Belgium convent, moved in with another WSPU member, the two women carved their initials on the post of the bed they shared. The couple would, like Radclyffe Hall's protagonist and Nina Boyle, later serve as medical volunteers on the Eastern Front, where Jack drove an ambulance.

Most of the tales about life at Eagle House come from the diaries of the colonel's daughter, Mary Blathwayt, who was among those to become besotted with Annie Kenney. A friend described Mary as an unquestioning heroine worshipper whose devotion never faltered. Mary painstakingly recorded complex and shifting relationships between the Pankhursts and the other WSPU icons, describing what sounded like giddy rounds of bed-hopping and one-night stands in Linley's garden house. One theory has it that Mary was briefly involved with the beautiful Christabel, who, like Kenney, aroused erotic feelings in many women, but was then supplanted by Kenney.

Certainly, Emmeline Pethick Lawrence described Kenney as Christabel's devotee "in a sense that was mystical … her devotion took the form of unquestioning faith and absolute obedience … No ordinary individual could have given what Annie gave … the surrender of her whole personality to Christabel." But it's up for debate how much we can trust Mary's account of free love and sexual rivalry among the suffragists, as is what exactly she meant by "sleeping with". Did the phrase have the same sexual connotation then as now? Or did it simply mean sharing a bed when accommodation was in short supply? And how much was Mary's judgement clouded by jealousy over Kenney's own obsession with Christabel?

Other suffragists added to the intrigue. The composer Ethel Smyth talked of her ardent affection for Emmeline Pankhurst and hinted at an affair between them, while Teresa Billington-Greig wrote that the intensity of feeling between Annie Kenney and Emmeline Pethick-Lawrence frightened her, calling it something unbalanced and primitive. But who knew? It all remains whispers in the dark in the pavilion.

PART IV

17

STICK TO IT AND YOU'LL WIN

Nina Boyle returned to London in the summer of 1917, shabby, penniless and exhausted. She had joined the staff of a small military hospital in a town called Vodena, perched on sheer dizzying cliffs, six hundred feet up in the Serbian mountains with streams running through its streets. It wasn't the obvious site for a medical unit, but the small British charity running it had had to take what they could get. The hospital itself was a large near-derelict house, thick with the fumes of the carbolic and paraffin deployed in a constant battle to kill off the swarms of lice and bed bugs. As Boyle was saying goodbye to her friends, a British doctor at Vodena, Dorothea Maude, jotted in her diary: "Rain, fog, rain, fog, three weeks *sans cesse*. Still continuing, hospital full and overcrowded with wounded."

When Boyle arrived in 1916, steeled for hardship and danger, she was both surprised and amused to be given the task of writing the menus for Christmas dinner—quite a good dinner, she noted. When this was followed by weeks of patching sheets and darning socks, however, frustration set in. She might as well have stayed at home and joined one of the sewing circles scorned by Mary Allen.

Even when she was appointed night sister despite her lack of nursing qualifications, this was still not the intrepid adventure she had anticipated, and at some point she left the hospital to join an ambulance unit. The details are unclear as, typically, Boyle would waste neither time nor ink chronicling her exploits or recording her feelings. The article that she wrote for *The Vote* about her experiences focused not on her own exploits but on the desperate situation of the Macedonian people.

She appears, for a while at least, to have served with an ambulance unit run by Lottie Despard's sister Katie Harley. The pair certainly ran into each other somewhere on the Eastern Front, for Boyle wrote to a friend: "Tell Mrs Despard that it was a real delight to see someone so like her in person and in spirit". Her last exploit was to accompany the battered Serbian army as it retreated all along the line down to the sea in the summer of 1917.

"Nina often talked to me of the sadness and fury of an army in retreat and the confusion and misery of the civilians left exposed to the enemy," Watson would recall.

They abandoned the ambulance when they reached the coast and escaped on a filthy cockroach-infested boat, dodging bombs and torpedoes and narrowly avoiding capsizing. Boyle arrived home in time for the last stages of the suffrage struggle, and the Women's Freedom League welcomed her back with another teetotal party. Katie Harley was not so fortunate. Harley, who had organised the "Great Pilgrimage" of 1913, a women's suffragist march from across England and Wales to Hyde Park, had died in Serbia in March 1917, a few weeks before Boyle left for home, killed by shellfire in what was by then enemy-occupied territory.

* * *

6th February 1918, nine months before the Armistice. After a knife-edge battle in the House of Lords, the Representation of the People Act passes into law. Over eight million women—those aged thirty and over with a property qualification—now have the right to vote. That is only about two-thirds of the total number of women in the UK, but it is surely only a matter of time before the rest follow. An important question remains, however: does this mean that women can also stand for Parliament?

Two months after the Representation of the People Act came into force, Sir Swire Smith, the Liberal MP for the constituency of Keighley in West Yorkshire, died suddenly and Boyle decided to settle the argument by putting herself forward as a candidate in the by-election. Her friend, the actress and writer Cicely Hamilton, thought her quite unsuited to the role: "She was too independent in thought and speech, too intolerant of any deviation from principle to make real and permanent success in a career that calls for patience as well as compromise."

The returning officer was inclined to allow Boyle to fight the Keighley seat, but then had to turn her down on technicalities: one of her sponsors wasn't on the electoral roll, while another lived outside the constituency. For Boyle, who had no chance of being elected and showed not the slightest desire to be an MP, this was of no consequence; she had proved her point. The Law Lords, however, took a different view. The Great Reform Act of 1832 specifically banned women from standing and there was nothing in the new legislation that changed that, their lordships said.

* * *

August 1918, three months before the Armistice. Sir Edward Henry is on holiday and the Metropolitan Police are on strike. The pickets take up their posts at midnight, and when the men arrive for their shifts all but a handful turn back. There follows a day of chaos. Tangles of carts and cars clog the streets, the drivers cursing and shouting, while the magistrates kick their heels on the benches and wait in vain for the prisoners to be delivered. Sylvia Pankhurst tells the strikers that they are now part of the working-class army: "Charwomen and work girls cheer you." She is right. As thousands of policemen march from Tower Hill to the West End demanding a pay rise, crowds gather to applaud them. The bus conductresses, stuck in the snarl-ups on the roads, are particularly feisty; according to one reporter, they shout: "Stick to it and you'll win, the same as we did." The bus girls, as they are known, had returned to work only days earlier after forcing the London General Omnibus Company to pay them the same as the men.

The officers did win—and quickly—but only because Lloyd George, who was now Prime Minister, stepped in. The Women's Freedom League congratulated "our old acquaintances" on their victory, but couldn't help contrasting the police officers' behaviour as protesters with the treatment they had meted out to the suffragettes when they attempted to do the same thing: "Last Saturday morning Downing Street was massed with policemen on strike. They sat upon Mr Lloyd George's garden wall and some of their number

followed in the wake of the suffragettes by speechifying from a wag-
gon, all within a stone's throw of the Prime Minister's residence."

The strike was a deep personal failure for Henry, and he resigned
the day after the settlement was announced. Of course, he had
originally planned to go in 1914, only staying on because of the war,
and was now nearly seventy and still suffering from the effects of his
bullet wound. It was a humiliating finale to his fifteen years in the
role and many saw him as a scapegoat. Months earlier he had warned
the Home Secretary, now Sir George Cave, about the low morale
among his men, but Cave had ignored him. Henry withdrew to his
Ascot seat in the beautiful Berkshire countryside where he became
a magistrate, resumed his finger-printing studies and joined the
committee of the NSPCC.

Henry's successor, Sir Nevil Macready, the man intended for the
role before the war intervened, was a stereotypical plain-speaking
army man. He had been born into an artistic and literary family; his
father William was an actor and theatre manager and his great-
grandfather was the artist William Beechey, who was knighted by
George III for his royal portraits. Macready himself was said to be a
talented singer but as a boy was far too lazy to apply himself to
drawing or painting, he explained in his autobiography, while his
father "would rather have seen a child of his in his coffin than on the
stage", following in his footsteps. According to his son, William
Macready had "endured agonies" trying to perfect his art and
attempting to raise the then lowly social status of the profession.
And so, Sir Nevil had rejected both the dramatic arts and the con-
cert hall in favour of Sandhurst.

Macready described the prospect of replacing Henry as "not a
pleasant one", and had had to be dragged out of the War Office and
into Scotland Yard kicking and screaming. When the Secretary of
State for War, Lord Milner, told him that Lloyd George had him
lined up as Commissioner, Macready said he wouldn't entertain the
idea. "I had attained a position in the army which had been the height
of my ambition, was egotistical enough to think that I knew the
work from A to Z, and wished to complete my time as Adjutant-
General, and then to retire into private life." He noted in his memoir that in 1914 he would have gladly accepted the offer, but had
changed his mind during the war years.

Milner reported back to Downing Street and that same afternoon Macready was summoned to the Cabinet Room, where he found assembled a high-profile reception committee including the Prime Minister, Milner, the Home Secretary and a sprinkling of assorted Cabinet Ministers. "I took a chair opposite Mr Lloyd George and then the fun began. For close on two hours I resisted the pressure to take up the Commissionership … I suggested other men, younger and equally fit for the post, to which the Prime Minister replied that it was necessary to have someone in whom the public would have confidence."

Lloyd George then played his ace: it was a matter of national importance that Macready should take the job. The soldier replied in his customary cut-to-the-chase manner: "I asked him if he really meant that, and had not said it as an extra little bit of gratifying whitewash. He said he did, on which, of course, I had nothing further to say, except that I would do my best to see the business through. The assent of the King was obtained through the telephone, and I left Downing Street at about seven pm in a very sad frame of mind." He spent a restless night thinking through the pros and cons and the next morning wrote to Lloyd George, begging the Prime Minister to think again. "Nothing, however, came of it."

When he arrived at his new command centre on the river, he found it a dreary workplace. Scotland Yard "could never exude cheerfulness—a settled atmosphere of nervousness and gloom seemed to have invested the place", he later wrote. Perhaps surprisingly, he contrasted the atmosphere with "the more light-hearted, optimistic mood at the War Office"; but then Macready was at home among the military men—his friends, he called them—in the great muscular bulk of a building on the corner of Horse Guards Avenue, while at the Yard he was an outsider, suspicious and regarded with suspicion.

Perhaps because of his experience commanding soldiers, however, Macready would turn out to be more solicitous of his men and more in touch with events on the ground than the administrator and political animal Sir Edward Henry; he ended up being quite popular. One of his first moves in his new job was to replace the superintendents' ponies and traps with motor cars, out-trumping Damer Dawson and Allen and their motorcycle combination.

"We wonder whether the new Commissioner will be more favourable than his predecessor to the appointment of women police on equal terms with men," *The Vote* mused.

18

TIME IS SHORT AND THE WORK IS COLOSSAL

Eleven o'clock on 11th November 1918. Lilian Wyles of the National Union of Women Workers is on duty when the sirens wail out across the vast industrial complex that sprawls the south-east bank of the Thames. The Royal Arsenal at Woolwich is from that moment redundant.

"From every gate of that vast establishment poured a seemingly endless stream of men and women; no more work for them on this longed-for day, for them rejoicing and merry-making," Wyles later wrote in an account of her life in the Met. She herself, though, was in a reflective mood: "Was this, then, the end of the women patrols and their work? Were we to retire to our homes and take up again a life of domesticity and gradually forget that we had been of some slight use to our country when it had been at war?"

She had joined the patrols only that summer, one of just a handful of Louise Creighton's recruits to be sent to a munitions factory. The daughter of a wealthy brewer from Lincolnshire, the thirty-three-year-old had been educated at a private school followed by a finishing school in Paris. Wyles had begun studying law, but a serious illness forced her to put her career plans on hold. Now, returned to health, she would never take up her studies again but neither would she give up work and surrender to domesticity.

* * *

The Armistice finds Edith Watson on the top of an open bus, cheering her way from Marylebone station to the East End, marvelling at the flags and the ecstatic crowds lining the route. "There prevailed everywhere an irresistible impulse to get into the streets and yell and sing and dance and weep, above all to make oneself supremely ridiculous," wrote one journalist.

By then Edith Watson was working nights as a telephonist in the civil service while going through another reconciliation with Eustace. The couple had moved into a commune with a group calling themselves The Communist Anarchists. They weren't Marxists, for while they believed in holding all property in common, they rejected state control. Watson described it as Christian Fellowship without the Christianity.

Eustace ended the war in the Royal Naval Air Service. He had joined up in 1916, when conscription was about to be introduced, in order to avoid being drafted into the infantry. This meant that the couple had been seeing each other only sporadically when he was on leave. The arrangement suited Watson perfectly; she much preferred to be racked with anxiety about him when he was away than having to listen to his interminable discussions when he was home. Her memoir records: "So, seeing each other intermittently, with me providing comfort, warmth, sympathy and love, while the RNAS gave him work, drill, a hard bed and badly cooked food [meant] that Eustace counted me among his blessings and we were both happy."

The pontificating, controlling Eustance was also out of town on Armistice Day, which must have added considerably to Watson's fun. She dined that night with a friend in the Regent Palace Hotel in Piccadilly. "After dinner we stood on tables drinking anyone's wine, glasses were smashed, plates broken … Sounds of dance music were coming from long windows on the first floor of a building and we started dancing and singing in the street. Suddenly the windows were thrown all the way up and the band came out onto the balcony and we were being conducted by Victor Sylvester."

* * *

Margaret Damer Dawson and Mary Allen were not to be found leaping around on restaurant tables swigging strangers' drinks or foxtrotting in the streets to the country's favourite dance band, but they were looking with pride and satisfaction at what for them had been a highly successful war. In Richmond, Allen's sister Dolly Hampton had proved a particular triumph, embodying how women's policing had proven itself during the war. An altogether steadier, more grounded character than Allen and free from the demons that urged her sister on in her chase for prominence and power, Hampton was clearly happy with routine day-to-day community police work. Part of her job was to support women in the magistrate's court where, like Edith Watson, she was often the only female present apart from the witness or the prisoner. As early as the spring of 1915, the Women's Local Government Association had started paying her a small salary, and when money began to run out, Sir Edward Henry had stepped in with thirty shillings a week, which he later topped up with a two-shilling war bonus and a grant for a winter coat and boots.

"When the WPS [Women's Police Service] was at the highest point of its efficiency," Allen would write, looking back in 1934, "when the organisation was handling grim police problems in the Metropolitan area [and] in the provinces, when policewomen were on guard at munitions works, on patrol duty in the streets, in hostels, canteens, parks and playgrounds, in soldiers' camps and recreation centres … came the sudden collapse of the German armies and the profound emotion and universal thanksgiving of Armistice Day".

Back in that turbulent summer of 1914, a doubtful Home Secretary and a Police Commissioner under pressure had reluctantly approved women police as a strictly temporary measure, but now, after four years of unstinting public service and with much of her fortune gone, Damer Dawson found it unthinkable that the Women's Police Service would be cast aside. Reflecting after the Armistice, Allen said that while she was not claiming that the women police's contribution had been more important than that of other women, the WPS had not only killed off the idea that women were unreliable in times of danger; they had also opened a door that could never be closed. Or so she thought.

* * *

As usual, Nina Boyle had something serious on her mind. Not only were women about to vote for the first time but, thanks to her test-run in Keighley, they were also standing for Parliament.

Just ten days after the Armistice, the Parliament (Qualification of Women) Act was passed. One of the shortest pieces of legislation on the statute book, it dealt with the issue raised by Boyle's spring candidacy in one sentence: "A woman shall not be disqualified by sex or marriage from being elected to or sitting or voting as a Member of the Commons House of Parliament".

Among the women standing in December's election was the now seventy-four-year-old Lottie Despard, fighting the Battersea North seat for the Labour Party where the League opened two tiny campaign offices. Canvassers were sought—"Do not delay! Time is short and the work is colossal"—and directions given: "36 Queen's Road, the motor bus 77 stops within two minutes and the little tram from Chelsea Bridge Road passes the door" and "171, Battersea Park Road, opposite Battersea Park Station; trams from the Embankment pass the door". However, despite the high hopes and intense efforts, Despard lost decisively to the Liberal Coalition candidate, garnering 5,634 votes to his 11,231.

One woman was elected. Constance Markievicz—formerly Constance Georgine Gore-Booth—had had a textbook high-aristocratic upbringing, complete with ancestral castle, grand tour of Europe, presentation as a debutante to Queen Victoria and marriage to a Polish nobleman, which made her Countess Markievicz. From an old Anglo-Irish family, she had then gone on to reinvent herself as a Fenian revolutionary, a poster figure for Irish republicanism with wild dark looks and a penchant for guns and military clothing, in her case though not peaked caps and breeches but guerrilla-style fatigues. She had been sentenced to death for her part in Dublin's 1916 Easter Rising, where she had fought British soldiers like Boyle's unfortunate fiancé Harry. Though she had been amnestied and released in 1917, by the time she was elected in the following December, she was again in Holloway over a new republican plot. Markievicz had won the constituency of Dublin St Patrick's with 66 per cent of the vote. In line with Sinn Féin's policy, however, on her release she refused to take her seat at Westminster.

The King, meanwhile, celebrated Armistice Day by cracking open a bottle of brandy to mark the end of his four years of enforced abstinence. He said it tasted musty.

19

WELL MEN, GIVE THEM A TRIAL

The 1919 New Year's Honours list was naturally heavy with military citations but this time there was a new award, introduced by the King in recognition of the thousands of people who had done their duty off the battlefield. The Officer of the Order of the British Empire, or OBE, went to over 1,500 civilians. On the list, along with Miss Gertrude Caroline Dixon, Secretary of the Wheat Executive; Captain Charles Leonard Conacher, from the Perivale Filling Factory; and Edward Jerome Dyer Esq, Honorary General Secretary of the Royal Navy's Vegetable Supply Committee; came Margaret Damer Dawson, Mary Allen and Louise Creighton's formidable patrol secretary Mary Carden, now aged sixty-nine. Six months later, in the King's Birthday Honours, there would be an MBE for Isobel Goldingham. Any convictions for assaulting police officers and causing criminal damage were clearly forgiven and forgotten.

But, just as the power within the women's policing movement had shifted decisively away from Nina Boyle and the Women Police Volunteers in 1915, Damer Dawson now found that the Women's Police Service was to be sidelined in the making of modern Britain.

* * *

In the summer of 1918, as the war drew near its end, the new Met Commissioner, Sir Nevil Macready, had called his men together at the Queen's Hall in Langham Place, a venue large enough to hold 3,000 but where his voice would carry. "I thought of approaching the management of the Drury Lane theatre but hesitated, [fearing] risking a failure on the boards which my father had trod with such distinction," he would explain.

As he wound up a somewhat rambling speech on the state of policing in the capital, Macready had raised the question of women and proceeded to both patronise and ridicule them, while at the same time claiming credit for giving them their chance. "And the last point is the inevitable female" he had begun—cue laughter—"Well men, give them a trial. They were invented by me. There is a certain class of social disability that I think these women could probably tackle as well as the men. I don't think it is quite the thing for a full-blown constable to go and stir up ladies and gentlemen lying around in parks. It had far better be done by the women police. Anyway it's an experiment. I thought, 'Let us try it and see if it turns out to be a farce'."

His men, however, had not been inclined to give them a trial, and instead "proclaimed their distaste loudly and forcibly", according to Lilian Wyles. The Home Secretary and the Commissioner, they said, must be deranged: "[The idea] was laughable, it was grotesque, not to be tolerated, and would give a frivolous tone to what had always been man's work."

Undeterred, Macready had ploughed on and in the autumn, an advertisement had gone out. Women between the ages of twenty-five and thirty-eight who were at least five feet four inches tall without their boots, who could read well, write legibly and had a fair knowledge of arithmetic, spelling and composition, were invited to apply to join the new Metropolitan Women Police Patrols. Even married women were eligible, provided they didn't have young children. The salary was thirty shillings a week, plus a twelve-shilling war bonus, with uniform and boots provided.

Macready was hiring a small corps on an experimental basis. Ten female sergeants would oversee one hundred policewomen under a female superintendent.

The women would still be called patrols, because no one was to be in any doubt about their status. Macready had proposed swearing them in as constables and giving them powers of arrest over women and children—only in exceptional circumstances would they be allowed to arrest men—but the Home Office had stamped firmly on this: "To do so would make them an integral portion of the

Metropolitan Police Force". The pay was paltry, which meant that women like Edith Watson, without a private income or a husband's wage, would struggle to live. And there was no pension. Even so, it was a significant step: for the first time women would be out on the streets of London wearing the full official uniform of the Metropolitan Police.

And so, just days after the Armistice, on a dismal late afternoon in November, twenty-five nervous young women sat perched in a line along a window seat at Scotland Yard, an eerie pall thrown over them by the clouds of mist swirling down the endless corridors.

Things had moved on since 1914 when Sir Edward Henry had sent the Women Police Volunteers and the National Union of Women Workers out onto the streets and told them to devise a role for themselves. Macready set out precisely what he expected of the first Metropolitan policewomen. Their principal role was to deal with "women and children ill, injured, destitute, homeless and those who have been the victims of sexual offences or are believed to be in danger of drifting towards an immoral life" but they could also be sent on observation duty and assist the Criminal Investigation Department, in plain clothes if necessary, in cases involving women.

In launching the Women Police Patrols, Macready decided not to reinvent the wheel but turned instead to Louise Creighton. He was not a particular admirer of her patrols, subscribing rather to Mary Allen's amateur welfare worker view, but bringing in Allen and Damer Dawson was unthinkable. He had come across them during his first few months in the job, so when he announced that his most important task in setting up his new force was to eliminate any women of extreme views—"the vinegary spinster or the blighted middle-aged fanatic"—no one was in any doubt about whom he had in mind. The truth was that he was personally revolted by the leaders of the Women's Police Service, whom he saw as aggressive, unwomanly and unnatural—in other words, lesbians. He had even heard that one of them had been seen wearing a sword, he said, although he hadn't seen it for himself. Allen said that was ridiculous.

But Creighton's patrols had evolved over the course of the war. Bright, ambitious women like Sofia Stanley, Dorothy Peto and Lilian Wyles had edged away from their founder's faith-based volunteer vision and, through Henry's temporary arrangement of paying some of them, they saw the NUWW as a way into policing as a career. Creighton herself had spent her war chairing committees and commenting on education, church matters and the needs of working women and children, much as she had always done. Nina Boyle was certainly in opposition to constituted authority, to quote Sir Edward Henry, while the establishment was Creighton's natural habitat. Yet the two women had several causes in common, and towards the end of the war, they separately campaigned for pensions for mothers, a minimum wage for women workers and emergency aid for famine-hit Russia.

Creighton had also remained true to the social purity campaign, writing pamphlets such as *Successful and Unsuccessful Marriages*, price four pence, one of a series along with Arthur Herbert Gray's *Purity* and Elma K. Paget's *In Praise of Virginity*, and she was more in demand than ever as a speaker, addressing packed houses around the country on subjects such as "Venereal Diseases and the Moral Cleansing of our Cities". Unlike Nina Boyle and Edith Watson, she had had the luxury of being able to leave the running of her organisation in the dependable hands of salaried professionals like Mary Carden.

Then, in the spring of 1918, the war for Creighton had become tragically personal. Her thirty-four-year-old son Oswin, the sixth of her seven children, had been ordained as a priest when he came down from Oxford and the declaration of war had found him ministering in the then infamous slums of Notting Hill. He had volunteered immediately as an army chaplain and was with the artillery in the Pas de Calais when his unit came under a massive shell attack. Men were ripped to pieces and their body parts flung far and wide over the flat sullen fields. Captain Creighton had gone out to try to recover their remains for burial when a shell burst close by, killing him instantly. Louise never recovered. She seldom spoke of his death, and her memoirs contain no mention of it, but she edited and published the letters that her son had been writing to her since he was a schoolboy of seventeen—amusing, affectionate and life-affirming.

* * *

By the time Macready set up his new unit, Sofia Stanley and Dorothy Peto had joined Lilian Wyles in London. Mary Carden had appointed Stanley as head of the London patrols the previous year, and Stanley, in turn, brought in Peto, who had helped set up a patrol school in Bristol. Peto had initially invited Margaret Damer Dawson to collaborate on a joint training programme, but the venture quickly collapsed when, entirely predictably, the NUWW found Damer Dawson too controlling and she accused them of being incapable of enforcing discipline. Stanley accepted Macready's offer at a salary of two hundred pounds a year, plus twelve shillings a week war bonus.

So Damer Dawson had been right: there was indeed a peacetime future for policewomen; it just didn't include her. Every minute of her waking life and most of her money for the past four years had been spent on the Women's Police Service. Buoyed by her success in the munitions factories, she had had no inkling of what was coming. Only three weeks earlier, Ellen Harburn had put out a call for seventy more "well-educated gentlewomen". The commandant and Allen had seen their OBEs as a mark of official acceptance, not as a gesture of thanks and farewell. Macready had even invited Damer Dawson into Scotland Yard in order to consult her about suitable recruits, back into that high round airy office where, four years earlier, she had schmoozed Sir Edward Henry and emerged triumphant.

It seemed, however, that it was Margaret Damer Dawson's very different performance at this encounter with Macready that had sealed her fate. He would never have given her a key role, but perhaps if she had played the tactful suppliant of 1914 she might have pulled some token advisory post from the wreckage. After four years of living and working alongside Mary Allen, however, raiding houses and running the munitions force, she was a flinty, confident figure who adopted a military pose and wore a uniform resembling that of an officer in the Royal Navy. This time then she chose to engage with the Commissioner on equal terms, as the leader of a respected national body applauded for its service to the Empire. It did not go down well.

Her organisation seemed to think that they were there to show how police work should be done, and to purify the male force, Macready huffed. He wanted nothing to do with them.

Damer Dawson was shattered, and her heartbreak made her uncharacteristically spiteful. Creighton's patrols—who, like those of Boyle and Watson's WPV, never enforced curfews or raided homes—knew nothing about real police work, she said. "They may be seen loitering about in unfrequented places in Hyde Park or looking hopelessly bored, leaning against the offices of the *Morning Post* in the Strand". Macready's "uniformed dummy" was absolutely not what people had had in mind when they had campaigned for policewomen.

These might have been Mary Allen's words. Perhaps they were. The pair put the blame entirely on Macready; his predecessor had always been so kind and charming. In fact, Henry, for all his impeccable manners and paternalism, had never lost his suspicion of the Women's Police Service, even after they had broken with Nina Boyle. The Commissioner's office was probably also influenced by Sofia Stanley, for during his last months in office, Stanley had been sending in regular reports of the NUWW's activities, never missing the chance to emphasise her team's sensitive, professional approach, unlike the crass, bossy WPS.

25th April—26th May 1918

Rochester Row "A" division

Patrols helped constable in trying to separate drunken soldiers who were fighting. Police constable knocked down insensible, patrols rendered first aid. Kept crowd back and blew their whistles.

Victoria "B" division

Two patrols on duty daily from 4–11pm without constable, 37 cautions for foolish behaviour, Canadian chaplain spoke to patrols and highly commended their work.

Tottenham Court Road "D" division

Patrols have been requested by manager of Oxford Music Hall to visit any time and call attention to any objectionable behaviour they might observe.

King's Cross "Y" division

Helped police constable to control crowd when returned British prisoners arrived.

Strand "E" division

Patrols had unpleasant scene with an "Inspector" of "Women Police Service" who came up to them and complained loudly of their action in assisting police to arrest two girls for soliciting and not also arresting some men they were with. Patrols made no attempt to argue but left the "Inspector" talking angrily to some of her companions.

August

Hyde Park "A" Division

On August 24th the patrols were stopped by a working-class man with a respectable-looking lady who accused them angrily of having interfered with the woman who he said was his wife. Patrols assured him they had never seen or spoken to this woman and on further enquiry found that the persons he wished to complain of were an "Inspector" and "Sergeant" of the "Women Police Service", who had apparently cautioned the women a few days before when she was waiting for her husband.

On August 30th and 31st the four women patrols spoke to forty-one couples about lying in a suggestive attitude. No one resented the action of the patrols and in every case complied with directions.

Of course, in addition to Stanley's public relations offensive, there was the inescapable fact that Louise Creighton was the widow of a former Bishop of London, as well as the close friend of the current incumbent, and came bearing the seal of approval of Her late Majesty the Queen. Social barriers might have taken something of a battering during the war, but they were still standing.

* * *

New Year's Eve 1919 and the mayor of Stalybridge, a fifty-eight-year-old widow called Ada Summers, swathed from head to foot in black but her face beaming, takes her seat at the local magistrates' court, the first woman in Britain to preside over a trial. A photograph taken to mark the event shows Summers at the centre of the bench, flanked to her left and her right by serious men with beards. (Unfortunately, the offences on that mild, momentous winter's day failed to match up to the occasion. All three men to appear before her—the delinquents as one newspaper called them—stood accused of allowing their chimneys to catch fire.) Summers, a rich philanthropist who would give her entire fortune to good causes, had been appointed by a group of women magistrates who had themselves only been sworn in on Christmas Eve with the instruction to select more of their sex. Among them was the best-selling novelist Mary Ward, founder of the Women's National Anti-Suffrage League and friend of Louise Creighton.

The new Sex Disqualification (Removal) Act, which had only become law on 23rd December, permitted women to enter professions and take up roles from which they had previously been banned, such as the law and the civil service. It was in this context that Ellen Harburn had put out a new recruitment ad for the Women's Police Service. Whoever wrote the ad was clearly conscious of the zeitgeist and had worded it shrewdly, for it promoted the WPS not only as a worthwhile career in itself, but also as a route into some of the new fields that were opening up, the kind that the Victorian-born intellectual Louise Creighton would surely have entered had she had the chance. "A unique opportunity is opened to women who intend later on to take up political and social reconstruction," the advertisement ran. "They will get a first-hand knowledge of actual conditions and of the needs of women … they will gain a practical insight that will add value to the theoretical training of universities and colleges, and give a firmer basis for future work, either in the political or social arenas, or in the fields of history, psychology and law."

By now, across the country the WPS and the NUWW, along with Macready's "trial" force of Met patrolwomen in London, were patrolling streets and parks, keeping watch on brothels and theatres and attending the courts, under a confusing tangle of arrangements. Some were still working on a voluntary basis while others were receiving small payments from police authorities, watch committees and charities. Some, like Edith Smith, had also gone through a swearing-in process which the Home Office continued to refuse to recognise. Dorothy Peto reasoned that the new law must surely mean that women could finally enter the police force on a permanent basis and on the same terms as men; however, policing wasn't specifically mentioned and at the Home Office confusion reigned. The Assistant Secretary believed that the legislation changed nothing, while the Permanent Secretary thought it just might. The government decided it was time to look into the whole question of women police, and in the spring of 1920 it announced an inquiry.

When Macready heard about it, he sent a tetchy note over to the now Home Secretary, Edward Shortt. Shortt had had an undistinguished career as a lawyer before being elected an MP but, in his case, lack of lustre had proved no bar to advancement. With his prim features, monocle, slicked-down hair and side parting, he looked like the sort of man who might be found causing trouble for Bertie Wooster. "I hope", wrote Macready, "if you have a committee on women police that Miss Damer Dawson or any of her satellites will not be included thereon, otherwise there will be considerable trouble over here". Shortt took the point and when the Baird committee began taking evidence in February 1920, Damer Dawson and Allen appeared merely as actors in a long cast of witnesses, with no more status than the deputy town clerk of Edinburgh.

The committee sat for eleven days and heard forty-seven witnesses, one of whom was Boyle and Watson's old bête noire Frederick Mead. In a 9,000-word grumble, the elderly magistrate got a few things off his chest, including his irritation with Sir Edward Henry; Edward Shortt; Shortt's predecessor Sir George Cave; women in court in indecency cases, "one's nature revolts from it"; women "frequenting the streets dressed as constables" and the "agitation over the equality of the sexes". He didn't dispute that women were intellectually equivalent to men, he said, although he did describe one NUWW patrol as the most stupid witness he had ever encountered, but he noted that there was no clamour for women to become seamen, "to go into stokeholds of ships and stoke the fires going through the Red Sea, for example".

Women, Mead said, were only fit for tasks that fell outside proper policing, such as helping people across the road. He then began reading word for word a long-running correspondence he had had with the Home Office and Scotland Yard. One letter that particularly upset him had arrived "while I was enjoying a holiday at the seaside". After about half an hour of this, a committee member Sir Francis Blake finally called a halt: "I don't wish to stop you reading anything you think is applicable ... I think that we quite see that you feel aggrieved ...".

But Mead's was now an isolated, anachronistic voice. There were differences among the senior police officers over details such as women's terms and conditions, and, above all, whether they should have powers of arrest, but it was clear enough that in the six years since their inception—notwithstanding fears in Westminster and Whitehall, opposition from the men, complaints from the public and a seismic split within the pioneers themselves—the women had proved their worth. A Met superintendent James Billings had initially been sceptical, he told the inquiry: "One would naturally have thought that they would hamper rather than help, but with trained women that is not the case ... I should like to see the scope of their employment very much enlarged."

John Henderson, Chief Constable of Reading, had employed six women who had been trained by Damer Dawson for the munitions factories: "That [experience] is why I am so glad I have got them," he said. The Chief Constable of Lancashire, Harry Lane, went further. He was facing an increasing problem from young prostitutes "of the lower classes" getting drunk and disorderly on the streets. Women were ideally placed to deal with them, he said, but they didn't have the legal status required to do the job. "That is why I say give them ... the same powers as the men, and the same pay, conditions of service, and everything." It was a call that resonated back to Bessie Moncrieff and beyond.

The Baird committee concluded that there was an urgent need for policewomen in those heavily populated areas where crime against women and children was high. They should be well qualified, highly trained and well paid. It seemed then that the tentative, temporary, ill-defined venture that Damer Dawson, Nina Boyle and Edith Watson had sent on its way in the face of war was now in peacetime endorsed at the highest level. But then came the catch: police authorities should be allowed to employ women if they chose, but should not be compelled to do so.

* * *

Three months after giving her evidence, Margaret Damer Dawson died from a heart attack at the age of forty-six, after what had been thought to be a mild illness. With her at Danehill Lodge in the Kent countryside was a shell-shocked Mary Allen. She described Damer Dawson's death as a deep personal grief to every woman who had worked with her. She certainly meant what she said but, presumably, to none more so than Allen herself. The chief had left her the house, together with what little was left of her money. The will had been made in 1915, just a few months after the couple first met. In the immediate aftermath of the tragedy, to Allen befuddled by shock and grief, it seemed inconceivable that the Women's Police Service could carry on. She would later recollect that the organisation seemed at risk of being pitched into limbo, but Damer Dawson's inspiration proved strong, and the paralysis was short lived: "If during her life we had been determined to maintain our organisation on a working basis, more than ever we were determined to persevere after the shock of her loss."

They did their poignant best to organise a funeral with the simple solemnity that they thought befitted a serving police officer. The coffin of unpolished oak was covered with a Union Jack, on which was laid a solitary laurel wreath and the WPS service ribbon. The cortege that travelled the short distance to the 11th-century St Stephen's Church consisted of a simple four-wheeled hearse drawn by a single horse, yet the escort was impressive. Mary Allen, Isobel Goldingham and Ellen Harburn led the way, followed by uniformed WPS inspectors, sergeants and constables from across the country.

Leading the civilian mourners was Damer Dawson's mother, the sixty-seven-year-old Agnes, Lady Walsingham; alongside her was General Frederick Hammersley, who had invited Damer Dawson to Grantham. "For all the Saints" was feelingly rendered, according to the *Folkestone Express*, after which the congregation moved into the churchyard where Damer Dawson's small body was lowered into the grave in a cemetery overlooking the marshes and the sea. The WPS then filed past, dropping sprigs of rosemary for remembrance onto her coffin. The place is now marked by a Celtic cross of rough grey stone.

"Those under her command paid tribute to their chief who was beloved by every one of them," said the *Folkestone Express*. "All showed in their demeanour that they had lost a true friend and the close of the committal service witnessed a striking and impressive display of affection." The pinched-faced, bespectacled little woman who liked to be addressed as Sir and Chief and Commandant, who cropped her hair and clipped about in jackboots and a peaked cap, who loved animals and children and couldn't bear to see suffering, had always been able to inspire affection in her staff. She had been supporting the children of several unmarried mothers at a time when to have a child put a single woman beyond the social pale; in tribute, the WPS opened the Damer Dawson Memorial Home for babies, a large airy house on the Kent coast.

The Times described her as "a woman of a naturally fastidious mind whose courage meant that her work was of far more use than that of a woman of coarser fibre would have been". Unlike Macready, the obituarist saw her as the most feminine of women, with a gentle voice and quiet manner, but added: "She yet went further than other uniformed women in adopting the outward symbols of male authority."

Mary Allen blamed the premature death of her partner and leader partly on the stress of running the WPS, but she believed that Damer Dawson had ultimately been broken by her treatment at the hands of the Metropolitan Police.

20

LADY SEARCHERS

May 1920, the Secretary of State for War and Air, Winston Churchill, makes a new appointment: the veteran Army officer Sir Ormonde de l'Épée Winter is to take over the brief of shaking up Britain's dysfunctional intelligence service in Ireland.

Winter was not the chivalrous, romantic figure that his name might suggest, but he was nevertheless a remarkable character. An official who worked with him described "O"—the code name by which he liked to be known—as a marvel: "He looks like a wicked little white snake, is as clever as paint, probably entirely non-moral, a first-class horseman, a card genius, knows several languages, is a super sleuth and a most amazing original. He can do anything." After the Armistice, Winter had taken what sounded like the quintessential desk job as the boundary Commissioner for Schleswig-Holstein but, based in Paris and with "very handsome emoluments", it was more attractive than it might first have seemed. Even so, Churchill's offer was far better suited to the Colonel's taste than border demarcations, so he took a pay cut and exchanged his luxurious hotel suite near the Champs Élysées for the dank formidable fortress of Dublin Castle—the British centre of command where Boyle's fiancé Harry had died during the Easter Rising. He unpacked his bags and set about applying his devious, maverick mind to the task before him.

The challenge was considerable. In one week during his first month, the IRA outrages, to use the British government's official term, included seven murders, ten shootings at the person, four aggravated assaults, seven cases of arson, and seventeen robberies of weapons. There had been no arrests.

When Churchill gave Winter the job, the old hands had been baffled. Winter was a distinguished soldier with a splendid war record, but he had no experience of espionage, only a Boy's Own penchant for cloak-and-dagger stunts—like putting on a wig and false moustache in order to steal IRA money from a Dublin bank, which was definitely not in his job description.

Not all of Winter's ideas were successful, including the magnificently insane plan to photograph the entire population of Ireland, both the front view and the back, while the fifty bloodhounds he imported from England proved useless. Nevertheless, the colonel showed himself to be a dangerous man. The mass raiding parties he unleashed across the country immediately upon his arrival—crashing into buildings, seizing guns, documents and suspects—were to be spectacularly effective. The plan took some time to work, however, partly due to an IRA tactic that confounded the conservative-minded British army and the police: deploying women.

* * *

Meanwhile, Mary Allen had persuaded herself that there was an upside to being dropped by Commissioner Macready. The Women's Police Service was now a totally autonomous, independent organisation, outside of any bureaucrat's control and needing no one's approval in order to function. She could run things as she saw fit and take the WPS in whatever direction she wished. "The bitterness of the first disappointment was soon vanquished and was even superseded by the realisation that I was free from an accumulation of petty tasks and anxieties," she said.

She and Damer Dawson had managed to keep going after the war despite the Commissioner's best efforts, but they had had to work hard to keep themselves in the public eye. They trumpeted their contribution to society at every possible opportunity, and set about persuading chief constables and other potential employers to take on the munitions force made redundant by the Armistice. Among those to write glowing testimonials were General Hammersley from Grantham and the chief of police in Gretna. The vicar of St Barnabas Church in Holloway, who praised the WPS for moving on "a large influx of undesirable women invading our poorer district", was already paying two policewomen out of the parish funds. By 1920 a considerable number had been placed, Damer Dawson had told the Baird inquiry, but the demand for jobs still outstripped the supply and when Mary Allen took over sole control of the WPS, she was open to any opportunity that might present itself.

* * *

Soon after taking up his appointment in Dublin, Winter appeared in Sir Basil Thomson's office at Scotland Yard with a request for help. Thomson was a fellow flamboyant spymaster, the former head of the CID, and now in charge of the Special Branch, working alongside MI5. In 1914, Thomson had helped to draft Nina Boyle's detested Defence of the Realm Act (DORA), and during the war he had interrogated the notorious, glamorous Mata Hari, later shot by the French as a German agent. The son of a former Archbishop of York, Thomson's career path had seen him become Prime Minister of Tonga at the age of twenty-eight, private tutor to the Crown Prince of Siam and governor of Dartmoor prison. He would later be arrested by his own officers in Hyde Park—where else?—for indecency with a prostitute.

Winter had encountered a major stumbling block for his raiding parties in Ireland: the rebel women who were carrying weapons and messages about their bodies, openly jeering at the powerless male officers and making a mockery of the new British stratagem. He wanted Thomson to supply him with fifty "trained and tested fearless women" to deal with them. The colonel obviously had a wildly exaggerated idea of the strength and resources of the Met's Women Police Patrols and Thomson had to tell him that he couldn't help, but thought he knew a woman who could.

Damer Dawson had died just as Winter was moving into his bleak new quarters behind the barbed wire at Dublin Castle, and so it was Mary Allen who got the call. The colonel's appearance in Allen's office came at precisely the right time and, with Macready having cut all ties with her, she was now free to make her own decisions. She agreed to Winter's request without a moment's hesitation, and set about arranging for a team to leave for Ireland immediately. Inspectors Jean Campbell and Olive Walton from Damer Dawson's

Chelsea circle were among those to go, with Campbell leading the first contingent of nine women.

Their orders stated that they were obliged to hold themselves in readiness, at any hour of the day or night, to accompany the Crown forces on raiding expeditions whenever the presence of uniformed women was considered desirable, and to assist in the search for firearms, military despatches, letters or papers likely to contain information useful to the Crown. It had echoes of Allen's original vision of the Women Police Volunteers as a trained, professional force, working full-time shifts.

Allen would later describe Ireland in 1920 as being in a state of civil war. Winter was certainly using the WPS for highly dangerous work, and the women were told to arrive in the country dressed as nuns for their own safety. They ignored it, not because it sounded fatuous, although it did, but because they thought it might expose them to greater danger. When they descended from the Dublin train in full uniform, the police sergeant waiting to greet them refused to let them leave the station until he had consulted Dublin Castle. It was eventually agreed that they would wear uniform on duty but travel in plain clothes.

Within hours, Campbell saw just what they were facing. At midnight, startled by loud explosions, they watched from their hotel window as an enormous fire blazed close by and listened to the screams and the gunfire. Towards three o'clock, the flames and the noise died down and search lights swept over the town. They were even more shocked the next morning when no one at the hotel thought the incident worth mentioning. Two days later, the young waiter who served their table was shot dead on the hotel doorstep.

* * *

Walton described a typical day in her diary. She and a colleague set off on a fifty-mile expedition across remote and treacherous terrain in a convoy of three lorries of heavily armed soldiers and police officers. They sat up next to the driver, an officer with his revolver at the ready alongside them. "At one point we left the lorries in the road and crossed fields through mud and water, over hedges and stone walls," Walton wrote. "It was good to be formed up and marched with the men. We kept up well. Several farmsteads were raised and searched. Returned safely at 6.30 pm."

All this marching had a purpose: to carry out Winter's raids across the country. On the 14th May 1921, for example, Special Branch sent the following request to the Royal Irish Constabulary:

> Please arrange for a big force with a woman searcher to raid Miss F Whelan 65 Eccles Street tonight at 7.45 and raid for documents and men on the run. Special instructions must be issued to the company commander to search thoroughly every person and every bit of property, luggage etc on the premises … Materials for assistance in escape from prison such as rope ladders may also be found.

In six months in the Dublin area alone, the raiding parties seized three hundred and ten revolvers, thirty-four rifles, twenty shotguns, thousands of rounds of ammunition, and large quantities of bombs, explosives and detonators. Sir Hugh Jeudwine, commanding the British Army's Fifth Division, wrote in his account of events in Ireland in 1920-21 that many more women should have been used. He believed that the effect on morale alone would have been considerable.

Allen would later acknowledge that some people found the idea of women searchers repugnant, but insisted that the process was carried out with the utmost consideration, and that sometimes those being searched were grateful that women were used. In one raid on a cottage, they came across a woman who had given birth just a few hours earlier. When the policewomen entered, she shouted, "Thank God it's you and not the men."

Ironically, while Sir Nevil Macready's despised Women's Police Service were risking their lives alongside the British Army and the Royal Irish Constabulary, Macready himself was now General Officer Commanding in Ireland, where his responsibilities included co-ordinating the work of the police and the military. Like his Scotland Yard posting, this was another job that he had taken on with great reluctance; he also had little regard for Ormonde Winter, who was not the man for the job, he said. In 1919 he had written to the newly appointed Chief Secretary for Ireland: "I cannot say I envy you for I loathe the country you are going to and its people with a depth deeper than the sea and more violent than that which I feel against the Boche."

When the Anglo-Irish peace treaty was signed in 1921, the "lady searchers" were sent home, but the agreement proved to be sadly misnamed and the following summer the new Ulster government asked Allen to send twenty women to Belfast.

PART V

21

THREE SILVER STRIPES

17th May 1919, Westminster Abbey. It is the memorial service for the three hundred and sixty officers and constables of the Metropolitan Police who fell in the conflict. 2,300 of their colleagues march from Horse Guards Parade to the Abbey to honour them. The Met's mass bands play Purcell's "When I am Laid in Earth", the choir sings Brahms' Requiem, the congregation sings "God Shall Wipe the Tears from their Eyes" and the Dean of Westminster gives the Solemn Address. Those in attendance include the Dowager Queen, Alexandra, her daughter Princess Victoria, the Prince of Wales, Sir Nevil Macready and Lilian Wyles, formerly of Louise Creighton's National Union of Women Workers' patrols.

Wyles was one of six women chosen to represent the Met's new Women Police Patrols. Mary Allen's Women's Police Service were far from the public eye in England as they worked with the counter-insurgency forces in Ireland, but the Met patrolwomen's presence at this high-profile event in the heart of the capital announced them to the world as officially part of the Metropolitan Police.

The day of the service was a momentous occasion in the Wyles' household, and they marked it with some ceremony. Early in the morning, Wyles emerged from her bedroom to face her family in their smart Bloomsbury apartment, assembled to see her in her full regalia. They were flanked, she remembered, by cook and the housemaid, saying, "My my" and "Fancy that". Her parents fussed about, straightening her tunic and adjusting her belt, and she then stepped out into the corridor where the porters were lined up like a guard of honour. The head porter, a retired guardsman called Thomas Vigers, gave her buttons a last polish before she pulled on a pair of white gloves and stumped into the lift and out into the street in her unforgiving boots.

She felt horribly self-conscious for, unlike the members of the Women Police Service, she wasn't used to being seen in uniform in public. "I lived in the heart of London, and within minutes I had left the friendly, encouraging district where the chemist, the dairyman, the newsagent and the greengrocer had known me from childhood, and turned into High Holborn. Men and women were hurrying to their places of business but they all had eyes on me, or so it seemed. I could feel people turning back to stare and small boys nudging each other as I went by, stepping firmly, a gleaming chain suspended from the second button of my tunic, ending in a whistle tucked cosily in my belt."

She reached the comforting gloom of Holborn tram station with relief and was steeling herself for the last lap of her journey when she spotted a familiar figure: "Mrs Morris, one of my own women" in the same uniform, adding a typically Wylesian comment: "except that on my sleeves I wore three silver stripes, while she had none on hers". The patrolwomen had run a sweepstake on who would be appointed their four sergeants; clearly Wyles had made an impression on Macready, for she had been chosen.

It was a glorious morning, with London lying under soft spring sunshine and the temperature at over 20 degrees. Officers and typists packed the windows of Scotland Yard to watch the women cross Parliament Square, and a couple of reporters waylaid their commander Sofia Stanley, trying in vain to persuade her to give an interview.

Settled in her seat in the Abbey, Wyles took a few surreptitious glances at the Queen and Princess and it seemed, to her at least, that the royals in turn were interested to see these women, dressed almost exactly as the men. At the end of the service the Queen gave them a sweet and encouraging smile, Wyles observed.

* * *

Wyles was not universally popular. She had a reputation as a snob, who looked down on those she considered her social inferiors and boasted about her influential connections. Her story about how she had come to join the NUWW, for example, asking her father to consult his friend, the Reverend Hugh Chapman, chaplain of the Royal Chapel of the Savoy, on whether the work was worth doing, didn't endear her to everyone.

Wyles could never have lived on the wages, she would note in her memoirs. Fortunately, she didn't have to; for her, the 42 shillings a week was pocket money. Beatrice Wills, a tall, strong-boned thirty-year-old Cornish woman with dark good looks, was one of the working-class patrolwomen. She had been working at the Plymouth dockyards when a friend had showed her Macready's recruitment ad in a newspaper. Her trip to London for the interview had been her first visit to the capital, so, she told an interviewer, she'd brought her mother with her "just in case". Thinking that she should dress neatly, she'd worn a blue suit with a small, matching hat.

The women queuing in the misty corridor after the Armistice that day had been summoned one by one, into a long, dimly-lit library where the invading fog had drifted up to the high ceiling, adding to the gloom. They found themselves facing three examiners, two from the NUWW and one from the Met: Sofia Stanley, looking pleased with herself, according to Lilian Wyles; a largely silent Mary Carden and, in the chair, Inspector Duncan from A Division. Duncan had policed all the suffrage protests but Creighton's patrols saw him as an ally. The questions had been few and to the point, and after just ten minutes each candidate had been sent back out to the corridor to await the verdict. Among them was Kate Summerton who, with Catharine Bagster, had stumbled across something shocking in the park.

Despite having no previous experience of police work, Beatrice Wills was one of just 50 such candidates to be successful out of 5,000 applicants.

Some of the patrolwomen who did have experience were ex-WPS as well as ex-NUWW. Macready's ban on the WPS applied only to their leaders but, like Sir Edward Henry, he was well aware of the animosity towards suffragettes at Scotland Yard, so the rank-and-file had been carefully vetted and anyone with a criminal record was out. The ordinary policeman was, after all, a very conservative person, Macready observed.

When asked about the women's backgrounds, the Commissioner said there were a few constables' wives who were in the domestic servant class, and he had taken on some of the bus conductresses who had stood in for the men during the war and were now out of a job—"I hardly know to what class they belong". He knew enough, however, to realise that many of the "bus girls", like the policemen's wives, had an advantage over the ladies: they understood the lives of the people they were dealing with. Overall, the women were a thoroughly mixed bunch of typists, nurses, "shop girls", teachers, a laundress and one or two university graduates. Macready was also looking for "the woman I can put into an evening dress with some diamonds or whatever she wears and send to a place to mix with people". This presumably was where the graduates and Lilian Wyles came in.

To begin their training, the first twenty-five recruits moved into the section house at 40 Beak Street in Soho, an ugly flat-fronted Edwardian building whose depressing exterior was matched by the spartan living conditions inside. Even for Beatrice Wills, from a working-class background, the place was primitive. The floors were bare boards, the bedroom furniture consisted of a small dressing table and a drop-down shelf, the pillows were described as hard as iron and the sheets doubled as tablecloths. Two weeks later, however, the classroom shifted to Peel House, the residential training centre for the entire Metropolitan Police, an altogether more imposing slab of a place, tucked away behind Vauxhall Bridge Road. Not surprisingly it was an overwhelmingly male establishment, complete with billiard room.

The women were drilled on the parade ground of Wellington army barracks on Birdcage Walk, 300 yards from Buckingham Palace, by a sergeant with the prerequisite thunderous lungs. His bellowing attracted crowds of passers-by, fascinated by the sight of lines of smartly dressed women falling over their feet.

* * *

It was being issued with their warrant cards that brought the new recruits' status home to the women themselves. And the air of officialdom would only increase. When they moved out of Peel House, red ribbons around their left arms to show that they had just been vaccinated, they were taken to Harrods for a uniform fitting.

The women regarded this outfit as a disaster; Wyles called it "unspeakable". It had been designed by Sofia Stanley, and Coco Chanel she was not. Stanley was only partly to blame, however; the Commissioner and the Home Secretary had also had a hand in selecting the clothing. The two middle-aged men, one a hardened military commander and the other a sober-minded lawyer and politician, had held a series of meetings where they solemnly studied the latest batch of sketches from London fashion houses and rejected them one by one, finally deciding that the Yard could do a better job itself. A team of Knightsbridge tailors had then set to work. When the women came into the store, the man in charge of pinning, cutting and ripping out ill-fitting sleeves was sighing and visibly exhausted, according to Wyles. She thought that he must be asking himself why it had fallen to him to have to make these dreadful garments, which would reflect little credit on his firm or himself.

Instead of being fashioned to suit the female body, the Stanley uniform, as it was known, was a tweaked version of the men's: heavy, cumbersome and made of coarse cloth that rubbed the skin. It was also, worst of all, hideous. It consisted of a single-breasted navy serge tunic with a high collar and silver metal buttons, a two-inch wide snake-clasp belt long enough to circle the waist of an average-sized woman twice over, a mid-calf-length navy skirt, a full-length navy double-breasted woollen overcoat, black woollen stockings, stiff black boots laced to the knee with one-inch heels and a helmet of cork and reinforced felt.

Wyles' unspeakable uniform arrived at the family apartment the day before the memorial service at the Abbey, and when her family had finally stopped laughing, she asked the ex-army head porter, Thomas Vigers, for advice on how to polish the buttons, belt and boots.

"He took a look, held up the belt and boots, sucked in his breath and said: 'Strewth. Pardon miss, but what could they have been thinking of?'". He then marched off clutching the tunic and helmet, the boots dangling and the belt draped around his neck. When he returned four hours later, his face usually red but now purple and his waxed moustache drooping dejectedly, he was cursing: "Them ruddy boots. They're beyond the polishing of any human. Divers' boots, that's what they are."

And as if the uniform itself wasn't enough, hair was to be "severely dressed" and make-up was strictly forbidden. Wyles shuddered when she saw herself in the mirror and for the first time had second thoughts about her choice of career. "I thought if only I could wear a pair of earrings and run a piece of white frilling along the top of the heavy stand-up collar of my tunic, how much better I should feel."

When the first Metropolitan Women Police Patrols appeared on the streets, however, they weren't all wearing the detested ungainly uniform. Harrods had run out of material.

22

WHETHER MISS ALLEN'S SKIRT
WAS FULLER THAN THAT OF MRS STANLEY

The 17th February 1922, and another of those dank, dark afternoons by the river. Sofia Stanley and Lilian Wyles are hunched over their paperwork when a smirking male sergeant marches in, brandishing a large worrying envelope marked "Strictly Confidential" in red capitals, which he presents to Stanley with a flourish. Wyles feels a quiver of fear run through her: "There was a look on his face of supreme enjoyment and he eyed me with a certain patronising pity."

* * *

In the three years since Stanley was appointed head of the Met's Women Police Patrols, she has done well. An astute, crisply competent woman with a talent for showing people—men especially, some say—the image of her that they want to see, she has worked to good effect on General Sir Nevil Macready. The Commissioner made it clear that he had no time for excitable or neurotic women, and whatever the enigmatic Stanley is, she is not that. There is a running joke among the patrols that Macready and Stanley are conducting a torrid affair up there in the turrets, tearing off their uniforms in an explosion of passion. It's funny because it's so ludicrously unthinkable, but at the same time it shows how close a relationship the women believe their superintendent has forged with Macready. Are the contents of the envelope about to shatter everything?

* * *

Cheyne Row might have been a smarter Chelsea address than Ixworth Place, but the latter's wide avenue, lined with fine early 20th-century apartment blocks, signalled respectability and good order, and No. 35 was a pleasant five-storey building of red and yellow-grey brick. Built originally as a police station and section house, Ixworth was now home to single women patrol members like Beatrice Wills. Unlike Beak Street, however, the pillows were soft and the tablecloths stayed on the tables. The common rooms had deep armchairs, bowls of flowers and well-stocked bookcases, and, despite being painted in the regulatory miserable Met colours of buff and dark green, it was cheerful. Here Stanley set aside one room where vulnerable women could get advice and support.

Beatrice Wills found Stanley an aloof figure who handed out the pay packets, her fingers thick with rings, without a word or a smile but, Wills added, she was very popular with the men. Lilian Wyles, however, described her as open and communicative, sensitive to the views of her staff, as well as "a most charming and cultured woman" and she went on to compare Stanley in weirdly poetic terms to "a flashing blade, exquisite in workmanship but dangerous to engage". Wyles was fond of the word cultured.

One of Stanley's triumphs was to smash a network of West End drug dealers. The Met had received a tip-off that what were described as lower-grade prostitutes were dealing cocaine in public lavatories. Tiny packets of drugs were being passed from dealer to pusher in what must have seemed like the perfect set-up, given that no man could enter the premises. It clearly never occurred to the gang that the Met would send in a woman. Stanley chose a patrol from another district unknown in the area, a dark, delicate-featured young woman who took on the disagreeable and potentially danger-ous job of hanging around women's lavatories in Piccadilly and Charing Cross for weeks. Sex workers used these large underground spaces as their dressing rooms, spending hours washing, changing their underwear, making up their faces and doing their hair. It took the policewoman a while to win their confidence but eventually she was offered drugs, which provided the evidence that the Met needed to break the entire operation.

At the same time, Stanley was training women in taking state-ments from the victims of child sex abuse, those children whose plight had helped fuel the start of the entire women's police movement. The work had begun on a small scale before Stanley's time with one woman, Elithe MacDougall—Scots and blunt of speech, according to Wyles—taking statements across the whole of the Met, but by 1922 Stanley had expanded this to at least six. She had also set up a welfare centre for the destitute women that the patrols encountered on their beats, and even persuaded Macready to pay for hostel places for the most desperate cases.

* * *

When Macready set up the Women Police Patrols, the Met must have hoped that they had seen the last of Margaret Damer Dawson and Mary Allen. Damer Dawson had died in 1920 but, despite the closure of the munitions factories and the army camps, Allen was still in business, and not only in Ireland. At home in London, the Women's Police Service was now operating out of a large Edwardian apartment block in Victoria Street, from where the hard-core old guard were still going out on the beat.

When Macready left for Dublin in April 1920, he was succeeded by another ex-military man, Brigadier William Horwood, who had a reputation for pomposity and was known at the Yard as The Chocolate Soldier—the title of a popular operetta—after a mentally ill man had tried to assassinate him with a box of arsenic-laced Walnut Whips.

Mary Allen had been a thorn in Stanley's side for a long time and, having failed to move Macready, Stanley now nagged Horwood to do something about her and she persuaded the new Commissioner to prosecute Allen for impersonating a policewoman. It was something that the magistrate Frederick Mead had tried to talk Sir Edward Henry into doing, but Henry hadn't been interested. There was nothing to stop anyone from patrolling the streets as a private citizen, offering assistance and advice, so long as they didn't claim to be authorised or annoy the public or pretend to be a police officer.

By this time, Stanley had already manoeuvred Allen's sister out of her job in Richmond. When Macready launched his Women Police Patrols, he wanted all of the women on the payroll to be members so Dolly Hampton, still in the WPS, completed the training and passed all of the entrance tests. She then discovered that Macready had no intention of employing her, even though Henry had been paying her a small salary out of the Met's budget for several years. Richmond didn't need a full-time sergeant, she was told, which was untrue. The borough was soon to have not only a full-time sergeant but three constables.

The vicar of Richmond demanded an explanation. Hampton was rejected, Stanley told him, because she was a Christian Scientist and must, therefore, refuse to take women and children for medical treatment. That was untrue too. Hampton had already taken many women to hospital to be treated for sexually transmitted diseases. Yet another story was then proffered: Hampton had criticised her superior officers. "I can say quite confidently that that was as untrue as the other two reasons," said the prominent local resident and moral purity campaigner Lady Nott-Bower: "She never criticises anybody." Stanley then claimed that she had only ever wanted Hampton to give up her role temporarily. Nott-Bower said that was another lie and they had copies of Stanley's letters to prove it. Nevertheless, Hampton lost her job.

On 7th March 1921, Miss Mary Allen OBE was once again up before a magistrate, this time charged not with breaking windows in Whitehall but summonsed under section 10 of the Police Act. Alongside her stood Superintendent Isobel Goldingham, Chief Inspector Edith Champneys, Inspector Mary Barnett and Sergeant Winifred Sims. They were accused of "Not being members of the Metropolitan Police Women Patrols or of the Metropolitan Police Force, they, without permission of one of his Majesty's Principal Secretaries State, wore uniforms having the appearance and bearing the distinctive marks of the uniform of the Metropolitan Police".

When Macready launched the Women's Patrols, he had been worried about section 10 to the extent that he had asked the Home Secretary for advice. As the women were not police constables, could it be that their uniform was not in fact authorised? It was odd that the Commissioner was in any doubt because, as the Home Office pointed out, the Act says: "if any person not being a member of a police force wears *without the permission of the police authority* [my italics] the uniform of the police force …". The statute then goes on to make it clear that people are free to dress up as policemen on the stage, in the music halls and even at the circus.

The man hearing the case at Westminster Magistrates' Court was the Dr Crippen look-alike Cecil Chapman, Conservative member

Fig. 27: *A Fair Cop*—this comic postcard by Fred Spurgin (c. 1916) shows a soldier's amusement as a policewoman administers law and order during wartime.

A FAIR COP.

Fig. 28: Patrolwomen from Louise Creighton's National Union of Women Workers with soldiers on leave, Euston Station, 1918.

Fig. 29: Edith Smith, the UK's first 'real' salaried policewoman, who was sworn in as a constable with powers of arrest in 1915. Here she is on duty in Grantham, home to a wartime military training camp, which was patrolled first by the Women Police Volunteers, then by the replacement Women's Police Service.

Fig. 30: The chief—Margaret Damer Dawson, commandant of the Women's Police Service, c. 1917. In 1915 she had broken with Nina Boyle and the Women's Freedom League to set up the WPS.

Fig. 31: Margaret Damer Dawson inspecting Mary Allen (left) and two other WPS officers, May 1915.

Fig. 32: Subcommandant Mary Allen (centre), flanked by four other WPS members, 1916. They are captured here by Britain's first woman photojournalist, Christina Broom.

Fig. 33: A war worker checking acid at the Gretna munitions factories. Conditions were hard and dangerous in all such facilities—a WPS sergeant known as Buckie, who campaigned for full policing powers, was among many made ill by acid fumes at a shell-filling factory.

Fig. 34: WPS inspectors lived on-site at Gretna, policing the women and girls on the factory floor and patrolling the perimeter after dark. In peacetime, this experience would serve Mary Allen and her policewomen well; they were deployed overseas by the War Office.

THE REFORM ACT
OF 1918

Full Text, Annotated with
Explanatory Notes

BY

J. RENWICK SEAGER, J.P.
Author of "Notes on Registration," &c.

With a Foreword by the

RT. HON. J. M. ROBERTSON, M.P.

AND

An Account of the Speaker's Conference
by the

RT. HON. SIR W. H. DICKINSON, M.P.

——

LONDON:
THE LIBERAL PUBLICATION DEPARTMENT,
42 PARLIAMENT STREET, S.W. 1.
1918.

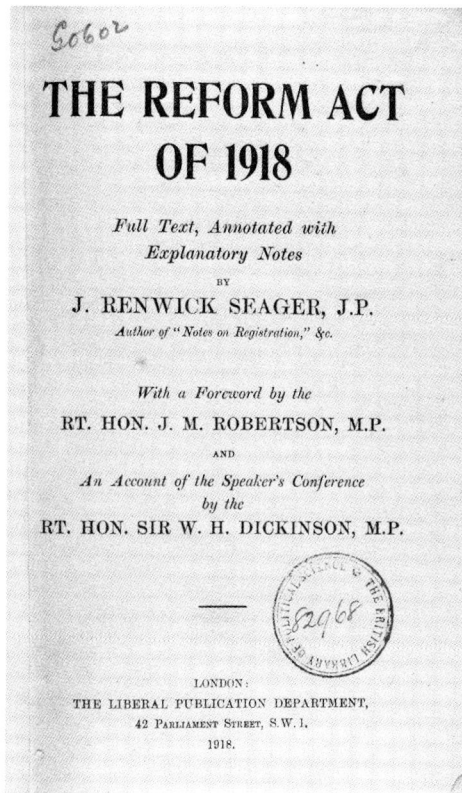

Fig. 35: The Representation of the People Act 1918, which finally gave the vote to most British women, nine months before war's end. Nina Boyle's prompt response—to stand for Parliament—hastened the passing of another law, clarifying that eligible women not only could vote, but could become MPs.

Fig. 36: Nancy Astor, the first woman to take her seat in the House of Commons, following the 1919 election campaign pictured here. That same year, the Metropolitan Women Police Patrols were set up on a trial basis; Astor would fight hard for them to be kept on and made permanent.

Fig. 37: The Women Police Patrols, c. 1919–20, with Superintendent Sofia Stanley front left (hands folded). In 1920, police forces nationwide were authorised, but not obliged, to employ women.

Fig. 38: Sofia Stanley had led Louise Creighton's NUWW patrolwomen in London towards the end of the war. For the new trial patrols, the Home Office and the Met turned to her—not to Mary Allen of the WPS. The two women ended up going to court over jurisdiction.

Fig. 39: Beatrice Wills, c. 1919. The working-class Cornishwoman was one of 5,000 women to apply for the Metropolitan Women Police Patrols in late 1918, and one of fifty with no previous experience to succeed.

Fig. 40: Lilian Wyles, c. 1919–21, in the 'Stanley uniform' she loathed. Wyles, a strong personality from a well-to-do family, went head-to-head with Stanley during the fight at Westminster and Scotland Yard over the future of the women's patrols. Only one of the two would survive with her career intact.

Fig. 41: Dorothy Peto became the first attested superintendent of Met policewomen in 1930, commanding them under her own branch from 1932 to 1946. She had joined the NUWW patrols back at the start of the war in 1914.

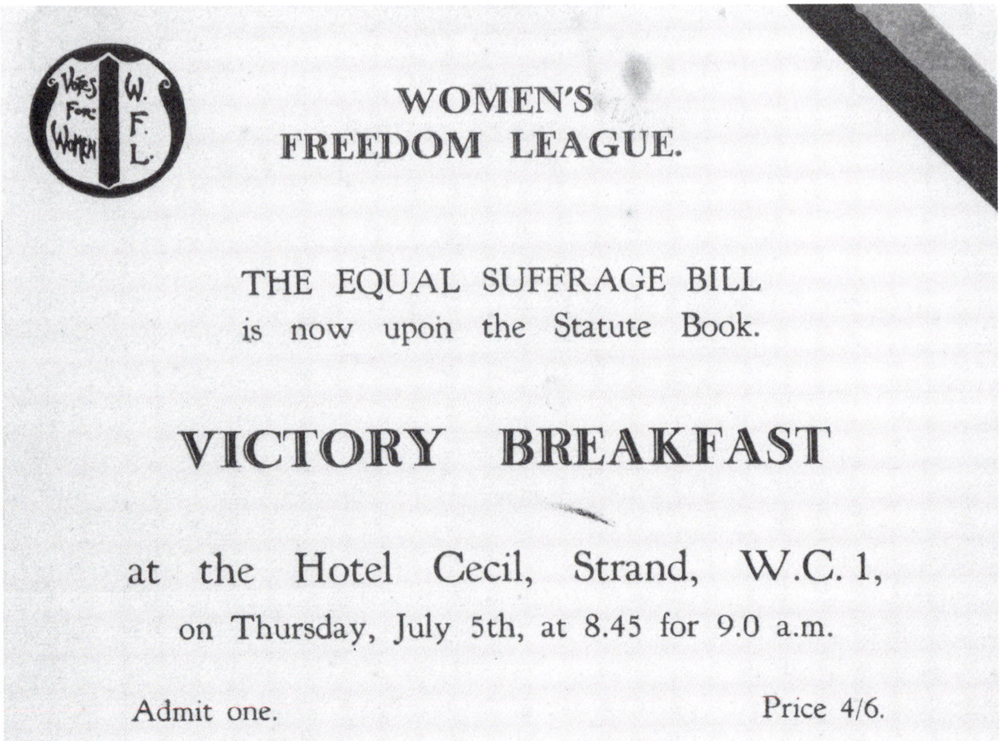

WOMEN'S
FREEDOM LEAGUE.

THE EQUAL SUFFRAGE BILL
is now upon the Statute Book.

VICTORY BREAKFAST

at the Hotel Cecil, Strand, W.C. 1,
on Thursday, July 5th, at 8.45 for 9.0 a.m.

Admit one.   Price 4/6.

Fig. 42: Invitation to a breakfast fêting universal suffrage under the Representation of the People (Equal Franchise) Act 1928. The Women Police Volunteers may not have lived to see all women receive the vote, but the Women's Freedom League that birthed the force did—and celebrated in style.

of Chelsea Council and described by Lilian Wyles as a family friend. Surprisingly perhaps, he was also an outspoken advocate of women's rights. Chapman's wife Adeline had had her own day in court in 1913 as one of a group of suffragettes who accused PC Henry Trudgell of assaulting them during a demonstration at the House of Commons. Alongside her was Edith Watson, who told the court that Trudgell looked very much like the constable who had punched her. When His Worship Mr Bennett commented: "That is a serious charge against the police", Watson replied: "Unfortunately, the police do not regard it as serious. They are never punished for it." As if to prove her point, Bennett dismissed the case.

The prosecution of Mary Allen, however, wasted no time in sliding into farce, which was probably inevitable given that it involved learned counsel bickering over items of women's clothing. In the witness box Stanley was forced to admit that her helmet was very different from Allen's headwear and when she got into a row with the WPS solicitor about whether Allen's skirt was fuller than hers, the lawyer announced that the question would soon be settled because the garments were about to be measured in court (Laughter). Sergeant Nicholls then described how he had put the defendants under surveillance for ten days, tramping glumly around the streets after them and hanging about in Victoria Street, studying their attire as they came in and out of Army and Navy Mansions, looking for signs that the public felt confused. Asked if he had ever mistaken Allen for a senior officer in the Metropolitan Police, he replied:

"No, sir." (More laughter.)

"Did you notice whether Miss Allen's skirt was fuller than that of Mrs Stanley?"

"No, I should think they were the same."

"Did you notice if their coats were lined with scarlet?"

"No sir. We did not look underneath." (Loud laughter)

Chapman fined the women a token 10 shillings and told them to modify their uniform and stop calling themselves police. Allen responded by changing the name to the Women's Auxiliary Service and adopting red shoulder straps. It was hardly the result for which Stanley had been hoping.

* * *

With the post-war economy shattered, Prime Minister David Lloyd George tasked the businessman Sir Eric Geddes with finding cuts of £100 million a year in government spending. Sir Eric proved horribly reliable. He proposed decimating the budgets for defence, health care, education, housing, pensions and benefits, and, following the principle that every little helps, he also scrutinised the Women Police Patrols and concluded that if they disappeared tomorrow, no one but the Treasury would notice. Home Secretary Edward Shortt agreed, throwing in a few disparaging remarks of his own. What the women did was not proper policing, and they kept down crime "only in the sense in which the schoolmaster keeps down crime, and the clergyman and the Sunday-school teacher".

Sofia Stanley opened the letter. Wyles saw her face pale and her lips tighten. She sat motionless for a moment and then silently handed it to Wyles. "It was, like most government commands, brief and brutally to the point," Wyles' memoirs recall. The Secretary of State for Home Affairs had decided with regret to disband the whole of the experimental women police force by the end of the following month.

23

THE MALE SOLIDARITY OF THE LOWER HOUSE

The dashing, unimaginably wealthy Lady Astor was an embarrassment. When she won a by-election in Plymouth in 1919, the forty-year-old had become the first woman to take her seat in the House of Commons. But for many of those who had endured police violence and force-feeding, their health now permanently damaged, it was a bitter irony that, after all those years of struggle, the honour had gone to a frivolous society hostess who had never shown the slightest interest in women's causes and had even presented herself as a stop-gap candidate, keeping the seat warm while her MP husband took a break. How much more fitting if that place in history had gone to a serious, worthy candidate such as Lottie Despard, Christabel Pankhurst or Nina Boyle.

Superbly dressed and heavy with glittering jewellery, Nancy Astor would pose at the top of the staircase of her great white Georgian confection of a house in St James's Square to greet her dinner guests, while the couple's sumptuous weekend parties at their country estate in the Thames Valley were a hot ticket. The celebrity guests to glide up the drive included Charlie Chaplin, George Bernard Shaw, Winston Churchill, Franklin D. Roosevelt, Lawrence of Arabia, Henry James and, bizarrely, Mahatma Gandhi. Perhaps he had confused the Astors with the Cistercians.

The leading portrait artist of the day, John Singer Sargent, painted Astor looking back over her bare shoulder with a glint of mischief, her hands clasped behind her as though about to prance out of the picture in her ivory silk ball gown. Louise Creighton might have had Astor in mind when in January 1918 she and the prime minister's wife, Margaret Lloyd George, had issued a manifesto in which they

185

urged the women of wartime Britain to embrace austerity. "We earnestly appeal to well-to-do women to lead the way," they wrote. "The example of many is counteracted by the ostentatious display of a minority. This is especially true with regard to dress. Changes of fashion imply serious waste of labour and material. We beg all women to deny themselves for the sake of victory."

Not all of the activists sneered at Astor, however. When she arrived in London to take her seat, a crowd of former suffragettes gathered at Paddington Station to cheer her. She made her way to the House of Commons, where she found her room piled high with hat boxes from fashionable milliners, hoping that she might be seen out and about in one of their creations. She'd sent them all back, however, opting instead for a severe black tricorn hat with not a flower nor a feather to be seen. She had also adopted a simple working outfit that became her trademark: a white blouse and a black suit with a white gardenia buttonhole. She looked neat and business-like and, importantly, she forced the press to concentrate on how she did the job rather than on her wardrobe. She would, after all, turn out to have her uses.

* * *

With just six weeks to save her service, Sofia Stanley worked fast. Louise Creighton set aside her social and charitable work to organise a protest meeting of more than 60 organisations, including the faith groups and The National Vigilance Association, but the purity movement had lost some of its muscle since 1914. Contrary to the many predictions, public decency and law and order had survived the war, but the previously cushioned middle-classes had been slammed up against a shocking reality over the past four years, and stomachs were not now so easily turned. Britain was a more pragmatic, more secular, less puritanical, less hierarchical place, and the battle to save the patrols would not this time be led by self-appointed guardians being ushered into Whitehall and Downing Street for a cosy chat over the Darjeeling. Stanley now had a weighty new ally at the centre of power.

By the time the campaign to save the women's patrols got underway in early 1922, Nancy Astor had surprised everyone, probably including herself. Women of all political persuasions across the country clearly regarded her as their personal representative at Westminster and, as they began writing to her in their hundreds every week, she turned her mind to their concerns. It proved so satisfying that she decided not to let her husband have his seat back after all.

So, while Creighton was once again given leave to head a line-up of the usual suspects into the Home Office, this time she was accompanied by Nancy Astor and Eleanor Rathbone, another pioneering politician who would go on to become an MP. Rathbone, from a family of social reformers, sat on Liverpool City Council, where she had gained first-hand knowledge of deprived social conditions. Unlike many people who claimed to speak for the labouring classes, she knew something about the lives of working women.

Shortt was in the chair. He had made clear his lack of enthusiasm by jotting resignedly in the file that he supposed he must receive them. It was notable that this time Astor rather than Creighton opened their case, and she talked politics rather than morality or the public good. While there had been no outcry in the House of Commons so far, enfranchised women throughout the country would be putting pressure on their MPs, she warned Shortt, and MPs, as he knew well, tended to take an entirely different view when their constituents made their voices heard.

The main proceedings began innocuously enough, with Rathbone telling Shortt that, while women's organisations tended to focus on those issues most relevant to educated and professional women, the patrols "went right home to the working woman who knows she is not able to provide for her young daughters the kind of protection that is provided for women of the more sheltered classes". Enid Tancred from the NUWW patrols was next. She had been looking at Geddes' calculations and she battered the Home Secretary with facts and figures, arguing that half of the so-called expenditure on women police was based on fixed costs. There was an amount for buildings, for example, but there were hardly any buildings specifically for policewomen. There was an amount for travel on police business, but the cost was the same whether it was a woman or a man doing the travelling. And without the preventative work with destitute girls, Tancred said, these young women would end up as a charge on the courts, the prisons and the workhouses, not to mention the risks to public health from sexually transmitted diseases and the cost to the public purse of treating them.

When Tancred finally wound down, the Mayor of St Pancras jumped in with an ominous prophesy: "If you carry out the [Geddes] committee's recommendation you will hear about it later somewhat disastrously," he told the Home Secretary.

By now Shortt was seething: "In spite of the threats from the Mayor of St Pancras, I am going to give you my views. Geddes did not describe the work of the women police as negligible but from the police point of view as negligible, and I have no doubt whatsoever that that is perfectly right. Further … we are bound, unless the country is to go bankrupt, to make very rigid cuts." He couldn't take issue with Tancred as he hadn't brought the figures with him, but he didn't agree with her in the least. And the women were not saving destitute girls from a life of crime but from a life of immorality, which was not policing. Policing was about maintaining law and order and preventing crime. These women were not doing that work. The delegation was then dismissed, it is fair to assume without the customary courtesies.

* * *

The old system of discussion behind closed doors, between gentlemen and ladies, hadn't worked. It seemed that Astor would have to take the fight to Parliament itself. For her first two years, Astor had been the lone female voice in the House of Commons, but in 1921 that had changed. The second woman to take her seat also lacked a respectable police record for assault, criminal damage or, at the very least, obstruction, but her credentials ticked a few boxes. Margaret Wintringham was active in the National Union of Societies for Equal Citizenship, Creighton's National Union of Women Workers, the Women's National Liberal Federation, the Women's Institute and the Townswomen's Guild. Born Margaret Longbottom—the name was reassuringly down-to-earth—she was a schoolmaster's daughter from Keighley in Yorkshire, the parliamentary seat that Nina Boyle had tried to fight. Her husband Thomas, a timber merchant, had been elected as the Liberal MP for

Louth in 1920. One August night a year later, he was in the House of Commons' reading room, waiting for the steak he had ordered to be cooked, when he gave a moan, slid to the floor and died on the spot from a heart attack. He was fifty-four.

In the by-election that followed, Margaret stood in his stead. She was known as the silent candidate because, being in mourning, she did no canvassing, but an energetic group of women, whom the press named "the ladies' flying picket", dashed around the constituency, drumming up votes. They came up against some formidable opposition from Astor's Conservative party, but when Wintringham won the seat Astor sent her a telegram saying: "Rejoicing over your victory; shall welcome you in the House of Commons". This probably didn't go down too well at Tory party headquarters.

Astor and Wintringham were the same age, and both had taken over their seats from their husbands, but they seemed to have little else in common. They came from wildly different backgrounds, with wildly different financial circumstances, political affiliations, temperaments and style—on the latter subject Wintringham said that Astor "went about her task like a high-stepping pony while I stumbled along like a cart horse"—but they became close friends and allies, and together they campaigned on nursery schools, widows' pensions, employment rights and safer childbirth. (In 1925 Astor would also introduce a bill aiming to put men and women on an equal footing under the law in offences such as soliciting and prostitution.) When Wintringham defended her seat in November 1922, Astor wired her again: "I am eagerly awaiting news of your election. I simply cannot go back without you."

Eighteen women were standing this time, and *The Illustrated London News* spread their photographs over two pages under the headline: "Women's Invasion of Parliament". Sadly, though, the paper had called it wrong. When the dust settled, Astor and Wintringham were still the only female MPs. One of the unsuccessful candidates was Mary Allen. She stood for the Liberal Party for the seat of Westminster St. George's, styling herself Commandant Mary Allen, but came in third in a three-horse race, taking only 1,300 votes of a turnout of 20,114 and losing her £150 deposit.

Nevertheless, two women MPs can still get a lot done. From the early spring of 1922 and on into the summer, Astor and Wintringham had been ambushing Shortt on the floor of the House in a series of ill-tempered spats. "Only those who knew Lady Astor in those early days of her parliamentary career can fully realise her impact on the male solidarity of the Lower House as she rose to open the debate," Dorothy Peto recalled. The Home Secretary did his best to smooth them over. There was no cause for concern because the bulk of the work would still be done by women, he said. The old police matrons were more than capable of stepping into the breach.

In other words, Astor retorted, the task would fall to policemen's wives; her sarcasm revealed a certain casual snobbery when she added: "No doubt policemen have delightful and charming wives, highly cultivated and qualified, but I do not believe they marry them because they will be able to deal with girls and women in a skilled way." And for all Shortt's insistence on saving money, Astor said, he had just increased the size of the mounted division to deal with riots and Bolshevism, "but the lives of children and young girls are just as important as the houses in Park Lane or the plate glass in Regent Street." On it went, punctuated by some lively theatrics from Astor, shaking her fist at Shortt and shouting "Oh, oh" in mock horror at some of his statements.

The two MPs had some support in the House. The Conservative Sir Arthur Steel-Maitland pointed out that the policewomen's limited powers were being used as an argument for getting rid of them, but if their powers were limited, whose fault was that? It was the Home Secretary who was refusing to give them powers of arrest. Likewise, when Shortt took issue with Wintringham over her use of the word disbandment—"This is not a question of disbanding"— Captain William Benn, father of Tony and grandfather of Hilary, shouted, "Abolishing them!".

Shortt liked that no better—"I object to the word 'abolishing,' and I have absolutely dissociated myself from it. I say 'reducing'."

Sir Donald Maclean shouted, "To zero?"

Shortt replied: "Zero, if you like. What does it matter if it can be restored at any moment?

Sir Murray Sueter told him: "If it be zero you cannot restore it".

Despite the drama and the semantics, the sackings began as planned at the beginning of April, but the protests continued to grow, both in the country as the news filtered out to the public, and from there back into the House, just as Astor had predicted. In a debate on 10th May, Wintringham observed: "A great many Members of Parliament have had a change of heart. That has possibly been due to the electors."

Even so, by the end of June half of the patrols were gone and, as the Astor and Wintringham bombardment thundered on, a curious subplot of subterfuge, bad faith and farce began to unfold that would suck in Parliament, the Government and the Metropolitan Police and make headlines in the national press.

24

A LARGE GARRISON IN AN ALIEN COUNTRY

As the Met's Women Police Patrols fought for survival, Mary Allen was on another journey. After the death of Damer Dawson, she had begun to express her sexuality more openly, and in the early 1920s she met another wealthy member of the now Women's Auxiliary Service. This time, though, the nature of the relationship soon became clear. Like Damer Dawson, Helen Bourn Tagart had grown up in some luxury—in her case in a Victorian mansion set in parkland in Bath—and like Damer Dawson, she was an accomplished pianist. She had inherited her money from her mother and her aunt, the daughters of a rich American, although there would be little left of it after her time with Allen. Tagart, a slim, upright figure with cheek bones sharp enough to slide plates off, moved into Danehill Lodge and presumably took over from Damer Dawson in supporting Allen, whose family allowance had long dried up. She was perhaps also helping to fund the Women's Auxiliary Service.

The prosecution for impersonating a police officer had achieved little except to make the Met look ridiculous, but Sofia Stanley and Dorothy Peto were determined not to be beaten, and they continued to goad the Commissioner every time Allen appeared to cross a line or a journalist made a mistake about her status. Horwood would then dash off his standard complaint to the editor: "Dear Sir, in an article which appears in your issue of … Miss Mary Allen of the Women's Auxiliary Service is described as Commandant Mary Allen, head of the London women police. I should be obliged if you would allow me to correct this much advertised misdescription. Miss Mary Allen has nothing whatever to do with the Women Police of London … and I am not aware by what right the title of Commandant is ascribed to her."

In an attempt to push her way back into public life, Allen took to dabbling in a little amateur detective work, investigating people she suspected were up to no good. It was not until August 1927, however, that Horwood thought that he had her when the landlady of a boarding house in Earl's Court called Amy Freemantle complained that Allen had been asking questions about her. It appeared that Allen suspected Freemantle of being an abortionist. Horwood was delighted to be able to inform the Home Office: "It would appear that Miss Allen is making enquiries about people which none but police officers are entitled to make. She is doing this under cover of a uniform that leads people … to believe her mission is official and she is collecting information and keeping dossiers of people which should not be in the possession of private persons … There is room for consideration whether the operations of this society [that is, the WAS] are not so manifold and so opposed to public interests as to justify a search warrant being applied for and the taking of steps as may put an end to these unauthorised activities."

His joy proved short-lived. The lawyers not only decided that there wasn't enough evidence to prosecute Allen, but they didn't believe there were even grounds for questioning her. The Home Office agreed. There was nothing to indicate that Allen was doing "substantial mischief". A prosecution would not only fail but would give the publicity-loving Allen "considerable openings for self-advertisement". And they were also suspicious of the landlady's original complaint, although they kept that to themselves. The wording of Freemantle's letter suggested that someone at the Yard had been coaching her on what to say. Horwood was forced to back off, and Allen emerged unscathed. She would survive Horwood, just as she had survived Macready, and the Commissioner would retire a year later in 1928 without ever managing to bring her to book.

With Grantham, Gretna and Ireland under her heavy military belt, Allen's conviction that her country needed her was not entirely delusional, and in 1923 there came another call for help. The British Second Army had entered Cologne in December 1918, three weeks after the Armistice, under torrential rain and watched by a large ominously silent crowd. They found themselves dealing with a population in shock who, as late as that summer, had expected to win the war. Soon, the city was spilling over with young British soldiers with money in their pockets and not enough to do, just as Grantham had been. Here though, instead of a settled, mostly sober-living, civilian population, there was the added complication of hundreds of single women and girls, many of them destitute and without identification, who had been displaced from countries across a chaotic and broken Europe.

In 1922, Lieutenant-General Sir Alexander Godley, General Officer Commanding of the British Army of the Rhine, faced the inevitable and familiar crisis. He had done his best to put the fear of God into his men. The chaplains were pumping out Biblical warnings, the medical officers were delivering stern lectures reinforced by magic lantern horror shows, and herds of soldiers were being force-marched around the venereal disease section of the German public health museum where, according to Godley, "all sorts of awful atrocities are exhibited". It hadn't worked. Cases of sexually transmitted diseases in the British Army of Occupation remained dangerously and intractably high.

The military's leading medical man was ordered to Cologne and instructed to come up with some recommendations, but Colonel Harvey returned with nothing of any practical use to suggest. When the problem then reached the desk of the Secretary of State for War, Godley received a pointedly courteous query from the Adjutant-General and was forced to account for himself—"My dear Philip ... The question has been exercising me very much ... I have been leaving no stone unturned ...".

It was at this point that the Liberal politician Margery Corbett Ashby arrived in the city. She had been among the first cohort of women running for Parliament in December 1918, losing to a fellow first-time candidate, Neville Chamberlain. A few days in Cologne were enough to convince her that something must be done. She returned to London and set about doing it. Her first move was to call upon Mary Allen, whom she knew by reputation, or, as Allen modestly put it: "... she at once drew me into consultation as one of the most experienced women in the social problems of Great Britain". Corbett Ashby's next stop was the War Office to request an official brief to go back to Cologne to investigate. Desperation meant that permission was readily granted. Back from Cologne for a second time, and now armed with evidence, Corbett Ashby did what she had already made up her mind to do before she went, which was to recommend that Allen be asked to supply a team of women to support the British military police. Lieutenant-General Godley agreed on the condition that the German civilian authorities approved. He was presumably keen not to antagonise an occupied population by imposing from on high a further level of control, particularly from a corps of British women in uniform.

After the Women's Police Service's success with the munitions factories, Allen was in good standing at the War Office, whatever the Home Office might think of her, so in March 1923 she too was sent to Cologne on a fact-finding visit.

She got off to an inauspicious start. Mistakenly leaving the train at the German frontier in the middle of the night, with the next train not due for 15 hours and a speech to give at the town hall the following day, she was forced to hitch a lift from a man who was towing a car. She clearly enjoyed the adventure and told the story with rare self-deprecation. "We left the inn just before 5am. The towed car was roped behind us but it had no driver. Whenever we came to a downward slope the driver depressed the accelerator of his big Benz as far as it would go and rushed away at top speed from the oncoming menace of the towed vehicle. I arrived in Cologne after more than fifty miles in this fashion to find the British authorities were searching the countryside, supposing I had been kidnapped or suffered some delay through the ill will of a fanatical German who had taken a dislike to my English police uniform. When I especially wanted to create a good impression I turned up ignominiously in front of a towed car."

But she arrived in time to deliver her speech, and when she finished, the audience of local dignitaries and women politicians voted in her favour. She was then taken on a whistle-stop tour of women's hospitals, prisons and hostels, sent out on raids with the military police—no doubt a nostalgic experience—and on inspections with the forbiddingly titled German Morals Police, and witnessed sex workers being examined for sexually transmitted diseases.

Back in Victoria Street, she set about training her team and, that summer, together with the German-speaker Ellen Harburn, she took her first six recruits to Cologne. They patrolled the streets in pairs, day and night, wearing their WAS uniforms, keeping an eye on the cinemas and cafes popular with British soldiers and working with a specialist Army unit which, the War Office said, had been set up "to combat the evils attendant upon the existence of a large garrison in an alien country". From their base in army headquarters, the women also found themselves running an agony aunt bureau as soldiers' wives and girlfriends began dropping in for advice about relationships and money, just as the young munitions workers had done at Gretna. By the end of 1923, Godley was praising their courage, tact and common sense. He said that they had had a particularly good effect on the class of women who came into contact with the police. And the rates of sexually transmitted diseases had gone down, although it was too early to say if it was due to the impact of the WAS. He recommended extending their contract by another six months. In fact, it would be continually renewed until 1925, when the British left the Rhineland.

25

THE POWERS, DUTIES, PRIVILEGES
AND RESPONSIBILITIES

A late summer's evening in Westminster, 1922. The uproar over the Women Police Patrols is at its height and James Olive, the sixty-six-year-old Assistant Commissioner of the Metropolitan Police and leading light of the Met's blacked-up minstrel band is issuing Sofia Stanley with orders in the street outside Scotland Yard. He tells her that a meeting with her and three of her team is scheduled for 11:30am the following day. Stanley phones Lilian Wyles, Inspector Charlotte Grace Dixon and Sergeant Violet Butcher. The women know the purpose of the meeting: Olive is about to offer them jobs as statement-takers in cases of sexual assault. Stanley already has a trained team on this, operating across the Met area, but these new roles are for civilians. She has been instructed to talk her own women into accepting their dismissal, in order, she suspects, to provide cover for the beleaguered Home Secretary, caught as he is between the campaign to keep the women patrols and the government agenda to make cuts.

If Stanley convinces Wyles, Dixon and Butcher to take the jobs, as she is supposed to, the three will no longer be policewomen.

* * *

According to Wyles, with her keen appreciation for social status, Dixon was a cultured, travelled gentlewoman. This did not necessarily bode well: Wyles had described Stanley too as most charming and cultured, but Olive's offer would soon see her painting the commander in a very different light. The three women were agi-

199

tated as they trooped into Olive's office the next morning, Stanley thought. Violet Butcher was in combative mode, saying that if Olive tried to put a gun to her head she would refuse. Charlotte Grace Dixon, however, an imposing woman with large haunting eyes who carried off the misshapen uniform with some style, was reluctant to turn down a job offer. She had a child to support.

According to the others, Wyles didn't commit one way or the other but she did say she hated welfare work and considered the posts a tremendous comedown. If she accepted, it would only be as a route to something better. She also wanted to consult her father, who was in Paris, and to talk it over with an old family friend, Cecil Chapman, the magistrate who had heard the case against Mary Allen. Wyles often name-dropped Chapman who, she told everyone, had been advising her ever since the disbandment was first announced early in the year.

The Yard must have been in something of a rush when they'd come up with the idea of statement-takers because Olive knew nothing about the terms and conditions but, anxious to push the deal through, he promised to get back to the women later that day. Commissioner Horwood immediately agreed to all of their demands on pay, pensions and leave, whereupon Dixon promptly added some more. That evening Wyles' brother Arthur gave Olive a call. Lilian desperately wanted the job, he claimed, but she was being intimidated into turning it down.

This picture of a timid, cowering Inspector Wyles—"almost hysterical", according to Arthur—was not someone anyone at the Met would have recognised, but Arthur said his sister frequently mentioned how afraid everyone was of Mrs Stanley, who boasted about her power over them. It doesn't seem to have occurred to Olive that Wyles might have been coveting Stanley's power more than she was scared of it or that ambition might be getting the better of honesty, and he invited Arthur in for a meeting.

The next morning, while her brother was with the Assistant Commissioner at Scotland Yard, Lilian went to ground, advising Dixon and Butcher to do the same. They should play for time, she said. So when Olive wanted her to come in and make a statement confirming what her brother had told him, there followed a comedic caper around London involving Superintendent Abbott—whom

Olive had dispatched to fetch her—and Stanley's clerk Agnes Morris who, trying to warn Wyles that Olive was on her trail, rushed round to her Bloomsbury flat under cover of posting a parcel for Stanley, but the inspector wasn't home.

Abbott eventually tracked her down to Bow Street Station, from where she was escorted across town to Scotland Yard to make her statement. She would be only too happy to transfer to a civilian role, she affirmed. It was her boss Stanley who was out to thwart the Met's plan.

The following day, when the Home Secretary rose to his feet to open what seemed set to be another punishing debate on the fate of the Met's patrolwomen, for once he had some good news to announce. He was pleased to be able to tell the House that three of the patrols were to be kept on. Nancy Astor jumped up. The women had turned the jobs down, seeing them for the obvious piece of camouflage that they were, she said. Shortt replied that as he understood it, they had all accepted, adding sarcastically: "Apparently the Honourable Member for Plymouth is better informed of what goes on confidentially in Scotland Yard than I am." Neither he nor the Commissioner can have been happy when Astor replied simply: "I am". While Sofia Stanley had been bringing her patrolwomen to talks about their decommissioning, it appeared that she had also been keeping their allies in Parliament well informed of the Met's manoeuvres.

Shortt thought he had the key to seeing off Astor and Stanley's version of events, and he proceeded to read to the House Lilian Wyles' statement, accusing Stanley of bullying. It's hard to piece together who was lying about what and why in this affair, but if Stanley and Wyles really did share the goal of saving the patrols and refusing this civilian proposal, then the allegations must have infuriated Stanley.

The first she knew of them was when she saw them in the newspapers the following day. Asked why Wyles would want to lie about her, she replied: "I have been aware for some time that Miss Wyles was anxious to supersede me as superintendent and would not be very particular as to the means she would use to obtain her end."

Under fire yet again, this time for presenting Wyles' defamatory and entirely uncorroborated accusations to Parliament as if they

were proven fact, the egregious Shortt ordered the Met Commissioner to look into what had been going on among the women.
Horwood delegated the task to Deputy Assistant Commissioner
Lieutenant-Colonel Percy Laurie, ex-Royal Scots Greys and best
known for organising spectacular displays of horsemanship when he
was head of the mounted branch.

Laurie proceeded to pick his way through a heap of conflicting
statements before submitting a narrative via Horwood to Shortt of
mind-numbing tedium of the "she said, she said" variety. His conclusions fizzed with misogyny as he painted the senior ranks of the
women's patrols as a stereotypical bunch of gossiping, vindictive
females. The women were not "merely carrying out their duties in
a pure spirt of patriotism for the public good", Laurie said, "… but
intrigue and jealously exist[ed] to a considerable degree … and
behind the whole conglomeration of assertation by one and denial
by another lies the sinister fact that the confidential transactions of
Scotland Yard are by no means preserved as official secrets but, in
accordance with mood or mentality … divulged to certain individuals who have nothing to do with this department and, in some cases,
no connection with any department of state whatsoever."

There was more. If this was how these women behaved to each
other and to their commanding officer, then "grave doubts must be
entertained about their reliability". Wyles was "a woman of rather
boastful disposition, who has probably bandied the names of persons
of position with a view to impressing those with whom she worked
with her social connections and superiority". That, at least, was a
description that some people would have recognised.

In fact, when Arthur Wyles was later asked if Chapman was a
friend of his sister, he would reply: "My sister has never mentioned
his name to me and has not consulted him to my knowledge. I don't
think my sister knows Mr Chapman, who is certainly not a friend of
the family." And when Dixon was asked if she would be surprised
to learn that Chapman had never met Miss Wyles, she replied that
she would not: Wyles had, at various times, claimed that her father
was a Guards Officer, a member of the secret service and a Home
Office official.

Unsurprisingly, Laurie found that everyone had a credibility
problem, but he concluded that Stanley had been the most economi-

cal with the truth. The prevailing view at the Home Office was that the Met would be well rid of all four women, but here too Stanley came in for most of the blame. They suspected her of sharing information with "outsiders", meaning Nancy Astor. Certainly someone at the Yard had been leaking, and the Home Office now started taking a particular interest in Stanley, looking into her contacts and trying to work out her next moves. She was associating with the secretary of a women's political association, according to their file, and had confided to her that she planned to retire in the autumn and stand for Parliament. They were also monitoring a former inspector called Elinor Robertson, who had been sacked in the first stage of the cull and was now thought to be briefing Margaret Wintringham.

Meanwhile, Astor and Wintringham were keeping up what one newspaper called their endless fire, and Shortt began to wobble. First, he made a vague promise that he would keep on a nucleus of women and then announced that this would amount to twenty, with the numbers to be increased to fifty as soon as he had the funds. In reporting his decision, the *Sheffield Daily Telegraph* commented that he had made it "after shifting his ground repeatedly, eating his former statements and no doubt finding them a bitter pill to swallow". Wyles, Dixon and Butcher were all kept on.

The Women Police Patrols emerged battered and much diminished in number, but their future within the Metropolitan Police was secure. This time, however, the clever Sofia Stanley had overreached herself and she was sacked. If she had ever planned to enter politics, she now changed her mind. She returned to the India of her youth, where she took a job with the Royal Society for the Prevention of Cruelty to Animals and also worked with the Calcutta police as a volunteer, fighting child prostitution. Wyles' only public comment was that Stanley's departure had come about because she had listened to the wrong people. Wyles would go on to serve for thirty years.

* * *

Christmas 1922, and there is a new Home Secretary. After agreeing to keep twenty patrolwomen in post, Shortt has left politics to take a job as president of the British Board of Film Censors, despite having no interest in cinema and positively disliking the new "talkies". He will distinguish himself by banning 120 films in his first five years and then going on to break a record by cutting scenes out of 382 productions in a single year.

His replacement, the Conservative MP Viscount Bridgeman, writes to Horwood about women being sworn in. The question had come up yet again, Bridgeman said, and he could see no objection: "In fact, I think it is preferable to place these women on exactly the same footing as men." The Commissioner played for time. Why not schedule a meeting in the New Year to discuss it, he suggested. The problem was that the people pushing for the move didn't understand the implications. The women would have to take on the full duties of a constable, which they were physically incapable of doing.

Bridgeman, however, had already made up his mind and in the spring of 1923, the Home Office and the Metropolitan Police caved in over a move they had been resisting since 1914. On the 19th April the women whom Edward Shortt had kept on as a gesture were sworn in as constables with "all the powers, duties, privileges and responsibilities" that went with the office.

Sergeant Violet Butcher was the first to sign the attestation book, followed by Inspectors Grace Dixon and Lilian Wyles, the latter posted to the CID as their sex crime statement-taker thus becoming one of the country's first female detectives. "The majority are spinsters," the *Dublin Evening Telegraph* told its readers, adding that, despite what Horwood had told the Home Secretary, they would not be expected to perform any duties that were beyond their physical capacity. In 1925, their numbers were increased as Shortt had promised.

Some twenty years later, on a New Year's Eve during the Second World War, Superintendent Dorothy Peto, now commander of the Met's Women Police, dropped in at the air raid shelter in the crypt of St Martin-in-the-Fields, Trafalgar Square. She had come to sing Auld Lang Syne with the displaced and the dispossessed. Here she discovered, on duty and in charge, a member of the Women's Auxiliary Service. The woman was probably, Peto thought, the last remaining survivor of Margaret Damer Dawson's Women's Police Service.

EPILOGUE

The 20th of April 1924 and Mary Allen makes a grand entrance into New York harbour on board the President Harding. She is wearing navy-blue breeches and gleaming knee-high black boots. Her peaked cap is heavy with silver braid, and a monocle is jammed into an eye socket. Waiting to greet her is the chief of the city's one hundred policewomen and a crowd of reporters for, as head of the British women's police force, Allen is an important visitor. Except, of course, that she isn't the head of the British women's police force but a private citizen in a martinet's outfit of her own devising. The Americans have misunderstood her status and she is not about to disabuse them.

In the 1920s and 30s, increasingly marginalised at home and with the Women's Auxiliary Service now faded into insignificance, Allen spent much of her time overseas being fêted, usually accompanied by Helen Bourn Tagart. In 1930, she was in Egypt posing for pictures on a camel alongside the chief of the Pyramids Police, with the Sphinx as a backdrop. On the occasions when she gave a talk on British soil, Edith Watson would often turn up to challenge her over the Women Police Volunteers. Allen was always gracious in acknowledging the role that she and Boyle had played when the subject was raised, Watson said, but she never mentioned it unprompted.

Christmas 1931 found Allen and Tagart at the home of the scandalous celebrity couple, Marguerite Radclyffe Hall, author of *The Well of Loneliness*, and her partner, Una Troubridge. Radclyffe Hall and Troubridge were also friendly with Isobel Goldingham, or Toto as they called her. Extraordinarily, Allen had exchanged her beloved regimentals and jackboots for fawn breeches, a red golf coat and patent leather pumps. Despite her jaunty outfit, however, Allen was depressed because she no longer had an official role in public life. She told her hosts that she was reduced to praying for a national

205

emergency, such as a transport strike, that would force the government to call upon her services once again.

She was thinking back to 1926 and the General Strike when, for nine glorious days, she had helped to organise thousands of women volunteers—"from peeresses to factory girls"—who stepped in, just as they had during the war, to keep the country going. Nancy Astor and a group of society ladies had turned up in Hyde Park in trench coats and military-style armbands, preparing food for the police and the volunteers.

A particular high point for Allen had been a surprise phone call. She recorded: "I picked up the receiver and heard the voice of Mrs Emmeline Pankhurst, my own former suffragette leader, putting her services entirely at my disposal". She was perhaps thinking back to her first meeting with Pankhurst when, as a young woman joining the Women's Social and Political Union, she had urged Pankhurst to use her in whatever capacity she thought best. She doesn't appear to have taken up her former leader's offer, however, for soon after Pankhurst took herself off on a tour of the city slums, organising meetings and concerts for women, trying to dissuade the working classes from causing their betters any more trouble. Still, the years had not blunted Allen's adulation: "Fearlessly this grand woman ... addressed sullen gatherings, doing the work of two ordinary people and soothing down some of the bitterest elements in our population."

Allen told Radclyffe Hall and Troubridge that the authorities were against her because she was an invert, hardly an irrational view given Sir Nevil Macready's opinions on the subject. Troubridge said it was clear that only "fluffy" policewomen were acceptable.

Soon after this conversation, Allen wrote to the incoming Metropolitan Police Commissioner, Horwood's successor, Lord Trenchard, perhaps hoping to inveigle her way in before Dorothy Peto, who had been the superintendent of women police since 1930, had had a chance to warn him off. Intriguingly, Allen said she had been asked to lay "certain facts" before the Commissioner and she asked for the privilege of a face-to-face meeting. She signed off as "Commandant", probably not a sensible move.

The mysterious certain facts turned out to be nothing more than that the residents of an unnamed district somewhere in London were asking for more policewomen. Unfortunately for Allen, Trenchard took the letter straight to Peto who described it as a try-on: under no circumstances should Allen be allowed to set foot in Scotland Yard, she said. Trenchard decided that the best way to deal with her was by "masterly inaction".

While Allen struggled to let go of her life with Margaret Damer Dawson, trying to reprise her former role leading a police force and continuing to remember her old chief in her writings and speeches, it was Annie St John Partridge who, in 1933, had a bird bath placed in Chelsea Embankment Gardens dedicated to Margaret. Running around the base is a quote from Samuel Taylor Coleridge's 'Rime of the Ancient Mariner': "He prayeth best who loveth best all things both great and small".

As well as coming out about her sexuality, Allen would soon find the perfect outlet for her political inclinations, and at some point in the 1930s she joined Sir Oswald Mosley's British Union of Fascists. At that time, the fascist movement was taking off in parts of Europe, notably in Spain and Italy, partly as a response to the rise of Communism after the Russian Revolution. Many former activists from the Women's Social and Political Union admired fascism's brand of authoritarianism under a strong, charismatic leader. Mary Richardson, famous for slashing the Rokeby Venus in the National Gallery, saw in Mosley's "Blackshirt" followers: "the courage, the action, the loyalty, the gift of service and the ability to serve that I had known in the suffragette movement". Another player in this story who at least appeared to espouse the fascists was Ormonde de L'Épée Winter. After he left the army in 1924, the colonel became director of the extreme organisation British Fascisti. There were rumours, however, that he was an MI5 plant and, where Winter was concerned, no one could ever be quite sure.

In 1934, Allen and Tagart flew to Berlin to discuss women police with Chancellor Adolf Hitler and his minister Hermann Göring. When Allen arrived in the Reich, back in uniform, clutching a briefcase, she was now fifty-six, a bulky, jowly figure. She would record her first impressions of Hitler in her memoirs: "In private he is a charming man, courteous, quiet and patient. He was much interested in my arguments in favour of Nazi police-women." She had been influenced by British government propaganda to expect that Hitler would be "ruthless in his power and impatient of everything except the progress of his own advancement", but instead discovered "a patriot whose sincerity and faith in his country's future enabled him to mould the passions of nearly one hundred million people and whose first-hand experience of trench warfare makes him one of the greatest factors in preserving European peace today".

When, in 1940, she refused to criticise the patient, peace-preserving Führer, her home was raided, ironically under a reincarnation of the Defence of the Realm Act, the legislation that had allowed her and Damer Dawson to raid women's homes in Grantham nearly thirty years earlier. By then, she was living a down-at-heel life with Tagart and an inevitable pack of dogs at the end of a muddy little track in Penwith, Cornwall, three miles from the nearest shop. It was here that Sergeant Martin found British Union of Fascists membership cards along with antisemitic propaganda, including a book by Arnold Leese, an expert on camels who had moved on to set up the Imperial Fascist League. Its flag was a Union Jack, crested by a British Lion, with a swastika at its heart.

Allen was considered for internment, but in the end the Home Office decided that she wasn't a serious security risk, merely "a terribly conceited women, a crank with a tremendous grievance … trailing round in a ridiculous uniform". Instead, she was confined to a five-mile radius of her home and banned from using cars, bicycles, telephones and radios. Imprisonment along with the likes of Sir Oswald Moseley would have given her a martyr's grandeur and the standing that she craved, preferable certainly to being dismissed as a risible figure of no consequence and left to potter around her shrunken little world without so much as a bike or a phone.

After the war, Allen sank further into isolation and obscurity, dying in 1964 in a Croydon nursing home, aged eighty-six, with a niece at her bedside. Tagart had died of cancer in 1956. It was a pitiful end for the young woman who had left the family home and set off with such courage and good intentions, but whose rigidity, vanity and downright stupidity had taken her down such a flawed and degenerate path.

* * *

In the summer of 1919, Edith Watson gave birth to a much-wanted child, although when the midwife told her she had delivered "a beautiful boy", she replied: "Bother. I wanted a girl".

With no financial support forthcoming from Eustace, she was forced to exchange the Old Bailey and the Strand for a job as a housekeeper in a boarding house, despite her loathing for domesticity. Throughout the 1920s, she continued as an unlikely landlady, supplementing her income and continuing her interest in politics by writing for left-leaning newspapers, scraping together the money to pay school fees. In 1924 she finally left her handsome, opinionated, flaky and occasionally cruel husband for good after discovering that he had been unfaithful to her during one of their periods of reconciliation. Her last word on the turbulent relationship would be: "No man was ever to mean to me all that he had meant. It was a sad ending to the great romance of my life."

Then, with her son Bernard John growing up, Watson broke free. First she took an apartment in Balcombe Street, Marylebone, a smart address near Regent's Park, and set herself up as a consultant on weight loss, skin problems, nervous conditions, insomnia and coping with troublesome children as well as "personal and domestic difficulties". Unsurprisingly, given that she had no training or experience in any of those fields, the venture was not a success. There followed six months working undercover for a trade union, investigating conditions at a Surrey psychiatric hospital, which was more her style, but then, abandoning seriousness altogether, she set off alone to see the world, travelling tourist class and supporting herself by writing travel articles. Throughout her wanderings, Watson's enquiring mind, along with her confidence and optimism, never deserted her, but while she was always able to earn a living, she lost that sense of purpose that Nina Boyle and the Women's Freedom League had given her.

* * *

While Watson was occupied with motherhood, Nina Boyle took off on another of her mercy missions. With her was the famous hunger-striker Lilian Lenton, who had gone on the run up and down the country dressed as a boy, in the Cat and Mouse days. The Save the

Children Fund had been set up in 1919 by two British sisters to help feed the thousands of children starving to death across a devastated Europe, and when the Fund sent 600 tons of food to post-revolutionary Russia, Boyle travelled with the convoy through the pitiless winter to oversee the distribution. "We walked hand in hand with death once we got into that terrible country," Boyle wrote. In Moscow, where there were at least a few partially functioning hospitals, the mortuaries were at bursting point. Out of her party of nine, seven fell sick and another died. Boyle alone came home unscathed, with a loathing for Communism but with no attraction to fascism.

With the suffrage struggle over, she turned her attention to women in those parts of the British Empire whose plight was far worse than that of women back home. She would write extensively about women who were nothing but goods and chattels to be sold, bartered, beaten and murdered at will by their fathers, husbands and brothers. In particular, she campaigned against a rite practised on young girls that she had come across all those years ago in South Africa, although hardly anyone in Britain had heard of it. Katharine Stewart-Murray, Duchess of Atholl, had campaigned against women's suffrage alongside Mary Humphry Ward and Louise Creighton, but became an MP in 1923. She was sickened when she read one of Boyle's accounts, and she asked the Under-Secretary of State for the Colonies, Thomas Shiels, if he knew anything about a pre-marriage initiation ritual known as clitorectomy that involved great suffering and mutilation. If so, was anything being done about it?

The answer was yes to both questions, Shiels told her, but great caution was needed when it came to interfering with "native customs". The government's policy was to persuade those tribes using the more brutal form of what he referred to as "the operation" to tone down the violence. Stewart-Murray responded by reading the Honourable Members a revolting eye-witness account of a public ceremony in Kenya involving an old woman, scores of girls and a knife.

On 2nd July 1928 the Equal Franchise Act finally gave all women the same voting rights as men. It prompted Boyle to throw down a challenge about female slavery, but this time she was not addressing men in power: "I ask my fellow women, emancipated now and enfranchised, what are they going to do about it? Are they going to do for their sex what men did for theirs, set them free? Or are they going to do as so many would have them do—renounce crusading, proceed along the lines of least resistance and abandon the slaves to that long, dreary process of 'educating public opinion'?".

Sadly, the answer to that last question was yes. The Women's Freedom League, like Nina Boyle, changed its focus after British women gained the vote, turning to the status of women across the world, but the new causes lacked the clarity and immediacy of the suffrage campaign. In 1961, fifty-four years after breaking away from the Pankhursts' WSPU, the WFL membership voted to disband.

Boyle's last years were blighted by money worries—two world wars and the rise of socialism had made their mark on the wealth and privilege of the upper classes—while a fall left her in constant pain and confined largely to a basement flat in Chelsea. Her friend Cicely Hamilton, who dropped in regularly, wrote of her: "The fracture that left her permanently lame and dependent on crutches did more than cut her off from the platform on which she excelled and delighted; it left her also a legacy of pain. Her last few years were darkened by suffering as well as anxiety, while to one of her active temperament, inaction itself must have been a sore trial. But neither inaction, ill health or financial worry could break her stubborn courage or lessen her capacity for interest in the work of the world. Listening to her argument for this or that, I used to think that her mind, her temperament, had not aged a bit since I first knew her. To the end she was a fighter, a jester, an enthusiast. Robert Louis Stevenson once described his wife as 'steel-true and blade straight' and it is not flattery of Nina Boyle's memory to borrow the terms for her use."

Boyle and Watson both died in nursing homes at the age of seventy-eight; Boyle in 1943 and Watson in 1966.

* * *

One 21st-century commentator writes of Louise Creighton: "She appeared to grow more progressive as she grew older yet she could never quite let go of her Victorian outlook." Creighton herself was clearly aware of the context in which she lived and how this coloured her views. Her autobiography is entitled *Memoir of a Victorian Woman*.

The prospect of writing it raised no fears of revisiting the past, she said. "My life has been a very happy one. I shall be glad to live it all over again in thought."

In the years following the war, she turned her attention increasingly to church matters, including questioning herself about why she was opposed to women priests. With the intellectual rigour and bent for self-examination that had led her to change her position on women's suffrage and that was so tragically lacking in Mary Allen, Creighton concluded that her views were rooted purely in prejudice and that there was no reason why women should not be ordained.

In 1927, after twenty-six years at Hampton Court, she moved back to Oxford with her long-serving cook, where she found a comfortable two-storey house near her daughter Gemma. As she grew increasingly frail, her grandchildren would push her around the city in a wheelchair, including to council meetings at one of the women's colleges, Lady Margaret Hall, where, in 1879, the first nine students had been admitted. She died in 1936, aged eighty-six, and her ashes were buried in her husband's grave in St. Paul's Cathedral as she had requested.

The Times obituarist wrote: "Her whole mind was set upon righteousness. Downright in manner and speech … she appeared at times uncompromising and even formidable. But … behind all this lay unflinching sincerity and a deep fund of sympathy. With her characteristic honesty she once said to a friend of widely differing character from her own: 'As the years go on I must grow gentler and you must grow sterner'."

Louise Creighton's National Union of Women Workers still exists today as the National Council of Women, and describes its aim as to ensure that women play a full role in society.

KEY SOURCES

The details of this book's account are drawn entirely from the superbly rich historical record, without any speculation or fictionalisation on the author's part. The gestures that Edith Watson made in court, the words she exchanged with Nina Boyle, Mary Allen's thoughts on what the WPV should be—all can be found in the women's own writings about this movement and their part in it.

Chapter 1

No Nice Woman

Manchester Courier, 23rd July 1913.
The Women's Library. Papers of Edith Mary Watson, 7EMW.
The Vote, multiple issues, 1913, 1914.

Chapter 2

The Most Awful Cockney

The Women's Library. Papers of Edith Mary Watson, 7EMW.

Chapter 3

Vixens in Velvet

Biggs Waller, Sharon. 'Dining Suffragette Style'. *Corsets, Cutlasses & Candlesticks*, 20th November 2013. https://corsetsandcutlasses.wordpress.com/2013/11/20/dining-suffragette-style/

Crawford, Elizabeth. 'Suffragettes and Tea Rooms: The Gardenia Restaurant'. *Woman and Her Sphere*, 6th September 2012. https://womanandhersphere.com/2012/09/06/suffrage-stories-suffragettes-and-tea-rooms-the-gardenia-restaurant/

Murphy, Gillian. 'Dare to be Free—the Women's Freedom League'. *LSE Blog*, 17th October 2018. https://blogs.lse.ac.uk/lsehistory/2018/10/17/dare-to-be-free-the-womens-freedom-league/?from_serp=1

National Archives. HO 144/1194/220196—236 to 500.

Old Bailey Archive. t19120514-54: Emmeline Pankhurst. Frederick William Pethick Lawrence. Emmeline Pethick Lawrence. Damage damage no detail. 14th May 1912. Digitised at https://www.oldbaileyonline.org/record/t19120514-54?text=t19120514-54

Oxford Dictionary of National Biography. Boyle, Constance Antonina [Nina] (1865–1943).

The Times, 14th July 1914.

The Women's Library. Papers of Edith Mary Watson, 7EMW.

Treves, Frederick. *The Tale of a Field Hospital*. Cassell and Company, 1912.

Chapter 4

The Consolation Which One Female Might Give Another

Balgarine, Florence. *A Plea for the Appointment of Police Matrons at Police Stations*. 1894.

National Archives. HO 45/9998/A47548: Employment at Police Stations of Women as Searchers and Matrons.

National Archives. MEPO 2/180: Women Prisoners: Employment of Matrons.

The Standard, 19th June 1890.

Chapter 5

A Body of Uniformed, Trained Women

Allen, M. *The Pioneer Policewoman*. Heyneman, J. (ed.). Chatto and Windus, 1925.

Allen, M. *Woman at the Crossroads*. Heyneman, J. (ed.). Unicorn Press, 1934.

Allen, M. *Lady in Blue*. Stanley Paul, 1936.

Damer-Dawson, Miss M. 'Evidence to The Committee on the Employment of Women on Police Duties [Baird]'. HMSO, 1921. Cmd. 1133.

National Vigilance Association Archives. The Women's Library. GB 106 4NVA.

Oxford Dictionary of National Biography. Dawson, Margaret Mary Damer.

Stead, W.T. 'The Maiden Tribute of Modern Babylon'. *Pall Mall Gazette*, 6th–7th July 1885. https://www.attackingthedevil.co.uk/the-maiden-tribute-of-modern-babylon/

The Times. 'Victims of the War at Folkestone'. 7th September 1914.

The Times. 'The Great Flight to England'. 8th September 1914.

The Times. 'Guests of the Nation'. 11th September 1914.

The Vote. 13th August 1914.

Chapter 6

You Will Get Yourself Knocked on the Head

Atkinson, D. *The Suffragettes in Pictures*. Sutton, 1996.

Damer Dawson, Miss M. Evidence to The Committee on the Employment of Women on Police Duties [Baird]. HMSO, 1921. Cmd. 1133.

Fido, M; Skinner, K. *The Official Encyclopaedia of Scotland Yard*. Virgin, 1999.

National Archives. HO 45/10806: Women Police and Women Patrols.

National Archives. HO 45/12915: Prisons and Prisoners: Fingerprinting of prisoners.

National Archives. MEPO 2/1608: Women Patrols under Supervision.

Oxford Dictionary of National Biography. Henry, Sir Edward Richard.

Chapter 7

To Follow a Vision

Allen, M. *The Pioneer Policewoman*. Heyneman, J. (ed.). Chatto and Windus, 1925.

Allen, M. *Woman at the Crossroads*. Heyneman, J. (ed.). Unicorn Press, 1934.

Allen, M. *Lady in Blue*. Stanley Paul, 1936.

Boyd, N. *From Suffragette to Fascist*. The History Press, 2013.

Kenney, A. *Memories of a Militant*. E. Arnold, 1924.

National Archives. HO 144/5521/185732: Prison and Prisoners. Other: Suffragettes—treatment in Bristol Prison.

Oxford Dictionary of National Biography. Allen, Mary Sophia.

Pankhurst, Emmeline. *Suffragette: My Own Story*. Hesperus Press, 2016.

The Times, 20th October 1913.

The Women's Library. Papers of Edith Mary Watson, 7EMW.

Chapter 8

Influencing and, If Need Be, Restraining

Carpenter, S.C. *The Biography of Arthur Foley Winnington-Ingram, Bishop of London, 1901–1939*. SPCK, 1959.

Colson, P. *Life of the Bishop of London*. Jarrolds, 1935.

Creighton, L. *Memoir of a Victorian Woman*. Covert, J. (ed.). Indiana University Press, 1994.

Ealing Gazette, 24th October 1914.

Farr, M. *Reginald McKenna: Financier among Statesmen*. Routledge, 2018.

MacKenzie, N.; MacKenzie, J. (eds). *The Diary of Beatrice Webb*. London School of Economics and Political Science, 1983.

National Archives. HO 45/10806/309485. Women Police and Women Patrols (1914–1918).

Oxford Dictionary of National Biography. Creighton [née von Glen], Louise Hume.

Oxford Dictionary of National Biography. Creighton, Mandell.

Oxford Dictionary of National Biography. Winnington-Ingram, Arthur Foley.

The Sketch, 26th August 1914.

The Times, 10th August 1914.

The Times, 13th October 1914.

To the Women and Girls of England, by Mrs Creighton. The League of Honour, 1914.

Wilkinson, A. *The Church of England and the First World War*. SCM Press, 1996.

Winnington-Ingram, A.F. *The Potter and the Clay*. Wells Gardner, Darton & Co., 1917.

Winnington-Ingram, A.F. *Fifty Years' Work in London, 1889–1939*. Longmans, 1940.

Chapter 9

I Could Easily Get a Man Down and Sit on Him

Allen, M. *The Pioneer Policewoman*. Heyneman, J. (ed.). Chatto and Windus, 1925.

Allen, M. *Woman at the Crossroads*. Heyneman, J. (ed.). Unicorn Press, 1934.

Allen, M. *Lady in Blue*. Stanley Paul, 1936.

Atkinson, D. *Rise up, Women*. Bloomsbury, 2019.

Callana, M; Heffernan, C; Spenn, A. 'Women's Jujitsu and Judo in the Early Twentieth-Century: The Cases of Phoebe Roberts, Edith Garrud, and Sarah Mayer'. *The International Journal of the History of Sport*, 2018 (35:6).

National Archives. HO 45/24665: Suffragettes: Amnesty of August 1914: index of people arrested, 1906–1914.

National Archives. HO 144/1194/220196: Disturbances: Suffragettes' demonstration. Imprisonment. Forcible feeding.

National Archives. HO 144/1236/230251. Disturbances: Ella Stevenson alias Ethel Slade, Suffragette, subject to the conditions of the Prisoners (Temporary discharge for ill health) Act, 1913.

National Archives. HO 144/1305/248506: Prisons and Prisoners— Other: Forcible feeding. Objections by the Bishop of London.

National Archives. HO 144/1721/233014: Prisons and Prisoners: Forcible feeding of prisoners.

Nottingham Evening Post, 17th February 1914.

Purvis, June. *Emmeline Pankhurst: A Biography*. Routledge, 2002.

The Times, 17th November 1913.

The Times, 31st January 1914.

The Times, 6th July 1914.

The Vote, 28th August 1914.

UK Parliament. '1913 Cat and Mouse Act'. Digitised version of Parliamentary Archives, HL/PO/PU/1/1913/3&4G5c4, https://www.parliament.uk/about/living-heritage/transformingsociety/electionsvoting/womenvote/case-study-the-right-to-vote/the-right-to-vote/winson-green-forcefeeding/cat-and-mouse-act/

Wilkinson, A. *The Church of England and the First World War*. SCM Press, 1996.

Women's Suffrage database. 'Miss Agnes Olive Beamish', n.d. https://www.suffrageresources.org.uk/database/1577/miss-agnes-olive-beamish

Women's Suffrage database. 'Miss Rachel Peace', n.d. https://www.suffrageresources.org.uk/database/2317/miss-rachel-peace

Chapter 10

They Are Not All Suffragettes

Damer Dawson, Miss M. 'Evidence to The Committee on the Employment of Women on Police Duties [Baird]'. HMSO, 1921. Cmd. 1133.

Levine, P. '"Walking the Streets in a Way No Decent Woman Should": Women Police in World War 1'. *The Journal of Modern History*, 1994 (66:1).

Grantham Journal, 12th September 1914.

Grantham Journal, 1st December 1914.

Grantham Journal, 12th December 1914.

Grantham Journal, 19th December 1914.

The Times, 27th February 1915.

The Vote, 16th October 1914.

The Vote, 6th November 1914.

The Vote, 9th April 1915.

The Women's Library. Papers of Edith Mary Watson, 7EMW.

White, J. *Zeppelin Nights*. Bodley Head, 2014.

Chapter 11

These Drinking Women

Duncan, R. *Pubs and Patriots: The Drink Crisis in Britain during World War One*. Liverpool University Press, 2013.

Fraser, Helen. 'Chapter XII: The War and Morals', *Women and War Work*. G. Arnold Shaw, 1918. Digitised at https://www.gutenberg.org/files/14676/14676-h/14676-h.htm

Lomas J. '"Delicate duties": issues of class and respectability in government policy towards the wives and widows of British soldiers in the era of the great war', *Women's History Review*, 2006 (9:1).

Meyer, J. (ed.). *British Popular Culture and the First World War*. Brill, 2008.

National Archives. HO 185/258: Women's Advisory Committee: reports and correspondence. Women's Service Committee: reports.

Pugh, M. *Lloyd George*. Longman, 1988.

The Times, 6th October 1914.

The Vote, 6th November 1914.

Votes for Women, 18th December 1914.

White, J. *Zeppelin Nights*. Bodley Head, 2014.

Chapter 12

Loitering and Soliciting

Aberdeen Journal, 15th August 1914.

Allen, M. *The Pioneer Policewoman*. Heyneman, J. (ed.). Chatto and Windus, 1925.

Cheney, D. 'Dr Mary Louisa Gordon (1861–1941): A Feminist Approach in Prison'. *Feminist Legal Studies*, 2010 (18).

Creighton, L. *Memoir of a Victorian Woman*. Covert, J. (ed.). Indiana University Press, 1994.

Dundee Courier, 27th April 1915.

Grantham Journal, 12th December 1914.

Justina [Nightingale, Florence]. 'Miss Garrett on the Contagious Diseases Acts'. *Pall Mall Gazette*, 18th March 1870.

Kennan, C. 'Mistaken identity: Elizabeth Burley and the Contagious Diseases Acts'. National Archives blog, 14th March 2019. https://blog.nationalarchives.gov.uk/mistaken-identity-elizabeth-burley-and-the-contagious-diseases-acts/#return-note-42870-11

National Archives. HO 45/10552/163497: Prisons And Prisoners. (1) Prisons Staff and Office Questions: Dr. Mary Gordon—the first Lady Inspector of Prisons.

National Archives. HO 45/10724/251861: Military: Suppression of 'camp followers' suffering from venereal disease.

Old Bailey Archive. t18871024-1058: Bowen Endacott. Deception; perjury. 24th October 1887. Digitised at https://www.oldbaileyonline.org/browse.jsp?div=t18871024-1058

Oxford Dictionary of National Biography. Gordon, Mary Louisa.

Pankhurst, E. *Suffragette: My Own Story*. Hesperus Press, 2016.

Royal Commission on Venereal Diseases. *First report of the commissioners*. 1914 Command Paper 7474

Sealey, J. '"A Thing in Petticoats": Nurses and the Contagious Diseases Acts of Britain'. Museum of Healthcare at Kingston blog, 14th October 2023. https://museumofhealthcare.blog/a-thing-in-petticoats-nurses-and-the-contagious-diseases-acts-of-britain/

The Vote, 11th November 1911.

The Vote, 20th June 1913.

Votes For Women, 18th December 1914.

Western Mail, 2nd December 1914.

Western Morning News, 22nd September 1914.

UK Parliament. 'Chapter 29', *Defense of the Realm Act, 1914*. Digitised at https://digitalarchive.parliament.uk/book/view?bookName=Defence%20of%20the%20Realm%20Act&catRef=HL%2fPO%2fPU%2f1%2f1914%2f4%265G5c29&mfstId=9b9eb18c-5411-40d9-9c20-a6a546e0bc8e#page/n2/mode/2up

UK Parliament. *Hansard* HC Deb 31st October 1911. Vol. 30, cc. 710–711.

UK Parliament. *Hansard* HC Deb 19th June 1918. Vol. 107, cc. 444–73.

UK Parliament. 'Defence of the Realm Act 1914'. N.d. https://www.parliament.uk/about/living-heritage/transformingsociety/parliament-and-the-first-world-war/legislation-and-acts-of-war/defence-of-the-realm-act-1914/

Chapter 13

The Keeping of a Pure Tone

Covert, J. *A Victorian Marriage: Mandell and Louise Creighton*. Hambledon, 2000.

Creighton, L. *Memoir of a Victorian Woman*. Covert, J. (ed.). Indiana University Press, 1994.

Holmes, M. *Lydia Becker. A Cameo Life-Sketch*. Women's Freedom League, 1913.

National Archives. MEPO 3/2778: Personal files of Woman Superintendent D. O. G. Peto, OBE.

National Archives. HO 45/10806/309485 Police—Metropolitan: Women Police and Women Patrols. (1914–1918).

Oxford Dictionary of National Biography. Peto, Dorothy Olivia Georgiana.

Oxford Dictionary of National Biography. Stanley, Sofia Annie.

Peto, D. *The Memoirs of Dorothy Olivia Georgiana Peto*. Organising Committee for the European Conference on Equal Opportunities in the Police [for] Metropolitan Police Museum, 1993.

Williams, J. *The Great Miss Lydia Becker*. Pen and Sword, 2004.

Chapter 14

No Order, However Distasteful

Allen, M. *The Pioneer Policewoman*. Heyneman, J. (ed.). Chatto and Windus, 1925.

Allen, M. *Woman at the Crossroads*. Heyneman, J. (ed.). Unicorn Press, 1934.

Allen, M. *Lady in Blue*. Stanley Paul, 1936.

Boyd, N. *From Suffragette to Fascist*. The History Press, 2013.

Cree, V. '"Khaki Fever" during the First World War: A Historical Case Study of Social Work's Approach towards Young Women, Sex and Moral Danger'. *The British Journal of Social Work*, 2016 (46).

Damer Dawson, Miss M. 'Evidence to The Committee on the Employment of Women on Police Duties [Baird]'. HMSO, 1921. Cmd. 1133.

Grantham Journal, 12th December 1914.

National Archives. HO 45/10806/309485: Women Police and Women Patrols.

National Archives. MEPO 2/1708: Gross Indecency in Hyde Park—question of women patrols giving evidence.

The Vote, 19th February 1915.

The Women's Library. Papers of Edith Mary Watson, 7EMW.

Woodeson, A. 'The first women police: a force for equality or infringement?'. *Women's History Review*, 1993 (2:2).

Woollacott, A. '"Khaki Fever" and Its Control: Gender, Class, Age and Sexual Morality on the British Homefront in the First World War'. *Journal of Contemporary History*, 1994 (29:2).

Chapter 15

Those Smiling Khaki-Clad Girls

Brader, C. *Timbertown Girls: Gretna Female Munitions Workers in World War I*. University of Warwick, 2001.

Daily Mirror, 12th May 1915.

Hamilton, P. *Three Years or the Duration*. Peter Owen, 1978.

Imperial War Museum. Documents.7142—The Private Papers of Miss G.M. West.

Imperial War Museum. Emp 43/102: HM Factory Gretna: The Day's Work of the Policewomen.

Imperial War Museum. 831 17/1: Recollections of the Great War by Miss. O.M. Taylor.

Lucy, H.W. *The Diary of a Journalist: Fresh Extracts*. Vol. III. Royal Institution, 1923.

McLaren, B. *Women of the War*. Hodder and Stoughton, 1917.

National Archives. HO 45/10806/309485: Women Police and Women Patrols.

National Archives. MEPO 2/1608: Women Patrols under Supervision.

National Archives. MUN 7/34: Agreement between Women's Police Service and the Ministry on provision of women police for Ministry factories.

Purvis, June. *Emmeline Pankhurst: A Biography*. Routledge, 2002.

The Times, 19th July 1915.

Williams, B. *The Best Butter in the World: A History of Sainsburys*. Ebury, 1994.

Woollacott, A. *On Her Their Lives Depend*. University of California Press, 1994.

Chapter 16

Close Association and Intimate Friendship

Daily Herald, 14th September 1928.

Derry, C. 'Lesbianism and Feminist Legislation in 1921: the Age of Consent and Gross Indecency Between Women'. *History Workshop Journal*, Volume 86, Autumn 2018, pp. 245–267, https://doi.org/10.1093/hwj/dby021

Derry, C. 'Lesbianism and the criminal law of England and Wales'. The Open University, 10th February 2021. https://www.open.edu/openlearn/society-politics-law/law/lesbianism-and-the-criminal-law-england-and-wales

Dobbie, B. *A Nest of Suffragettes in Somerset: Eagle House*. Batheaston Society, 1979.

Dundee Courier, 30th April 1914.

Iglikowski-Broad, V. 'LGBTQ+ history: Maud Allan and "unnatural practices among women"'. National Archives blog, 14th February 2019. https://blog.nationalarchives.gov.uk/lgbtq-history-maud-allan-unnatural-practices-women/

Kenney, A. *Memories of a Militant*. E. Arnold, 1924.

National Archives. CRIM 4/1398: Extract from the Central Criminal Court Indictments, 23rd April 1918.

National Archives. HO 45/22797: Entertainments: Theatre clubs: private performances of unlicensed plays.

National Archives. HO 144/22547: Publications: The Well of Loneliness by Miss Radclyffe Hall: obscene publication; order by Chief Magistrate for destruction.

Oxford Dictionary of National Biography. Blathwayt, Mary.

Oxford Dictionary of National Biography. Bodkin, Sir Archibald Henry.

Oxford Dictionary of National Biography. Holme, Vera Louise.

Pugh, M. *The Pankhursts*. Allen Lane, 2001.

Sheffield Independent, 17th November 1928.

Simkin, J. 'Basil Thomson'. *Spartacus Educational*, January 2020. https://spartacus-educational.com/SSthomson.htm

Spartacus Educational. 'Women's Suffrage', n.d. https://spartacus-educational.com/women.htm

Staveley-Wadham, R. '"The Well of Loneliness"—An LGBTQ Book on Trial'. *The British Newspaper Archive blog*, 15th June 2020. https://blog.britishnewspaperarchive.co.uk/2020/06/15/the-well-of-loneliness/

Suffragette Stories. 'Vera "Jack" Holme. N.d. https://suffragettestories.omeka.net/bio-vera-jack-holme

The Times, 3rd January 1958.

The Times Literary Supplement, 2nd August 1928.

UK Parliament. *Hansard* HL Deb 29th April 1914. Vol. 15 cc. 1111–1135.

UK Parliament. *Hansard* HL Deb 20th July 1914. Vol. 17 cc. 25–53.

UK Parliament. *Hansard* HL Deb 27th July 1914. Vol. 17 cc. 182–185.

Chapter 17

Stick to It and You'll Win

Dundee Courier, 3rd November 1921.

Macready, N. *Annals of an Active Life*. Hutchinson, 1924.

Mulvihill, M. *Charlotte Despard: A Biography*. Pandora, 1989.

Nina Boyle by Cicily Hamilton. The Nina Boyle Memorial Committee, 1940s [exact date unknown, according to the British Library].

The Vote, 6th September 1918.

The Women's Library. Papers of Edith Mary Watson, 7EMW.

Wellcome Collection. Nasmyth, Dorothea Clara. Early life and war diaries. GC/219/6, GC/219/7, GC/219/8.

Chapter 18

Time Is Short and the Work Is Colossal

Macdonagh, M. *In London during the Great War*. Eyre & Spottiswoode, 1935.

Mulvihill, M. *Charlotte Despard: A Biography*. Pandora, 1989.

The Women's Library. Papers of Edith Mary Watson, 7EMW.

Wyles, L. *A Woman at Scotland Yard*. Faber and Faber, 1952.

Chapter 19

Well Men, Give Them a Trial

Allen, M. *The Pioneer Policewoman*. Heyneman, J. (ed.). Chatto and Windus, 1925.

Allen, M. *Woman at the Crossroads*. Heyneman, J. (ed.). Unicorn Press, 1934.

Allen, M. *Lady in Blue*. Stanley Paul, 1936.

Covert, J. *A Victorian Marriage*. Hambledon, 2000.

Damer Dawson, Miss M. 'Evidence to The Committee on the Employment of Women on Police Duties [Baird]'. HMSO, 1921. Cmd. 1133.

Folkestone Express, 29th May 1920.

General Sir Nevil Macready. 'Evidence to The Committee on the Employment of Women on Police Duties [Baird]'. HMSO, 1921. Cmd. 1133.

Macready, N. *Annals of an Active Life*. Hutchinson, 1924.

Magistrates' Association. 'History of the Magistracy'. N.d. https://www.magistrates-association.org.uk/about-magistrates/history-of-the-magistracy/

National Archives. HO45/10962/343889—The Employment of Women Police.

National Archives. HO45/11067/370521: POLICE: Metropolitan Police Women Patrols—formation of.

The Times, 25th May 1920.

Chapter 20

Lady Searchers

Allen, M. *The Pioneer Policewoman*. Heyneman, J. (ed.). Chatto and Windus, 1925.

Allen, M. *Woman at the Crossroads*. Heyneman, J. (ed.). Unicorn Press, 1934.

Allen, M. *Lady in Blue*. Stanley Paul, 1936.

Hart, P. *British Intelligence in Ireland, 1920–21*. Cork University Press, 2002.

McMahon. *British Spies and Irish Rebels: British Intelligence and Ireland*. Boydell Press, 2008.

National Archives. CO 904/44/14: Ireland: Dublin Castle Records. Judicial Proceedings.

National Archives. CO 904/114: Ireland: Dublin Castle Records. Police Reports. Inspector General's and County Inspectors' monthly confidential reports.

National Archives. CO 904/150: Ireland: Dublin Castle Records. Police Reports.

National Archives. WO 35/86B: Irish Situation: Raid and Search Reports: Special Intelligence and Military Reports.

National Archives. WO 35/214: Report on the Intelligence Branch of the Chief of Police, Dublin Castle.

O'Brien, P. *Havoc: The Auxiliaries in Ireland's War of Independence*. Collins, 2017.

Oxford Dictionary of National Biography. Thomson, Sir Basil Home.

Winter, Ormonde de l'Épée. *Winter's Tale*. Richards Press, 1955.

Chapter 21

Three Silver Stripes

General Sir Nevil Macready. 'Evidence to The Committee on the Employment of Women on Police Duties [Baird]'. HMSO, 1921. Cmd. 1133.

Macready, N. *Annals of an Active Life*. Hutchinson, 1924.

National Archives. HO45/11067/370521: Police: Metropolitan Police Women Patrols—formation of.

National Archives. MEPO 2/2678: Reports of committees on the employment of Women Police 1920–1928.

Wyles, L. *A Woman at Scotland Yard*. Faber and Faber, 1952.

Chapter 22

Whether Miss Allen's Skirt Was Fuller than That of Mrs Stanley

Mrs Stanley. 'Evidence to The Committee on the Employment of Women on Police Duties [Baird]'. HMSO, 1921. Cmd. 1133.

National Archives. HO45/11067/370521: Metropolitan Police Women Patrols—formation of.
UK Parliament. *Hansard* HC Deb 11th July 1922. Vol. 156 cc. 1042–3.
Wyles, L. *A Woman at Scotland Yard*. Faber and Faber, 1952.

Chapter 23

The Male Solidarity of the Lower House

Dundee Courier, 9th August 1921.
National Archives. HO45/11067/370521: Police: Metropolitan Police Women Patrols—formation of.
Oxford Dictionary of National Biography. Wintringham [née Longbottom], Margaret.
The Times, 21st September 1921.
UK Parliament. *Hansard* HC Deb 23rd February–29th June 1922. Vol. 150 c. 2148–vol. 155 c. 2318.

Chapter 24

A Large Garrison in an Alien Country

Allen, M. *The Pioneer Policewoman*. Heyneman, J. (ed.). Chatto and Windus, 1925.
Allen, M. *Woman at the Crossroads*. Heyneman, J. (ed.). Unicorn Press, 1934.
Allen, M. *Lady in Blue*. Stanley Paul, 1936.
National Archives. HO45/10806/309485: Police—Metropolitan: Women Police and Women Patrols.
National Archives. HO45/11067/370521: Police: Metropolitan Police Women Patrols—formation of.
National Archives. MEPO 3/2441—Activities of "Women Police Service" a private organisation.
National Archives. WO 32/3562: Overseas: Europe (Code 0(V)): Visit of Commandant Mary Allen (Women's Auxiliary Service) to the British Army of the Rhine in connection with use of Policewomen.
Pawley, M. *The Watch on the Rhine*. I.B. Tauris, 2008.
Peto, D. *The Memoirs of Dorothy Olivia Georgiana Peto*. Organising Committee for the European Conference on Equal Opportunities in the Police [for] Metropolitan Police Museum, 1993.

Chapter 25

The Powers, Duties, Privileges and Responsibilities

Berry-Waite, L. 'Tracing the experiences of the Metropolitan Police Women Patrols'. National Archives blog, 27th May 2022. https://blog.nationalarchives.gov.uk/20speople-tracing-the-experiences-of-the-metropolitan-police-women-patrols/

Dublin Evening Telegraph, 24th April 1923.

National Archives. HO 45/11067/370521: Metropolitan Police Women Patrols—formation of. 1918–1922.

Peto, D. *The Memoirs of Dorothy Olivia Georgiana Peto*. Organising Committee for the European Conference on Equal Opportunities in the Police [for] Metropolitan Police Museum, 1993.

Sheffield Daily Telegraph, 1st September 1924.

UK Parliament. *Hansard* HC Deb 23rd February–29th June 1922. Vol. 150 c. 2148–vol. 155 c. 2318.

Wyles, L. *A Woman at Scotland Yard*. Faber and Faber, 1952.

Epilogue

Allen, M. *Lady in Blue*. Stanley Paul, 1936.

Boyd, N. *From Suffragette to Fascist*. The History Press, 2013.

Creighton, L. *Memoir of a Victorian Woman*. Covert, J. (ed.). Indiana University Press, 1994.

National Archives. MEPO 3/2441: Activities of Women Police Service—A private organisation.

National Archives. HO 144/21933: DISTURBANCES: Mary Allen, Commandant of unofficial Women's Auxiliary Service: detained under Defence Regulation 18B for fascist sympathies.

Pugh, M. *Hurrah For the Blackshirts!*. Jonathan Cape, 2005.

Purvis, June. *Emmeline Pankhurst: A Biography*. Routledge, 2002.

The Women's Leader, 13th September 1929.

The Women's Leader, 20th September 1929.

The Women's Leader, 27th September 1929.

The Women's Library. Papers of Edith Mary Watson, 7EMW.

The Times, 6th April 1936.

UK Parliament. *Hansard* HC Deb 11th December 1929. Vol. 233 cc. 599–615.

LIST OF ILLUSTRATIONS

1. Suffragette Nina Boyle, editor-in-chief of *The Vote*. Public domain / The Women's Library via Flickr.

2. Nina Boyle and Edith Watson, Women Police Volunteers.

3. Women's Social and Political Union meeting, 1900s. Public domain / The Women's Library via Flickr.

4. Suffragettes at the Blathwayts'. Public domain / The Women's Library via Flickr.

5. 'Roll of Honour' for suffragettes jailed, including Mary Allen. Public domain / The Women's Library via Flickr.

6. Margaret Damer Dawson and Mary Allen, women police commanders. Public domain / Crown copyright.

7. *Louise Creighton, Wife of Mandell Creighton, Bishop of London* by Glyn Warren Philpot. Artepics / Alamy Stock Photo.

8. Arthur Foley Winnington-Ingram, Bishop of London. Chronicle / Alamy Stock Photo.

9. Crowds wait for Mrs Pankhurst, Bow Street Magistrates' Court. Public domain / The Women's Library via Flickr.

10. Mrs Pankhurst lifted off her feet, arrested at Buckingham Palace. Chronicle / Alamy Stock Photo.

11. Arrest of Dora Thewlis. Public domain / Huddersfield Exposed via Flickr.

12. Arrest of Dora Marsden, photographed by Manchester City Police. Public domain / Crown copyright.

41. Dorothy Peto, superintendent of Met policewomen, photographed by the London Metropolitan Police. Public domain / Crown copyright.

42. Invitation to WFL equal suffrage breakfast. Public domain / The Women's Library via Flickr.

INDEX

abortion, 194

Albemarle, George Granville, 1st Duke, 54

alcohol, 22, 53, 72, 77–87

Aldrich, Verna, 134

Aldwych, Westminster, 16, 25

Alexandra Palace, Haringey, 25

Alexandra, Queen consort, 173, 174

Allan, Maud, 132–4, 137

Allen, Margaret, 41–2, 49

Allen, Margaret 'Dolly', *see* Hampton, Margaret

Allen, Mary, 41–51, 103, 143, 157, 181, 205–8
  Armistice (1918), 150–51
  Baird Committee (1920), 161
  Cologne, policing in (1923), 195–7
  Damer Dawson, relationship with, 131–2, 147, 162–3, 164, 193, 207
  death (1964), 208
  detention (1940), 208
  Freemantle investigation (1927), 194
  general election (1922), 189
  General Strike (1926), 206
  Grantham, policing in (1914), 72–3, 105–9, 114, 208

  Hitler, meeting with (1934), 207–8
  Holloway prison sentence (1909), 46–8, 63, 105, 138
  Ireland, policing in (1920–21), 167–70
  munitions factories, policing of, 122, 127
  New York visit (1924), 205
  Parliament break-in attempt (1909), 46
  Police Act charge (1921), 182–3, 193
  prison visit (1915), 127
  sexuality, 131–2, 193, 205, 206, 207
  swearing-in affair (1915), 121
  Tagart, relationship with, 193, 205
  Women Police Patrols establishment (1918), 155, 157, 158, 166
  Women Police Volunteers, joining of (1914), 49–51, 70, 71

Allen, Thomas, 41–2, 49

allowances, 77–87

Amazons, 63–4

Anderson, Elizabeth Garrett, 96, 102

233

INDEX

Cuff, Herbert, 25
curfews, 95, 97, 107

D'Abernon, Edgar Vincent, 1st
  Viscount, 85–6
Dacre Fox, Norah, 67
Daily Herald, 138
Daily Mirror, 80, 120
Daily Telegraph, 132
Damer Dawson, Margaret 25, 27–
  31
  Allen, relationship with, 131–
    2, 147, 162–3, 164, 207
  Armistice (1918), 150–51
  Baird Committee (1920), 161,
    167
  death (1920), 162–4, 167, 193,
    207
  Grantham, policing in (1914),
    72–3, 105–8, 114, 208
  munitions factories, policing
    of, 121–2, 124–30, 162
  prison visit (1915), 127
  swearing-in affair (1915), 121
  vote of confidence (1915),
    108–9
  Women Police Patrols estab-
    lishment (1918), 155, 157
  Women Police Volunteers
    establishment (1914), 35–9,
    50–51, 55–6, 69, 70, 71
  Women's Police Service
    establishment (1915), 110,
    120
Damer Dawson, Richard 30, 31
Damer Dawson Memorial Home,
  Kent, 164
Danehill Lodge, Kent, 162, 193

Darlington, County Durham, 124
Darwin, Charles, 102
Davison, Emily Wilding, 16
De Boyville family, 13
Defence of the Realm Act
  (1914), 89, 95, 97, 167, 208
Denmark, 31
Department of Munitions and
  Supply, 119
Despard, Charlotte, 17, 55, 56,
  81, 82, 97, 122, 138, 144, 152
Dickens, Charles, 43
Dixon, Charlotte Grace, 199–
  202, 203, 204
Dixon, Gertrude, 153
domestic servants, 8
Douglas, Alfred, 132, 134
Dover, Kent, 96
Doyle, Arthur Conan, 128, 129
Drummond, Ada, 5
Drury Lane theatre, Covent
  Garden, 153–4
Dublin Evening Telegraph, 204
Dublin, Ireland, 113, 152, 165,
  167
Duckworth, George, 119
Duncan, Agnes, 56
Dundee Courier, 77
Dunning, Leonard, 120–21
Dyer, Edward, 153

Eagle House, Batheaston, 112,
  138
Ealing, Middlesex, 42
Easter Rising (1916), 113–14,
  152, 165
Edinburgh, Scotland, 49, 64–5,
  71, 93, 126

237